THE
WISDEN
CRICKET QUIZ BOOK

THE
WISDEN
CRICKET QUIZ BOOK

compiled by
STEVEN LYNCH

Published by John Wisden & Co Ltd,
13 Old Aylesfield, Golden Pot,
Alton, Hampshire GU34 4BY

JOHN WISDEN & CO LTD
13 Old Aylesfield, Golden Pot, Alton, Hampshire GU34 4BY
enquiries@johnwisden.co.uk
www.cricinfo.com

THE WISDEN CRICKET QUIZ BOOK
Compiled by Steven Lynch

Typeset in Slimbach and Univers by Nigel Davies
Cover photograph by Patrick Eagar
Printed and bound in Great Britain by Clays Ltd, St Ives plc

"Wisden" and its woodcut device are registered trademarks of John Wisden & Co Ltd

© John Wisden & Co Ltd 2004
Published by John Wisden & Co Ltd 2004

10 9 8 7 6 5 4 3 2 1

ISBN 0-947766-92-8

Distributed by Macmillan Distribution Ltd

My thanks go to Christopher Lane of John Wisden & Co, who commissioned and edited the book; to Albért Sanders and Cris Freddi, who road-tested most of the questions and suggested some others; to Will Webb of Bloomsbury, who designed the cover; to Nigel Davies of Wisden, who designed and typeset the inside pages; to Gordon Burling, Wisden's proofreader; and to my colleagues at Wisden Cricinfo, who put up with having random questions fired at them, and occasionally suggested better ones in return.

Steven Lynch
Epsom, Surrey   September 2004

CONTENTS

CONTENTS

CONTENTS

CONTENTS

HOW TO PLAY

Each quiz contains 11 themed questions, with easier ones at the top of the batting order and harder ones lurking lower down. Then comes the googly, a tough question usually connected with that page's theme. Often it's quirky – occasionally it's plain unbelievable.

Every question has four alternative answers: one correct and three red herrings. The best way to play is to persuade someone to ask you the questions and – if you're stuck – then give you the suggested answers. If you're playing on your own, try holding a postcard over the alternatives and running it down the page if you need a hint or two.

You score four runs for each question you answer correctly without help, and two for each one you get right after you've been given the alternative answers. If you get the googly right, score a big six – or three if you need the suggestions.

So if you get everything right in one quiz entirely off your own bat, you score a Wisden half-century. And if you manage it twice running, consider yourself a Wisden century-maker. If you're slightly less of a cricket mastermind, you can still aim for an impressive Wisden fifty across a pair of facing pages.

And the umpire says "Play"…

SLOW STARTERS

1 Who made a pair of ducks on debut for England in 1975, but ended up with 8900 Test runs?
A Graham Gooch B Ian Botham C Mike Gatting D David Gower

2 Who only took one expensive wicket on his Test debut in 1991-92, but reached 500 Test wickets a dozen years later?
A Muttiah Muralitharan B Shane Warne C Courtney Walsh D Glenn McGrath

3 Which Australian captain didn't score a century until his 30th Test, but finished up with 10 in 62 matches?
A Allan Border B Bill Lawry C Bobby Simpson D Kim Hughes

4 Who had 0 for 110 on his debut in 1972-73, but took 33 wickets in an Ashes series two years later and finished up with 200 Test wickets?
A Bob Willis B Jeff Thomson C Phil Edmonds D Dennis Lillee

5 Who made his Test debut in 1958, but didn't score his first Test century until 1969, by which time he was England's captain?
A Mike Smith B Ted Dexter C Colin Cowdrey D Ray Illingworth

6 Which batsman scored only 12 runs in his first seven innings, but ended up captaining New Zealand in 18 of his 56 Tests?
A Bevan Congdon B Ken Rutherford C Geoff Howarth D John Reid

7 Which South African was forced to wait until he was 39 for his first Test cap, and was then dismissed by the first ball of his debut match in 1992-93?
A Clive Rice B Barry Richards C Jimmy Cook D Peter Kirsten

8 Which West Indian managed only one wicket on his debut, in India in 1978-79, and cried on the way back to the pavilion after being given out for a duck ... but finished up with 362 Test wickets?
A Michael Holding B Joel Garner C Curtly Ambrose D Malcolm Marshall

9 Who didn't score a single run in his first three Test matches for Australia, but finished up with the double of 1032 runs and 212 wickets in Tests?
A Ian Johnson B Richie Benaud C Keith Miller D Merv Hughes

10 Which future England captain toured South Africa in 1964-65, but didn't make his Test debut until 1976?
A Tony Lewis B Mike Brearley C Mike Denness D David Steele

11 Who made his debut for South Africa in 1902-03, and made his only Test hundred 19 years later, when he was 42?
A Aubrey Faulkner B Herbie Taylor C Bob Catterall D Dave Nourse

The Googly

Who opened the innings in his first Test alongside another debutant, scored 0 and 1, but retained his place (unlike his partner, who made 22 and 7 but was never selected again) and scored 100 in his next match, and a Test triple-century the following year?
A Andy Sandham B Bob Cowper C Garry Sobers D Len Hutton

Answers on page 172

ENGLAND v WEST INDIES: THE WISDEN TROPHY 2004

1 Who scored 221 for England in the first Test, at Lord's?

A Andrew Strauss B Andrew Flintoff C Robert Key D Graham Thorpe

2 Which 20-year-old West Indian made his debut at Lord's and scored 44?

A Dwayne Smith B Dwayne Bravo C Carlton Baugh D Darren Sammy

3 Who scored a century in each innings for England in the Lord's Test?

A Andrew Strauss B Michael Vaughan C Robert Key D Marcus Trescothick

4 Who was the only previous man to achieve that feat for England at Lord's?

A W.G. Grace B Geoff Boycott C Graham Gooch D Walter Hammond

5 And who was the first West Indian to do it at Lord's?

A Garry Sobers B Brian Lara C Everton Weekes D George Headley

6 Who narrowly missed joining them, with 128 and 97, both not out, at Lord's in 2004?

A Shivnarine Chanderpaul B Brian Lara C Ramnaresh Sarwan D Andrew Flintoff

7 Who scored a century in each innings in the second Test at Edgbaston, but was out for a second-ball duck in his next innings of the series?

A Chris Gayle B Marcus Trescothick C Graham Thorpe D Ramnaresh Sarwan

8 Who hit every ball of an over for four during the fourth Test at The Oval?

A Andrew Flintoff B Michael Vaughan C Chris Gayle D Dwayne Smith

9 Who took his 100th Test wicket when he dismissed Brian Lara at Lord's?

A Ashley Giles B Simon Jones C Andrew Flintoff D Matthew Hoggard

10 And who took his 100th Test wicket in the final Test at The Oval?

A James Anderson B Stephen Harmison C Corey Collymore D Jermaine Lawson

11 Who was the leading runscorer in the series, with 437?

A Michael Vaughan B Marcus Trescothick C Chris Gayle D Shivnarine Chanderpaul

The Googly

Andrew Flintoff smashed 167, including seven sixes, in the second Test at Edgbaston in 2004. One of his aerial shots was dropped in the crowd – who by?

A West Indies' 12th man B The video analyst on the England dressing-room balcony C His father Colin in the first row of the upper tier of the stand D A man dressed as the back end of a pantomime horse

Answers on page 172

IAN BOTHAM

1 In which Minor County was Botham born, in 1955?

   A Northumberland B Berkshire C Cheshire D Dorset

2 Against which country did Botham mark his Test debut with 5 for 74 in 1977?

   A Australia B India C Pakistan D West Indies

3 Which county did Botham join in 1987?

   A Yorkshire B Warwickshire C Worcestershire D Durham

4 On which ground was his famous 149 not out against Australia in 1981 played?

   A Edgbaston, Birmingham B Trent Bridge, Nottingham C Old Trafford, Manchester
   D Headingley, Leeds

5 For which Australian state did Botham play?

   A New South Wales B Queensland C Tasmania D Victoria

6 Against which country did Botham make his highest Test score of 208, at The Oval in 1982?

   A Australia B India C New Zealand D Pakistan

7 Botham reached 100 Test wickets in the then-record time of two years nine days. Which Indian was his 100th victim, in 1979?

   A Mohinder Amarnath B Bishan Bedi C Kapil Dev D Sunil Gavaskar

8 For which county did Botham's son Liam play?

   A Somerset B Surrey C Hampshire D Essex

9 Who was the flamboyant agent who promised that Botham would make it big in Hollywood?

   A Micky Most B "Lord" Tim Hudson C Max Clifford D Screaming Lord Sutch

10 Which New Zealander did Botham dismiss with his first ball back in Tests after a drug ban in 1986?

   A Ken Rutherford B Bruce Edgar C Jeff Crowe D Martin Crowe

11 Who were the opposition in Botham's final first-class match, for Durham in 1993?

   A Australians B Somerset C Oxford University D Worcestershire

The Googly

What record for an English first-class season did Ian Botham establish in 1985?

A Most wickets B Most catches C Most disciplinary breaches D Most sixes

Answers on page 172

STRANGE BUT TRUE

1 Why was the so-called Timeless Test between South Africa and England in 1938-39 left drawn and not played to a finish as planned?
A The ground was flooded **B** *The England team had to catch the boat home* **C** *No-one turned up to the tenth day's play* **D** *The ground was only available for ten days*

2 Why was the second scheduled day of the India v England Jubilee Test at Bombay in 1979-80 turned into a rest day?
A A total eclipse **B** *The Indian prime minister was shot* **C** *There was a general strike after unions received a reduced allocation of match tickets* **D** *Princess Anne's wedding*

3 What unscheduled interruption affected the 1973 England–West Indies Test at Lord's?
A A crowd invasion by anti-European campaigners **B** *An underground drain burst and flooded the outfield* **C** *The announcement of Garry Sobers's knighthood* **D** *A bomb scare*

4 Why was there an unscheduled rest day on what should have been the second day of the India-England Test at Madras in February 1952?
A The Queen's Coronation **B** *News of the ascent of Mount Everest* **C** *Jim Swanton was ill and unable to attend the match for the Daily Telegraph* **D** *The death of King George VI*

5 Why did the first match between England and the Rest of the World in 1970 start on a Wednesday, with a rest day on the Thursday?
A A royal wedding **B** *A royal funeral* **C** *A general election* **D** *The referendum on whether to join the Common Market*

6 How did Michael Angelow interrupt the 1975 Lord's Test against Australia?
A He parachuted into the ground **B** *He streaked naked across the ground* **C** *He broke his leg and had to be helicoptered to hospital* **D** *He staged a sit-down protest on the pitch*

7 And how did George Davis bring a premature end to the 1975 Headingley Test?
A He vandalised the covers – and then it rained **B** *He crashed his car through the main gates and abandoned it on the outfield* **C** *He held the umpires hostage in their dressing-room* **D** *Supporters claiming he had been wrongly arrested dug up the pitch*

8 Whose expulsion from Guyana in 1980-81, because of his "South African connections", brought about the cancellation of the scheduled Test there between West Indies and England?
A Tony Greig **B** *Geoff Boycott* **C** *Robin Jackman* **D** *Allan Lamb*

9 Whose non-selection for the Test against South Africa at Bridgetown in 1991-92 led to a boycott by locals angry at the absence of any Barbadian bowlers in the Test team?
A Anderson Cummins **B** *Ezra Moseley* **C** *Franklyn Stephenson* **D** *Malcolm Marshall*

10 Which student leader was selected for Pakistan v England in 1968-69, supposedly because if he hadn't played the authorities were worried the students would riot and stop the match?
A Aftab Gul **B** *Imran Khan* **C** *Younis Ahmed* **D** *Aftab Baloch*

11 What happened on the rest day of the second Test between Zimbabwe and New Zealand at Harare in 1992-93?
A They played a one-day international **B** *Both teams bungee-jumped at Victoria Falls* **C** *There was a general election in Zimbabwe* **D** *Nelson Mandela was released*

The Googly
What was responsible for a series of hold-ups in the second Test between Australia and England at Melbourne in 1924-25?
A Hundreds of seagulls "divebombing" the players **B** *Dust and debris from nearby forest fires* **C** *A batch of substandard balls that kept going out of shape* **D** *Firemen attending a blaze on the nearby railway line kept asking the groundsman for more water*

Answers on page 172

THE ASHES

1 Where is the Ashes urn traditionally kept?

A The Victoria & Albert Museum *B ICC headquarters* *C The Lord's Museum*
D The Bradman Museum

2 The Ashes legend was spawned after an exciting Test match, which ended when England, chasing only 85 to win, were bowled out for 77 – where was it played?

A Lord's *B The Oval* *C Melbourne* *D Sydney*

3 And in which year was that match played?

A 1877 *B 1882* *C 1884* *D 1893*

4 Who took 14 wickets for Australia in that match?

A Tom Garrett *B Hugh Boyle* *C Charles "Terror" Turner* *D Fred "Demon" Spofforth*

5 In which publication did the mock obituary appear, lamenting the death of English cricket and saying "the ashes [will be] taken to Australia"?

A The Sun *B The Daily Telegraph* *C The Sporting Times* *D Punch*

6 Which Australian captain twice regained the Ashes on his birthday?

A Allan Border *B Bill Woodfull* *C Richie Benaud* *D Don Bradman*

7 Which English captain, in 1970-71, was the first to regain the Ashes in Australia since the 1932-33 Bodyline tour?

A Mike Smith *B Ray Illingworth* *C Colin Cowdrey* *D Mike Denness*

8 Who captained England 32 times, but never in Australia, although he made five Test-playing tours there?

A Ted Dexter *B Mike Brearley* *C Colin Cowdrey* *D David Gower*

9 Who captained Australia in a record 29 Test matches against England?

A Allan Border *B Bob Simpson* *C Mark Taylor* *D Don Bradman*

10 And who captained England a record 22 times against Australia?

A Mike Atherton *B Mike Brearley* *C Archie MacLaren* *D W.G. Grace*

11 Which man, prominent in the Bodyline series, took 41 wickets in 11 Ashes Tests in Australia, but never played a home Test against Australia?

A Bill Bowes *B Bill Voce* *C Harold Larwood* *D Gubby Allen*

The Googly

What happened to Florence Morphy, one of the "ladies of Melbourne" who presented the Ashes urn to the Honourable Ivo Bligh, the England captain, in 1882-83?

A She perished in the Titanic disaster *B She married Bligh* *C She became the Governor of Queensland* *D She became the first lady president of the Melbourne Cricket Club*

Answers on page 172

WISDEN CRICKETER OF THE 20TH CENTURY: DON BRADMAN

1 What was Bradman's famous final Test average?

A 112.52 B 101.00 C 99.94 D 95.14

2 On which ground in England did Bradman start three of his four England tours with a double-century?

A Arundel B Bristol C Leicester D Worcester

3 Where is the Bradman Museum, in the New South Wales town in which Bradman grew up?

A Ashburton B Bowral C Cootamundra D Deniliquin

4 Of the distinguished panel of 100 which chose the Wisden Cricketers of the 20th Century, how many voted for Bradman?

A 52 B 66 C 91 D 100

5 On which ground did Bradman score two Test triple-centuries?

A Adelaide B Lord's C Melbourne D Headingley, Leeds

6 Who bowled Bradman for a duck in his last Test innings?

A Alec Bedser B Eric Hollies C Denis Compton D Doug Wright

7 With whom did Bradman share a partnership of 451, a Test record at the time, at The Oval in 1934?

A Bill Woodfull B Bill Ponsford C Stan McCabe D Jack Fingleton

8 Who exactly matched Bradman's score of 234 against England at Sydney in 1946-47?

A Lindsay Hassett B Sid Barnes C Arthur Morris D Keith Miller

9 Who was Bradman's first Test captain, in 1928-29?

A Jack Ryder B Herbie Collins C Bill Woodfull D Vic Richardson

10 On which ground did Bradman score nine Test centuries and average 128?

A Adelaide B Sydney C Melbourne D Brisbane

11 What score did Bradman make against South Africa at Adelaide in 1931-32?

A 99 B 99 not out C 199 D 299 not out

The Googly

Don Bradman never played first-class cricket anywhere except England and Australia – but he did tour overseas in 1932, and scored 3777 non-first-class runs at an average of 102.1 ... where was this?

A New Zealand B North America C Fiji and Tonga D India and Ceylon

Answers on page 172

WEST INDIES v INDIA

1 Who scored 2749 runs – and an unprecedented 13 centuries – in Tests between West Indies and India?

  A Sachin Tendulkar B Everton Weekes C Sunil Gavaskar D Garry Sobers

2 Who took 16 wickets on his Test debut against West Indies at Madras in 1987-88?

  A Anil Kumble B Narendra Hirwani C Maninder Singh D Arshad Ayub

3 And who broke the Test record with six stumpings in that match?

  A Kiran More B Bharat Reddy C Chandrakant Pandit D Jeff Dujon

4 Who started his Test career with 93 and 107 at Bangalore in 1974-75?

  A Viv Richards B Len Baichan C Gordon Greenidge D Desmond Haynes

5 Which West Indian fast bowler was sent home from the 1958-59 tour of India for bowling beamers?

  A Wes Hall B Roy Gilchrist C Charlie Griffith D Lester King

6 Whose 256 at Calcutta in 1958-59 was, until 2004, the highest Test score by a Guyanese batsman?

  A Rohan Kanhai B Basil Butcher C Clive Lloyd D Joe Solomon

7 Who took over as India's captain midway through the 1961-62 tour of West Indies, even though he was only 21 and the youngest player in the side?

  A Ajit Wadekar B Chandu Borde C Nari Contractor D Nawab of Pataudi junior

8 Who took 9 for 95 in only his second Test, at Port-of-Spain in 1970-71?

  A Arthur Barrett B Keith Boyce C Jack Noreiga D Uton Dowe

9 Which 6ft 6ins bowler, who took 5 for 68 at Bridgetown in 2000-01, was reportedly India's tallest Test cricketer?

  A Abey Kuruvilla B Venkatesh Prasad C Debasis Mohanty D Dodda Ganesh

10 Who, less than a month past his 20th birthday, hit a century in the 1978-79 Delhi Test?

  A Aunshuman Gaekwad B Dilip Vengsarkar C Sachin Tendulkar D Kapil Dev

11 Who scored 115 on his Test debut against India at Port-of-Spain in 1952-53?

  A Denis Atkinson B Bruce Pairaudeau C Clairmonte Depeiza D Roy Marshall

The Googly

What was unusual about India's second innings at Kingston in 1975-76?

A Five batsmen were absent hurt B It was India's lowest total in Tests C Four batsmen were out hit wicket – a first-class record D There were eight lbws, a Test record

Answers on page 172

THE MEN IN WHITE COATS

1 Who was the first umpire to stand in 50 Tests?

A David Shepherd **B** *Syd Buller* **C** *Steve Bucknor* **D** *Dickie Bird*

2 Who umpired in his 150th one-day international in 2004?

A Venkat **B** *Steve Bucknor* **C** *Rudi Koertzen* **D** *David Shepherd*

3 Which umpire stood in his 90th Test during 2004?

A Venkat **B** *Steve Bucknor* **C** *Rudi Koertzen* **D** *David Shepherd*

4 What's the real first name of the flamboyant New Zealand umpire "Billy" Bowden?

A Montague **B** *Brent* **C** *Claude* **D** *William*

5 Who played 26 Tests for England between 1976 and 1986, and had umpired in 25 by the end of 2003?

A Neil Mallender **B** *Mark Benson* **C** *Peter Willey* **D** *John Hampshire*

6 Which New Zealander umpired in exactly 100 one-day internationals before retiring in 2002?

A Brian Aldridge **B** *Fred Goodall* **C** *Doug Cowie* **D** *Steve Dunne*

7 Who was the popular Indian umpire of the late 1970s, notable for his ample girth?

A Swaroop Kishen **B** *Piloo Reporter* **C** *Hanumantha Rao* **D** *Ram Babu Gupta*

8 Which Worcestershire batsman lost an arm in the First World War, became an umpire, and stood in a then-record 48 Tests before retiring in 1953?

A Alex Skelding **B** *Syd Buller* **C** *Frank Chester* **D** *Hugo Yarnold*

9 Which umpire stood in the 1960-61 Tied Test, and later became chairman of the Australian Cricket Board?

A Phil Ridings **B** *Bob Merriman* **C** *Col Egar* **D** *Lou Rowan*

10 Who played cricket and rugby for New Zealand, and later umpired Tests and refereed rugby internationals as well?

A Brian McKechnie **B** *Eric Tindill* **C** *Eric Petrie* **D** *Merv Wallace*

11 Which Australian stood in his first Test in 1974, at Edgbaston, and gave Sunil Gavaskar out caught behind to the first ball of the match?

A Bill Alley **B** *Tom Brooks* **C** *Cec Pepper* **D** *Peter Wight*

The Googly

After a late withdrawal by the appointed official, Gerry Gomez umpired West Indies' Test against Australia at Georgetown in 1964-65. What was unusual about this?

A He was a Test selector at the time **B** *He'd never umpired before* **C** *He had played in the previous Test* **D** *His son was playing in the match*

Answers on page 173

DATELINES

1 In which year was the first official one-day international played at Melbourne?

A 1961 B 1967 C 1971 D 1977

2 And in which year was the first Test match played, also at Melbourne?

A 1864 B 1877 C 1880 D 1884

3 In which year was the one-day Gillette Cup introduced in England?

A 1939 B 1948 C 1956 D 1963

4 In which year was the first men's World Cup played?

A 1965 B 1975 C 1978 D 1979

5 The women beat the men to staging a World Cup – when was their first one?

A 1954 B 1964 C 1971 D 1973

6 In which year did Brian Lara break both the Test and the first-class batting record for the highest score?

A 1994 B 1995 C 1996 D 1998

7 When did Don Bradman score 974 runs in a five-Test series in England?

A 1930 B 1934 C 1938 D 1948

8 In which year was the Marylebone Cricket Club founded?

A 1737 B 1787 C 1814 D 1837

9 And in which year did MCC first admit women as members?

A 1919 B 1947 C 1992 D 1998

10 In which year was Twenty20 cricket started in England?

A 1997 B 1999 C 2001 D 2003

11 In which year was Test cricket's first Triangular Tournament played?

A 1899 B 1912 C 1939 D 1979

The Googly

In which calendar year did the record for the highest Test score change hands twice in just over three months?

A 1912 B 1930 C 1938 D 2003

Answers on page 173

BETTER THAN AVERAGE

1 Who made four tours of England, and topped the overall first-class batting averages each time?

   A Viv Richards B Allan Border C George Headley D Don Bradman

2 Who topped the English first-class batting averages in 1999 (for Essex) and 2003 (for Lancashire)?

   A Ronnie Irani B Stuart Law C Carl Hooper D John Crawley

3 Which overseas player topped the English first-class bowling averages four times between 1981 and 1987?

   A Andy Roberts B Joel Garner C Richard Hadlee D Malcolm Marshall

4 Who averaged more than 100 with the bat in both the 1971 and 1979 English seasons?

   A John Edrich B Geoff Boycott C Zaheer Abbas D Dennis Amiss

5 Which West Indian topped the English first-class batting averages in 1963 and 1966, and again in 1970?

   A Rohan Kanhai B Garry Sobers C Conrad Hunte D Basil Butcher

6 Which 19th-century England bowler took 112 Test wickets at the record-low average of 10.75?

   A George Lohmann B Johnny Briggs C Tom Richardson D Jack Hearne

7 Don Bradman averaged 99.94 in Tests – of those who played more than 15 matches and finished their career by 2000, who lies second, with 60.97?

   A Herbert Sutcliffe B Graeme Pollock C Javed Miandad D George Headley

8 Bradman averaged 95.14 in first-class cricket – who (of those who had finished their career by 2000) is second on that list, with 71.22?

   A Allan Border B Sachin Tendulkar C Vijay Merchant D Bill Ponsford

9 Who averaged 101.70 in first-class cricket in England in 1990?

   A Graham Gooch B Graeme Hick C Jimmy Cook D Mark Ramprakash

10 Who averaged 102, with the aid of 16 not-outs from 17 innings, on tour in England in 1953?

   A Sonny Ramadhin B Bill Johnston C Fazal Mahmood D Neil Adcock

11 Who is the only person who played more than a dozen Tests (before 2000) whose batting average never dipped below 60?

   A Javed Miandad B Don Bradman C Herbert Sutcliffe D George Headley

The Googly

Who topped the English first-class bowling averages in 1964, and won an FA Cup-winners' medal the same year?

A Graham Cross B Jim Standen C Chris Balderstone D Jim Cumbes

Answers on page 173

AUSTRALIA v PAKISTAN

1 When Pakistan were bowled out for 59 and 53 in a Test in 2002-03, which Australian scored more than their combined totals in his one innings of 119?

A Steve Waugh B Matthew Hayden C Ricky Ponting D Mark Waugh

2 Who, at Melbourne in 1978-79, took 9 for 86, including a spell in which he took seven wickets for one run?

A Abdul Qadir B Rodney Hogg C Sarfraz Nawaz D Imran Khan

3 What was Pakistan's margin of victory in the first Test at Karachi in 1994-95?

A An innings and 238 runs B One run C One wicket D Three runs

4 Who took 12 wickets to help Pakistan win the 1976-77 Sydney Test?

A Sikander Bakht B Iqbal Qasim C Sarfraz Nawaz D Imran Khan

5 Who dismissed Colin McDonald with his first ball in Test cricket, at Karachi in 1959-60?

A Intikhab Alam B Nasim-ul-Ghani C Mushtaq Mohammad D Mohammad Munaf

6 Who took a hat-trick on his Test debut for Australia at Rawalpindi in 1994-95?

A Jo Angel B Shane Warne C Paul Reiffel D Damien Fleming

7 Which batsman was the third victim in that hat-trick, after having scored 237?

A Aamir Sohail B Salim Malik C Saeed Anwar D Inzamam-ul-Haq

8 Who scored 166 on his Test debut for Pakistan at Karachi in 1964-65?

A Asif Iqbal B Billy Ibadulla C Majid Khan D Shafqat Rana

9 Who took 6 for 15, in only his second Test, as Australia pulled off a surprising victory over Pakistan at Sydney in 1972-73?

A Jeff Thomson B Max Walker C Dennis Lillee D Ashley Mallett

10 Who scored 210 not out, the highest Test score by a wicket-keeper at that time, at Faisalabad in 1979-80?

A Ashraf Ali B Taslim Arif C Rod Marsh D Salim Yousuf

11 Who, in December 1959, became the only American president known to have attended a Test match, the fourth day of the third Test at Karachi?

A John Kennedy B Richard Nixon C Lyndon Johnson D Dwight Eisenhower

The Googly

Pakistan's home Test series against Australia in 2002-03 was shifted to neutral territory because of concerns over security. Two of the matches were held in Sharjah, but where was the first Test played?

A Abu Dhabi B Dhaka C Colombo D Dubai

Answers on page 173

HAMPSHIRE

1 Which Australian Test player captained Hampshire in 2004?

A Simon Katich B Ricky Ponting C Michael Clarke D Shane Warne

2 Who scored 138 hundreds, and nearly 49,000 runs, for Hampshire between 1905 and 1936?

A George Brown B Philip Mead C Frank Woolley D Lionel Tennyson

3 Who captained Hampshire to their first County Championship title, in 1961?

A Roy Marshall B Peter Sainsbury C Colin Ingleby-Mackenzie D Richard Gilliat

4 Which player, who first appeared for Hampshire in 2000, is the son of a Hampshire player and the grandson of an England Test cricketer?

A Dimitri Mascarenhas B Liam Botham C Chris Tremlett D James Hamblin

5 Who took 2669 wickets in his career for Hampshire (1948-69) at an average below 19?

A Derek Shackleton B Peter Sainsbury C Vic Cannings D Bob Cottam

6 In which town have Hampshire played home games at a ground called Dean Park?

A Bournemouth B Basingstoke C Cowes D Portsmouth

7 Which Hampshire player scored 4236 runs in 62 Tests for England?

A Philip Mead B Robin Smith C Chris Smith D David Gower

8 In which year did Hampshire start playing at their new Rose Bowl ground?

A 1999 B 2000 C 2001 D 2002

9 Who captained Hampshire for ten years from 1985?

A Nick Pocock B Paul Terry C Mark Nicholas D Robin Smith

10 Which Hampshire batsman played one Test for England, in 1931, and won one international soccer cap for England too?

A Johnny Arnold B Jim Bailey C George Brown D Lofty Herman

11 Which Hampshire player captained England against Australia in 1921?

A Alex Kennedy B Lionel Tennyson C Freddie Gough-Calthorpe D George Brown

The Googly

Hampshire's lowest total is 15, against Warwickshire at Edgbaston in 1922. What was the result of the match?

*A Warwickshire won by an innings B It was a tie C Warwickshire won by 155 runs
D Hampshire won by 155 runs*

Answers on page 173

THE ASHES 1985

1 Which man, who eventually captained in five Ashes series, was in charge for his first in 1985?

A Allan Border B Steve Waugh C Mike Gatting D David Gower

2 Who was England's wicket-keeper throughout the series?

A Bob Taylor B Bruce French C Jack Richards D Paul Downton

3 Who scored 175 in the first Test, on his debut against Australia?

A Tim Robinson B Bill Athey C Chris Broad D Mike Gatting

4 And who scored 196 in the second Test at Lord's, which helped Australia square the series?

A Allan Border B Greg Ritchie C Graeme Wood D David Boon

5 Which 38-year-old took 5 for 68 in the Lord's Test?

A John Emburey B Bob Holland C Phil Edmonds D Murray Bennett

6 Who was Australia's wicket-keeper in this series, who was out in controversial circumstances in the fifth Test at Edgbaston?

A Rod Marsh B Steve Rixon C Wayne Phillips D Ian Healy

7 Who took his 200th Test wicket – his 100th against England – at Edgbaston?

A Terry Alderman B Jeff Thomson C Geoff Lawson D Dennis Lillee

8 Who played in the last two matches of the series, was on the winning side in both, but never played again for England?

A Arnie Sidebottom B Les Taylor C Richard Ellison D David Bairstow

9 Who scored a total of 732 runs in the series?

A Allan Border B Graham Gooch C Tim Robinson D David Gower

10 Who, in the final Test at The Oval, made his first century against Australia, in his 40th innings against them?

A Graham Gooch B Mike Gatting C John Emburey D Allan Lamb

11 Who played only his second Test against England, four years after making a hundred in his first ... both matches being at The Oval?

A Andrew Hilditch B Dean Jones C Greg Ritchie D Dirk Wellham

The Googly

Which man, who went on to play 87 one-day internationals for Australia, won only six Test caps – five of them in England in 1985?

A Greg Ritchie B Peter Taylor C Greg Matthews D Simon O'Donnell

Answers on page 173

DOUBLING UP

1 Who scored more than 1000 runs in Tests for both Australia and South Africa?

   A Alan Kippax B Peter Kirsten C Kepler Wessels D David Hookes

2 Who played one-day internationals for Scotland and a Test for England?

   A Gavin Hamilton B Peter Such C Dougie Brown D Mike Denness

3 Who scored a century on Test debut for England, and later captained India?

   A K.S. Ranjitsinhji B Douglas Jardine C K.S. Duleepsinhji D Nawab of Pataudi senior

4 Which man played one-day internationals for New Zealand, and was briefly the All-Blacks' leading rugby union try-scorer?

   A Jeff Wilson B Bruce Blair C Christian Cullen D Stu Wilson

5 And which rugby union All-Black was the non-striker when Trevor Chappell unfurled his infamous underarm delivery at the end of a one-day international in 1980-81?

   A Brian Lochore B Brian McKechnie C Bob Cunis D Jock Edwards

6 Which Test cricketer was a junior tennis champion, who at 16 beat Johan Kriek (the 1982 Australian Open champion), and after his Test career was over took up archery?

   A Jonty Rhodes B Graeme Pollock C Kepler Wessels D Jimmy Cook

7 Which Test regular of the 1990s was asked to make himself available for the South African hockey team at the 1996 Olympics, but declined?

   A Andrew Hudson B Jonty Rhodes C Hansie Cronje D Daryll Cullinan

8 Who captained South Africa at cricket in the 1950s, after playing rugby union for England?

   A Paul Winslow B Jack Cheetham C Clive van Ryneveld D Tony Harris

9 Who kept wicket for West Indies in New Zealand in 1951-52, emigrated there, and four years later kept wicket for New Zealand against West Indies?

   A Alfie Binns B Bruce Pairaudeau C Sammy Guillen D Clairmonte Depeiza

10 Which contemporary of W.G. Grace is the only man to play for England against Australia, and also for Australia against England, in Tests?

   A Jack Ferris B Billy Murdoch C Charlie Turner D Billy Midwinter

11 Who was banned from his native Sri Lanka for joining a rebel tour of South Africa, and later played for Holland in the World Cup?

   A Flavian Aponso B Johanne Samarasekera C Rohan Jayasekera D Roland Lefebvre

The Googly

India's Cota Ramaswami and Ralph Legall of West Indies are the only Test cricketers who have also done what in sport?

A Played hockey at the Olympics B Managed a national football team
C Played Davis Cup tennis D Won an event on the Asian golf tour

Answers on page 173

WISDEN CRICKETER OF THE 20TH CENTURY: GARRY SOBERS

1 On which Caribbean island was Sobers born?

A Antigua B Barbados C Jamaica D Trinidad

2 Sobers didn't make a century until his 17th Test, but when he eventually did, how many did he score?

A 174 not out B 198 C 226 D 365 not out

3 Where was that innings played?

A Kingston, Jamaica B Bridgetown, Barbados C St John's, Antigua D Georgetown, Guyana

4 Who was the bowler when Sobers became the first batsman to hit six sixes in an over in first-class cricket?

A Peter Walker B Barry Lloyd C Malcolm Nash D Don Shepherd

5 Who was Sobers playing for in that match?

A West Indians B Northamptonshire C Nottinghamshire D Rest of the World XI

6 How many of the distinguished panel of 100 which chose the Wisden Cricketers of the Century voted for Sobers?

A 70 B 80 C 90 D 100

7 With whom did Sobers share a partnership of 446 against Pakistan in 1957-58?

A Clyde Walcott B Everton Weekes C Conrad Hunte D Seymour Nurse

8 Where did Sobers play an innings of 254 for a World XI that Don Bradman said was the best innings he'd ever seen in Australia?

A Adelaide B Brisbane C Melbourne D Sydney

9 With which other batsman did Sobers bat through two whole days of a Test against England in 1959-60?

A Joe Solomon B Basil Butcher C Frank Worrell D Everton Weekes

10 Who was Sobers's Test-playing cousin, with whom he shared a match-saving stand in the 1966 Lord's Test?

A Conrad Hunte B Lance Gibbs C Charlie Davis D David Holford

11 For which Australian state did Sobers have two very successful seasons in the early 1960s?

A New South Wales B Queensland C South Australia D Western Australia

The Googly

Garry Sobers's first Test wicket, in 1953-54, was that of a man who later wrote a biography of him. Who was it?

A Richie Benaud B Trevor Bailey C Jim Laker D Ian Peebles

Answers on page 173

THE 1975 WORLD CUP

1   Which country won the inaugural World Cup?

   A Australia B New Zealand C Pakistan D West Indies

2   Who captained the winning team?

   A Rohan Kanhai B Ian Chappell C Clive Lloyd D Greg Chappell

3   Who was the Man of the Match in the final?

   A Ian Chappell B Roy Fredericks C Clive Lloyd D Dennis Lillee

4   Who was a late replacement in the West Indian squad for the injured Garry Sobers?

   A Rohan Kanhai B Keith Boyce C Maurice Foster D John Shepherd

5   How many Australians were run out in the final?

   A One B Three C Five D Seven

6   Who did West Indies beat in their semi-final at The Oval?

   A India B New Zealand C Pakistan D Sri Lanka

7   Who took 6 for 14 – and scored a vital 28 not out – in the low-scoring Headingley semi-final?

   A Jeff Thomson B Gary Gilmour C Max Walker D Dennis Lillee

8   Apart from Sri Lanka, which non-Test-playing team took part?

   A Holland B United States C Canada D East Africa

9   Who scored 78 for West Indies in their group match at The Oval, including a memorable assault on Dennis Lillee while wearing only a bright red floppy hat on his head?

   A Alvin Kallicharran B Gordon Greenidge C Viv Richards D Roy Fredericks

10   Who scored two not-out centuries in the tournament – 114 against India and 171 against East Africa?

   A Keith Fletcher B Glenn Turner C Zaheer Abbas D Dennis Amiss

11   Who scored a hundred before lunch in Australia's group match against Sri Lanka at The Oval?

   A Alan Turner B Rick McCosker C Greg Chappell D Doug Walters

The Googly

While Clive Lloyd was hurtling to a century in the final at Lord's, who remained scoreless for one period of 11 overs, while compiling a more sedate 55?

A Gordon Greenidge B Alvin Kallicharran C Rohan Kanhai D Deryck Murray

Answers on page 173

INDIA v PAKISTAN

1 Who scored the first triple-century in these matches, early in 2004?

   A Sachin Tendulkar **B** *Inzamam-ul-Haq* **C** *Virender Sehwag* **D** *Rahul Dravid*

2 Who took all ten wickets in an innings against Pakistan at Delhi in 1998-99?

   A Anil Kumble **B** *Javagal Srinath* **C** *Harbhajan Singh* **D** *Venkatesh Prasad*

3 Who scored 231 and shared a record-equalling partnership of 451 with Javed Miandad at Hyderabad in 1982-83?

   A Mohsin Khan **B** *Mudassar Nazar* **C** *Qasim Omar* **D** *Salim Malik*

4 Who, in successive innings in the 1978-79 series, scored 176, 96 and 235 not out?

   A Javed Miandad **B** *Sunil Gavaskar* **C** *Dilip Vengsarkar* **D** *Zaheer Abbas*

5 Who took 99 wickets in Tests between India and Pakistan?

   A Abdul Qadir **B** *Bishan Bedi* **C** *Kapil Dev* **D** *Imran Khan*

6 How many successive draws did India and Pakistan play out between 1952-53 and 1960-61?

   A 10 **B** *12* **C** *16* **D** *19*

7 And how many years elapsed between 1960-61 and the next series?

   A 12 **B** *15* **C** *18* **D** *21*

8 Who was no-balled for throwing during the 1960-61 Bombay Test?

   A Haseeb Ahsan **B** *Jasu Patel* **C** *Fergie Gupte* **D** *Mahmood Hussain*

9 Who captained India for the only time during the 1989-90 series in Pakistan?

   A Sandeep Patil **B** *Ravi Shastri* **C** *Kris Srikkanth* **D** *Kiran More*

10 And who captained Pakistan for the only time in Tests in the 1979-80 series, and retired when they lost?

   A Asif Iqbal **B** *Mushtaq Mohammad* **C** *Majid Khan* **D** *Zaheer Abbas*

11 Who, in 1952-53, was the first Indian to score a century on his Test debut against Pakistan?

   A Madhav Apte **B** *Vijay Manjrekar* **C** *Kripal Singh* **D** *Deepak Shodhan*

The Googly

Why did the umpires, Shakoor Rana and Khalid Aziz, hold up play for 11 minutes at the start of the final day in the Test between Pakistan and India at Faisalabad in 1978-79?

A They said the Indian captain had sworn at them **B** *There were no bails*
C There were no balls **D** *The TV cameras were not switched on*

Answers on page 174

WORCESTERSHIRE

1 Which Worcestershire player, later their chairman, was also a famous batmaker?

   A Stuart Surridge **B** *Gray Nicolls* **C** *John Newbery* **D** *Duncan Fearnley*

2 Which Worcestershire player scored 158 in the 1968 Oval Test against Australia?

   A Tom Graveney **B** *Don Kenyon* **C** *Peter Richardson* **D** *Basil D'Oliveira*

3 Which Worcestershire player scored 106 in a one-day international for England at The Oval in 2003?

   A Gareth Batty **B** *Vikram Solanki* **C** *Ben Smith* **D** *Graeme Hick*

4 Who took 2143 wickets for Worcestershire between 1930 and 1955?

   A Roly Jenkins **B** *Fred Root* **C** *Reg Perks* **D** *Dick Howorth*

5 Who captained Worcestershire from 1959 to 1967, and led them to their first two Championship titles?

   A Tom Graveney **B** *Ken Graveney* **C** *Martin Horton* **D** *Don Kenyon*

6 Who hit 180 not out in a NatWest Trophy match for Worcestershire in 1994, and 160 in a Sunday League game in 1991?

   A Damian D'Oliveira **B** *Ian Botham* **C** *Tim Curtis* **D** *Tom Moody*

7 Which wicket-keeper made 100 dismissals for Worcestershire in 1964?

   A Laurie Johnson **B** *Roy Booth* **C** *Rodney Cass* **D** *Gordon Wilcock*

8 In which town have Worcestershire staged home games at a ground called Amblecote?

   A Stourbridge **B** *Kidderminster* **C** *Hereford* **D** *Evesham*

9 Who took two hat-tricks in the same Championship match for Worcestershire in 1949?

   A Roly Jenkins **B** *Dick Howorth* **C** *Reg Perks* **D** *Jack Flavell*

10 Which South African Test fast bowler took 67 wickets for Worcestershire in 2003?

   A Justin Kemp **B** *Andy Bichel* **C** *Andrew Hall* **D** *Nantie Hayward*

11 Which Worcestershire player was Man of the Match in the first Gillette Cup final in 1963, even though he finished on the losing side?

   A Tom Graveney **B** *Norman Gifford* **C** *Len Coldwell* **D** *Basil D'Oliveira*

The Googly

Who resigned as Worcestershire's captain in the middle of a match in 2004?

   A Graeme Hick **B** *Ben Smith* **C** *Tom Moody* **D** *Steven Rhodes*

Answers on page 174

DATELINES 2

1 In which year did Brian Lara break the world-record Test score for the second time?
   A 1994 B 1998 C 2003 D 2004

2 In which year did Kerry Packer's World Series Cricket disrupt the game?
   A 1968 B 1977 C 1980 D 1982

3 In which English season did Denis Compton score 3816 first-class runs?
   A 1937 B 1947 C 1951 D 1955

4 In which year did Sussex win the County Championship for the first time?
   A 1898 B 1998 C 2001 D 2003

5 In which year did Geoff Boycott score his 100th first-class century in a Test?
   A 1971 B 1973 C 1977 D 1981

6 In which year did Graham Thorpe score a century on his Test debut?
   A 1993 B 1995 C 1997 D 1999

7 Which was the only year in the 20th century when England beat Australia at Lord's?
   A 1902 B 1934 C 1968 D 1985

8 In which year did Scotland play in their first cricket World Cup?
   A 1983 B 1996 C 1999 D 2003

9 In which year did W.G. Grace play his final Test match, when he was 50?
   A 1882 B 1894 C 1899 D 1905

10 In which year were England "blackwashed" 5-0 at home by West Indies for the first time?
   A 1973 B 1976 C 1980 D 1984

11 In which year did England play the Rest of the World in a series of five unofficial Tests?
   A 1960 B 1965 C 1970 D 1973

The Googly
In which year were eight-ball overs used in English first-class cricket for the only time?
A 1914 B 1919 C 1939 D 1946

Answers on page 174

AUSTRALIA IN TESTS

1   On which Australian ground was the first Test of all played?

   A Adelaide B Brisbane C Melbourne D Sydney

2   Who captained Australia in the 1981 Ashes series in England?

   A Allan Border B Kim Hughes C Greg Chappell D Graham Yallop

3   Which Australian Test player is the brother-in-law of England's Craig White?

   A Andrew Symonds B Justin Langer C Darren Lehmann D Matthew Hayden

4   Who took 5 for 84 on his Test debut in 1970-71, and finished up with 355 Test wickets?

   A Ashley Mallett B Max Walker C Jeff Thomson D Dennis Lillee

5   Which man played 79 Tests for Australia but captained them for the only time at Lord's in 1961?

   A Neil Harvey B Norman O'Neill C Ray Lindwall D Richie Benaud

6   Which batsman, who made his Test debut in 1993, was out in the nineties nine times in Tests?

   A Mark Taylor B Michael Slater C Mark Waugh D Steve Waugh

7   Who took over as Australia's captain after Don Bradman retired in 1948?

   A Bill Brown B Keith Miller C Ian Johnson D Lindsay Hassett

8   Which Australian batsman scored 307 against England at Melbourne in 1965-66?

   A Bill Lawry B Bob Simpson C Bob Cowper D Doug Walters

9   Which Australian fast bowler of the 1970s started life with the surname "Durtanovich"?

   A Dennis Lillee B Len Pascoe C Geoff Dymock D Jeff Thomson

10   Where in Australia is the Test ground called the Marrara Oval?

   A Hobart B Canberra C Cairns D Darwin

11   Which Australian was the first bowler from any country to take 200 Test wickets?

   A Clarrie Grimmett B Bill O'Reilly C Fred Spofforth D Ray Lindwall

The Googly

Who stepped in as a makeshift opener after an injury in Australia's third Test in England in 1972 and scored 170 not out in only his second Test, so was duly selected to open in the next match ... and bagged a pair?

A Graeme Watson B Bruce Francis C Ross Edwards D Rick McCosker

Answers on page 174

ENGLISH DOMESTIC CRICKET

1 Which county won a record 30th Championship title in 2001?

A Essex B Nottinghamshire C Surrey D Yorkshire

2 Which county won seven successive Championship titles in the 1950s?

A Kent B Lancashire C Surrey D Yorkshire

3 Which county won the first two limited-overs Gillette Cups (1963-64)?

A Essex B Kent C Sussex D Warwickshire

4 And which county won the first two Sunday League titles (1969-70)

A Essex B Lancashire C Middlesex D Worcestershire

5 Which county joined the Championship in 1992?

A Durham B Herefordshire C Leicestershire D Somerset

6 And which was the previous county before them to join, in 1921?

A Cambridgeshire B Essex C Glamorgan D Northamptonshire

7 Which county won the Championship, the Sunday League and the Benson & Hedges Cup in 1994?

A Essex B Somerset C Warwickshire D Worcestershire

8 Which county won all three domestic one-day competitions in 2000?

A Glamorgan B Gloucestershire C Surrey D Warwickshire

9 Which county won the Sunday League for the first time in 1983 – but were also bottom of the Championship for the first time in their history?

A Derbyshire B Middlesex C Surrey D Yorkshire

10 Which side won the Minor Counties Championship four years running from 1994?

A Cheshire B Devon C Lincolnshire D Staffordshire

11 In which year were batting and bowling bonus points introduced to the Championship?

A 1928 B 1948 C 1968 D 1982

The Googly

Which man, who was killed in the Second World War, played only ten seasons of first-class cricket, yet won seven County Championship titles in that time?

A Ken Farnes B Maurice Leyland C Hedley Verity D Maurice Turnbull

Answers on page 174

WISDEN CRICKETER OF THE 20TH CENTURY: VIV RICHARDS

1 On which Caribbean island was Richards born?

A Antigua B Barbados C Grenada D St Lucia

2 What is Richards's rarely used first name?

A Ian B Irving C Isaac D Immanuel

3 At which other sport did Richards represent his island in internationals?

A Football B Basketball C Clay-pigeon shooting D Volleyball

4 Richards played county cricket for Somerset and which other side?

A Glamorgan B Gloucestershire C Sussex D Durham

5 Where did Richards score 291 against England in 1976?

A St John's, Antigua B Trent Bridge, Nottingham C The Oval D Georgetown, Guyana

6 And where did he hammer 189 not out in a one-day international against England in 1984?

A Lahore B Headingley, Leeds C Old Trafford, Manchester D Kingston, Jamaica

7 What's the name of Richards's son, who was on the Middlesex staff in 2004?

A Viv junior B Mali C Courtney D Denali

8 Against whom did Richards score 192 not out, his maiden Test century, in 1974-75?

A Australia B India C New Zealand D Pakistan

9 Against whom did Richards score a county-record 322 for Somerset in 1985?

A Derbyshire B Essex C Warwickshire D Worcestershire

10 Which two teams compete for the Sir Vivian Richards Trophy?

*A Antigua and Barbuda B West Indies and South Africa C Somerset and Glamorgan
D West Indies and Pakistan*

11 Which bowler dismissed Richards for 60 in his last Test innings, at The Oval in 1991?

A Phil Tufnell B Ian Botham C Chris Lewis D David "Syd" Lawrence

The Googly

Which newsreader wrote an "authorised biography" of Viv Richards in 1984?

A Jeremy Paxman B Reginald Bosanquet C Trevor McDonald D David Dimbleby

Answers on page 174

THE 1979 WORLD CUP

1 Who won the second World Cup?

   A Australia *B England* *C India* *D West Indies*

2 Who captained the winners?

   A Viv Richards *B Graham Gooch* *C Clive Lloyd* *D Mike Brearley*

3 Who was the Man of the Match in the final?

   A Joel Garner *B Viv Richards* *C Colin Croft* *D Desmond Haynes*

4 Who blasted a rapid 86 in the final at Lord's?

   A Gordon Greenidge *B Clive Lloyd* *C Collis King* *D Ian Botham*

5 Which team did Sri Lanka beat, for their first victory in an official one-day international?

   A India *B New Zealand* *C Pakistan* *D England*

6 Apart from Sri Lanka, which non-Test-playing country took part?

   A East Africa *B Bangladesh* *C Canada* *D Zimbabwe*

7 Who took 5 for 38 in the final?

   A Mike Hendrick *B Ian Botham* *C Colin Croft* *D Joel Garner*

8 Which team did England bowl out for 45?

   A India *B New Zealand* *C Canada* *D Sri Lanka*

9 Who were the two beaten semi-finalists?

   A New Zealand and Pakistan *B Pakistan and India* *C India and Sri Lanka*
   D Sri Lanka and New Zealand

10 Who scored the only hundred in the tournament apart from Viv Richards's in the final?

   A Glenn Turner *B Gordon Greenidge* *C Majid Khan* *D David Gower*

11 Who captained Pakistan, as he had in 1975, even though he still hadn't skippered them in a Test match?

   A Asif Iqbal *B Imran Khan* *C Mushtaq Mohammad* *D Zaheer Abbas*

The Googly

For the last ball of West Indies' innings in the 1979 final at Lord's Viv Richards sauntered across his stumps and flicked the ball high into the Mound Stand for a nonchalant six over square leg. Who was the disbelieving bowler?

A Ian Botham *B Bob Willis* *C Mike Hendrick* *D Chris Old*

Answers on page 174

ONE-DAY SPECIALISTS

1 Who played 94 one-day internationals for Australia before finally making his Test debut in March 2004?

    A Andrew Symonds *B Michael Bevan* *C Ian Harvey* *D Martin Love*

2 And who played 76 one-dayers for Australia before making his Test debut in 1999-2000?

    A Adam Gilchrist *B Andy Bichel* *C Michael Bevan* *D Darren Lehmann*

3 Who took 108 one-day wickets for Australia – but only six in Tests?

    A Tom Moody *B Peter Taylor* *C Carl Rackemann* *D Simon O'Donnell*

4 Who played his first Test for India in 2003-04, after winning 73 one-day caps?

    A Mohammad Kaif *B Hemang Badani* *C Rohan Gavaskar* *D Yuvraj Singh*

5 Which medium-pacer played 55 one-dayers for New Zealand before winning his first Test cap in 1994?

    A Rod Latham *B Gavin Larsen* *C Chris Harris* *D Chris Pringle*

6 Who played his second Test for West Indies in May 2004 – and won his 100th one-day cap later in the year?

    A Wavell Hinds *B Ryan Hinds* *C Ricardo Powell* *D Ian Bradshaw*

7 Who kept wicket for England throughout the 1983 World Cup, but never did play in a Test?

    A Geoff Humpage *B David Bairstow* *C Ian Gould* *D Bobby Parks*

8 Who played 54 one-dayers for Sri Lanka, but only four Tests, despite scoring a double-century on his debut?

    A Sidath Wettimuny *B Brendon Kuruppu* *C Ruwan Kalpage* *D Uvaisul Karnain*

9 Who played 66 one-dayers for Pakistan before his first Test, which was in 1998-99?

    A Abdul Razzaq *B Shoaib Malik* *C Azhar Mahmood* *D Shahid Afridi*

10 Which future umpire played ten one-dayers for England, all in 1982-83, but never won a Test cap?

    A John Steele *B Jack Birkenshaw* *C Trevor Jesty* *D Barry Dudleston*

11 Who played 29 one-dayers for South Africa, scoring a then-record 169 not out in one of them, but never won a Test cap?

    A Adrian Kuiper *B Justin Kemp* *C Alan Dawson* *D Dave Callaghan*

The Googly

Who averaged over 50 with the bat in his 93-Test career, but played only one one-day international, in which he was out for 0?

    A Geoff Boycott *B Bill Lawry* *C Colin Cowdrey* *D Garry Sobers*

Answers on page 174

THE FIRST TIED TEST

1 On which ground was the Tied Test between Australia and West Indies played in 1960-61?

   A Adelaide B Brisbane C Georgetown D Sydney

2 Who was Australia's captain?

   A Neil Harvey B Bill Lawry C Bob Simpson D Richie Benaud

3 And who captained West Indies?

   A Garry Sobers B Frank Worrell C Rohan Kanhai D John Goddard

4 Who scored a memorable century in West Indies' first innings?

   A Garry Sobers B Conrad Hunte C Rohan Kanhai D Frank Worrell

5 Which player scored 100 runs and took 10 wickets in the match?

   A Alan Davidson B Garry Sobers C Richie Benaud D Frank Worrell

6 Who smashed 181 in Australia's first innings?

   A Colin McDonald B Peter Burge C Norman O'Neill D Neil Harvey

7 Who was the West Indian wicket-keeper in the match?

   A Gerry Alexander B Deryck Murray C Rohan Kanhai D Cammie Smith

8 Which famous commentator missed the end of the match, after assuming it would be a draw and taking an early flight home?

   A Alan McGilvray B Brian Johnston C Jack Fingleton D Jim Swanton

9 Who bowled the fateful last over of the match?

   A Alf Valentine B Garry Sobers C Frank Worrell D Wes Hall

10 Whose side-on throw from square leg broke the stumps to run out the last Australian batsman and force the tie?

   A Cammie Smith B Basil Butcher C Conrad Hunte D Joe Solomon

11 And who was the batsman run out going for the winning single?

   A Ian Meckiff B Wally Grout C Lindsay Kline D Ken Mackay

The Googly

Which man, who played in the first tied Test, was involved in an official capacity in the next tied Test, between India and Australia at Madras in 1986-87?

A Richie Benaud B Bob Simpson C Wes Hall D Alan Davidson

Answers on page 174

GROUNDS AROUND THE WORLD

1 On which Australian Test ground would you find The Hill?

   A Adelaide B Brisbane C Melbourne D Sydney

2 And on which one would you find the huge Great Southern Stand?

   A Adelaide B Brisbane C Melbourne D Sydney

3 On which Test ground in England might someone bowl from the Kirkstall Lane End?

   *A Edgbaston, Birmingham B Headingley, Leeds C Old Trafford, Manchester
   D Bramall Lane, Sheffield*

4 And on which one is there a Radcliffe Road End?

   A Lord's B Trent Bridge, Nottingham C Chester-le-Street D The Oval

5 At which ground in the Caribbean might you sit in the George Headley Stand?

   *A Georgetown, Guyana B Bridgetown, Barbados C Kingston, Jamaica
   D Port-of-Spain, Trinidad*

6 Which ground held its first Test, a match between Pakistan and West Indies, in 2002 –
nearly 18 years after first staging a one-day international?

   A Sheikhupura B St George's, Grenada C Sharjah D Sialkot

7 Where in South Africa is Springbok Park, which staged its first Test match in October
1999?

   A Kimberley B Bloemfontein C Potchefstroom D East London

8 Which English county ground has a Nackington Road End?

   A Leicester B Canterbury C Chelmsford D Derby

9 Which ground, in 1981, became West Indies' first new Test venue for more than 50 years?

   *A St John's, Antigua B Beausejour Stadium, St Lucia C Kingstown, St Vincent
   D St George's, Grenada*

10 Which team played a one-day international at Lord's for the first time in 2004?

   A West Indies B Bangladesh C New Zealand D Holland

11 Which Test ground in England has a two-sided stand that faces the cricket ground on one
side and a rugby ground on the other?

   A Lord's B Edgbaston, Birmingham C Headingley, Leeds D Old Trafford, Manchester

The Googly

Which is the only ground to have staged home Tests for two different countries, a neutral
Test in which neither country was at home, and several one-day internationals?

   *A Sharjah Stadium B Harare Sports Club C Old Trafford, Manchester
   D Bangabandhu National Stadium, Dhaka*

Answers on page 175

DATELINES 3

1 In which year did Shane Warne win a World Cup winners' medal?

   A 1987 B 1996 C 1999 D 2003

2 In which year did South Africa play their first Test after readmission to international cricket?

   A 1986 B 1988 C 1990 D 1992

3 In which year did Kenya beat West Indies in the World Cup?

   A 1987 B 1992 C 1996 D 1999

4 In which year did Graham Gooch score 333 against India at Lord's?

   A 1990 B 1992 C 1994 D 1996

5 In which year did England play simultaneous Test matches against New Zealand and West Indies?

   A 1912 B 1926 C 1930 D 1939

6 In which year did Jim Laker take 19 Australian wickets in the same Test?

   A 1948 B 1953 C 1956 D 1959

7 In which year did MCC celebrate their bicentenary with a gala match against the Rest of the World?

   A 1987 B 1990 C 1992 D 1995

8 In which year did Pakistan win a Test in England for the first time?

   A 1954 B 1971 C 1974 D 1982

9 In which year was the women's World Cup final played at Lord's for the first time – England won?

   A 1973 B 1988 C 1993 D 1996

10 In which year was the first Test match played in England, at The Oval?

   A 1876 B 1878 C 1880 D 1882

11 In which year did David Steele endear himself to the public with his plucky displays against Australia?

   A 1975 B 1977 C 1979 D 1981

The Googly

In which year did England have four Test captains in the course of one five-Test series against West Indies?

A 1950 B 1976 C 1988 D 1995

Answers on page 175

WICKET-KEEPERS

1 Who kept wicket for Australia in both Centenary Tests, and later became an England selector?

A Steve Rixon B Rod Marsh C Wally Grout D Richie Robinson

2 Who was the first keeper to make 300 dismissals in one-day internationals?

A Adam Gilchrist B Mark Boucher C Ridley Jacobs D Nayan Mongia

3 Who was the first keeper to play in 100 Tests?

A Alan Knott B Ian Healy C Rod Marsh D Godfrey Evans

4 Who set a new Test record at Johannesburg in 1995-96 by taking 11 catches in the match?

A Alec Stewart B Mark Boucher C Jack Russell D Dave Richardson

5 Who was the first Pakistani to make 200 Test dismissals?

A Salim Yousuf B Imtiaz Ahmed C Moin Khan D Wasim Bari

6 And who was the first New Zealander to make 200?

A Adam Parore B Lee Germon C Ken Wadsworth D Ian Smith

7 Who is the only keeper to make 50 stumpings in Tests?

A Les Ames B Bert Oldfield C Godfrey Evans D Syed Kirmani

8 Who made a record 1649 first-class dismissals in a 28-year career behind the stumps?

A Herbert Strudwick B Bob Taylor C John Murray D Godfrey Evans

9 Who established a new first-class record in 1995-96 by making 13 dismissals in a match – in which he also scored 99 and 99 not out?

A Tahir Rashid B Wayne James C Tim Zoehrer D Darren Berry

10 Which recent England keeper called his autobiography *Taking It From Behind*?

A Steven Rhodes B Paul Downton C Richard Blakey D David Bairstow

11 Who was the first wicket-keeper to take 100 catches in Tests before he made a stumping?

A Jeff Dujon B Salim Yousuf C Alec Stewart D Dave Richardson

The Googly

When Bob Taylor was pulled out of the hospitality tent to keep wicket in the 1986 Lord's Test against New Zealand, who was the original wicket-keeper whose injury while batting led to the call for Taylor?

A Jack Richards B Bobby Parks C Bruce French D Paul Downton

Answers on page 175

DURHAM

1 Who was Durham's first captain in the County Championship?

A Tom Graveney B David Graveney C Ian Botham D Paul Parker

2 And who was Durham's first official overseas player?

A Manoj Prabhakar B Craig McDermott C Anderson Cummins D Dean Jones

3 What's the name of Durham's purpose-built ground at Chester-le-Street?

A The Rose Bowl B Reebok Stadium C The Riverside D The Stadium of Light

4 Which Australian captained Durham from 1997 to 1999?

A David Ligertwood B Allan Border C David Boon D Dean Jones

5 Which former Middlesex bowler, who became a TV commentator, played for Durham in the 1990s?

A Mike Selvey B Angus Fraser C Phil Tufnell D Simon Hughes

6 Before Durham gained first-class status, which county side did they upset in the 1973 Gillette Cup?

A Lancashire B Middlesex C Surrey D Yorkshire

7 Which Pakistan Test player made his debut for Durham in 2003?

A Shahid Afridi B Shoaib Akhtar C Shabbir Ahmed D Shadab Kabir

8 Which Durham bowler won his only Test cap against Pakistan at Lord's in 1996?

A Mike Smith B Phil Bainbridge C Simon Hughes D Simon Brown

9 Which hard-hitting England batsman of the 1960s was born in County Durham?

A Colin Cowdrey B Colin Milburn C Tom Graveney D Roger Prideaux

10 What's the name of the supposedly haunted castle that overlooks the ground at Chester-le-Street?

A Lumley Castle B Barnard Castle C Castle Howard D Fountains Abbey

11 Who made the highest score (81) in Chester-le-Street's inaugural Test match in 2003?

A Michael Vaughan B Alec Stewart C Travis Friend D Anthony McGrath

The Googly

What was unusual about Chris Scott's dropped catch for Durham against Warwickshire at Edgbaston in 1994?

A It broke his jaw B It dropped onto the wicket and the batsman was stumped instead C It cost 483 runs D It bounced off his cap and went for four

Answers on page 175

WISDEN CRICKETER OF THE 20TH CENTURY: JACK HOBBS

1 On which ground are the Hobbs Gates, which mark his distinguished service for his county?

A Leicester B Lord's C The Oval D Hove

2 In which Minor County was Hobbs born, in 1882?

A Staffordshire B Berkshire C Cambridgeshire D Lincolnshire

3 What was Hobbs's rather unusual middle name?

A Blaxland B Berry C Blundell D Barford

4 With whom did Hobbs share 15 century opening partnerships in Test matches, 11 of them against Australia?

A Wilfred Rhodes B Patsy Hendren C Herbert Sutcliffe D Frank Woolley

5 With whom did Hobbs share an opening stand of 352 against Warwickshire in 1909?

A Bobby Abel B Bill Brockwell C Tom Hayward D Donald Knight

6 And with which opener did he share a county stand of 428 in 1926?

A Andy Sandham B Percy Fender C Alfred Jeacocke D Douglas Jardine

7 Who was Hobbs's captain on his first tour of Australia, in 1907-08?

A Arthur Jones B Stanley Jackson C Pelham Warner D Johnny Douglas

8 And who was in charge on his last, in 1928-29?

A Arthur Carr B Arthur Gilligan C Percy Chapman D Ronny Stanyforth

9 How old was Hobbs when he played his final Test?

A 45 B 47 C 49 D 51

10 On which ground did Hobbs score more than 1000 Test runs – the first batsman to do this outside his own country?

A Johannesburg B Melbourne C Sydney D Durban

11 According to *Wisden*, Hobbs scored 197 centuries in first-class cricket. How many of them came after he was 40 years old?

A 13 B 46 C 71 D 98

The Googly

What was the name of the organisation founded by John Arlott to celebrate the life of his friend Hobbs with an annual dinner?

A The Master's Club B The Hobbs Society C The 197 Club D The Hobbits

Answers on page 175

NEW ZEALAND v INDIA OR PAKISTAN

1   Who scored 329 for Pakistan against New Zealand at Lahore in 2002?

   A Abdul Razzaq B Younis Khan C Inzamam-ul-Haq D Yousuf Youhana

2   Which player, who later coached India, scored 185 against them at Christchurch in 1989-90?

   A David Trist B John Bracewell C Geoff Howarth D John Wright

3   Who marked his debut for New Zealand with 109 and 5 for 68 against India at Calcutta in 1964-65?

   A Vic Pollard B Bruce Taylor C Bob Cunis D Ross Morgan

4   Who scored a century before lunch for Pakistan on the first day of the 1976-77 Karachi Test against New Zealand?

   A Asif Iqbal B Sadiq Mohammad C Majid Khan D Zaheer Abbas

5   Who took 7 for 52 (and 11 wickets in the match) for New Zealand against Pakistan at Faisalabad in 1990-91, but later admitted that he'd scratched the ball with a bottle-top?

   A Danny Morrison B Derek Stirling C Chris Cairns D Chris Pringle

6   Who scored New Zealand's first double-century against Pakistan, at Christchurch in 2000-01?

   A Nathan Astle B Stephen Fleming C Lou Vincent D Mathew Sinclair

7   Who scored 107 and 56 on his Test debut against Pakistan at Auckland in 1972-73 – and never played another Test?

   A Richard Anderson B Murray Parker C Peter Coman D Rodney Redmond

8   Which 19-year-old Pakistani scored 163 on his Test debut, against New Zealand at Lahore in 1976-77?

   A Mudassar Nazar B Javed Miandad C Wasim Raja D Zaheer Abbas

9   Which bowler, who later became an umpire, took 7 for 99 on his Test debut for Pakistan against New Zealand at Karachi in 1969-70?

   A Mohammad Nazir B Javed Akhtar C Shakoor Rana D Mahboob Shah

10 Which Indian batsman emulated his father in scoring a century on Test debut, against New Zealand at Auckland in 1975-76?

   A Aunshuman Gaekwad B Surinder Amarnath C Sanjay Manjrekar D Pronob Roy

11 Who scored two double-centuries against New Zealand in India in 1955-56?

   A Polly Umrigar B Vinoo Mankad C Vijay Manjrekar D Pankaj Roy

The Googly

Which Pakistani scored a century on debut against New Zealand at Lahore in 1996-97, and later went to live in New Zealand?

A Ali Naqvi B Basit Ali C Mohammad Wasim D Zahid Fazal

Answers on page 175

TEST BOWLING RECORDS

1 Who was the first bowler to take all ten wickets in a Test innings, in 1956?

   A Ray Lindwall **B** *Richie Benaud* **C** *Fred Trueman* **D** *Jim Laker*

2 And who was the second man to do it, more than 42 years later?

   A Shane Warne **B** *Muttiah Muralitharan* **C** *Anil Kumble* **D** *Devon Malcolm*

3 Which two bowlers were tied as Test cricket's leading wicket-taker, with 527, for a few weeks in 2004?

   A Walsh and Muralitharan **B** *Walsh and Warne* **C** *Muralitharan and Warne*
   D Wasim Akram and Warne

4 Who was the first South African to take 200 – and 300 – Test wickets?

   A Allan Donald **B** *Peter Pollock* **C** *Shaun Pollock* **D** *Hugh Tayfield*

5 Who was the second New Zealander after Richard Hadlee to take 200 Test wickets?

   A Danny Morrison **B** *Daniel Vettori* **C** *Chris Cairns* **D** *Lance Cairns*

6 Who bowled a record-breaking 98 overs in an innings for West Indies against England at Edgbaston in 1957?

   A Alf Valentine **B** *Lance Gibbs* **C** *Sonny Ramadhin* **D** *Garry Sobers*

7 Which bowler once took 49 wickets in a four-Test series?

   A Dennis Lillee **B** *Sydney Barnes* **C** *Imran Khan* **D** *Hugh Trumble*

8 Who took more than 40 wickets in an Ashes series in England in the 1980s ... twice?

   A Terry Alderman **B** *Geoff Lawson* **C** *Jeff Thomson* **D** *Dennis Lillee*

9 Who took four wickets in five balls, separated by a no-ball, for England against Pakistan at Edgbaston in 1978?

   A Geoff Arnold **B** *Bob Willis* **C** *Chris Old* **D** *Mike Hendrick*

10 Who became only the third Sri Lankan to take ten wickets in a Test, with 10 for 210 against Australia at Cairns in July 2004?

   A Lasith Malinga **B** *Nuwan Zoysa* **C** *Upul Chandana* **D** *Chaminda Vaas*

11 Who took ten wickets in each of three successive Tests in South Africa in 1935-36 ... and never played for Australia again?

   A Tim Wall **B** *Bill O'Reilly* **C** *Clarrie Grimmett* **D** *Bert Ironmonger*

The Googly

Who took his 100th wicket in his 90th Test, the most matches to reach this landmark?

A Ravi Shastri **B** *Garry Sobers* **C** *Carl Hooper* **D** *Greg Chappell*

Answers on page 175

THE ASHES 1986-87

1 Who captained England on this successful tour?

  A Graham Gooch B Ian Botham C Mike Gatting D David Gower

2 Who scored three hundreds for England in the series?

  A Bill Athey B David Gower C Chris Broad D Allan Lamb

3 Who hit a rapid 138, including 22 off one Merv Hughes over, in the first Test?

  A Allan Lamb B Ian Botham C Mike Gatting D David Gower

4 Who made his debut for England in the first Test, and scored 133 in the second?

  A Wilf Slack B Bill Athey C Jack Richards D Phillip DeFreitas

5 Which Australian made his debut in the final Test, after playing only once for his state in the season, and took 6 for 78?

  A Peter Sleep B Peter Taylor C Craig McDermott D Peter McIntyre

6 Who, during this series, became the tallest player to appear in Ashes Tests, at 6ft 8ins?

  A Graham Dilley B Bruce Reid C Chris Matthews D Tony Greig

7 Who kept wicket for Australia in four of the five Tests?

  A Ian Healy B Wayne Phillips C Tim Zoehrer D Greg Dyer

8 Who scored 110 in the first Test, his first match against England?

  A Greg Matthews B David Boon C Geoff Marsh D Dean Jones

9 Who took 7 for 78 in the final Test at Sydney, which remained his best Test bowling figures?

  A Merv Hughes B Phil Edmonds C John Emburey D Bruce Reid

10 Which Englishman played what turned out to be his only Test match at Adelaide?

  A James Whitaker B Mark Benson C Joey Benjamin D Phil Newport

11 Who came into the England side for the fourth Test, took five wickets in the first innings, and held the catch that clinched the Ashes in the second?

  A Neil Foster B Phil Edmonds C John Emburey D Gladstone Small

The Googly

Apart from the Ashes, England completed what became known as a "Grand Slam" on this tour by winning the regular Australian triangular one-day series, and another one-day competition in Perth, which was staged to celebrate what?

*A The 200th anniversary of the founding of Perth B 100 years of cricket at the WACA ground
C The first staging of the America's Cup yachting in Australia D The centenary of the Sheffield Shield*

Answers on page 175

THE 400 CLUB

1 Who was the first person to score a quadruple-century in a Test match?

    A Garry Sobers *B Graham Gooch* *C Brian Lara* *D Matthew Hayden*

2 Who scored 405 not out for Worcestershire v Somerset in 1988?

    A Glenn Turner *B Graeme Hick* *C Tim Curtis* *D Phil Neale*

3 Who was the first man to pass 400 in first-class cricket twice?

    A Bill Ponsford *B Bill Woodfull* *C Walter Hammond* *D Don Bradman*

4 How was Hanif Mohammad out when he scored 499 in 1958-59?

    A Stumped *B Bowled* *C Caught on the boundary* *D Run out*

5 Who was the first man to score 400 runs in a Test match (two-innings total)?

    A Andy Sandham *B Graham Gooch* *C Garry Sobers* *D Don Bradman*

6 Who scored 452 not out in a Sheffield Shield match in 1929-30?

    A Archie Jackson *B Bill Woodfull* *C Jack Badcock* *D Don Bradman*

7 Which is the only English ground on which two quadruple-centuries have been scored in first-class cricket?

    A Edgbaston, Birmingham *B Fenner's* *C Taunton* *D The Oval*

8 Who scored 424 in the County Championship in 1895?

    A Arthur Shrewsbury *B W.G. Grace* *C K.S. Ranjitsinhji* *D Archie MacLaren*

9 Who was left stranded on 443 not out in a domestic match in India in 1948-49 when his opponents forfeited the match?

    A Mushtaq Ali *B Bhausaheb Nimbalkar* *C C.K. Nayudu* *D Vijay Merchant*

10 Which county was on the receiving end of the first two Championship quadruple-centuries?

    A Glamorgan *B Northamptonshire* *C Somerset* *D Derbyshire*

11 Who scored 428 in a Pakistan domestic match in 1973-74, and later found himself in Room 428 while on tour in England?

    A Aftab Baloch *B Hanif Mohammad* *C Zaheer Abbas* *D Mansoor Akhtar*

The Googly

Who is the only man known to have witnessed both Hanif Mohammad's 499 and Brian Lara's 501 not out?

    A Mushtaq Mohammad *B Dickie Bird* *C Bob Woolmer* *D Zaheer Abbas*

Answers on page 175

SOUTH AFRICAN DOMESTIC CRICKET

1 What was the name of the trophy competed for by South Africa's provincial sides from 1889-90 to 1989-90?

    A Sheffield Cup   *B Botha Bowl*   *C Currie Cup*   *D Rhodes Bowl*

2 Which side won it a record 24 times?

    A Natal   *B Eastern Province*   *C Western Province*   *D Transvaal*

3 Which trophy replaced it in 1990-91?

    A Standard Bank Trophy   *B Benson & Hedges Cup*   *C Castle Cup*   *D Yellow Pages Cup*

4 And which province won it in 1992-93, their first domestic championship?

    A Boland   *B Border*   *C Griqualand West*   *D Orange Free State*

5 Which dominant team of the 1970s was known as the "Mean Machine"?

    A Natal   *B Transvaal*   *C Eastern Province*   *D Western Province*

6 Which future Test player scored 102 for Eastern Province in January 1961, a month before his 17th birthday?

    A Ali Bacher   *B Barry Richards*   *C Eddie Barlow*   *D Graeme Pollock*

7 And which future Test player broke that record by about a month, with 106 not out for Border in January 1984?

    A Andrew Hudson   *B Jonty Rhodes*   *C Hansie Cronje*   *D Daryll Cullinan*

8 For which provincial side did Allan Donald and Hansie Cronje play?

    A Natal   *B Orange Free State*   *C Transvaal*   *D Northern Transvaal*

9 Which provincial side played its home matches at Port Elizabeth?

    A Boland   *B Eastern Province*   *C Natal*   *D Transvaal*

10 Who broke the record for South African domestic cricket with 337 not out for Transvaal in 1993-94?

    A Trevor Lazard   *B Adrian Kuiper*   *C Daryll Cullinan*   *D Gary Kirsten*

11 Which bowler, who also played for Hampshire, took 10 for 59 in a South African domestic match in 1987-88?

    A Neil Johnson   *B Steve Jefferies*   *C Hugh Page*   *D Robin Smith*

The Googly

The 1996 *Wisden* records that "fried calamari stopped play" during a South African domestic match at Paarl in February 1995. What happened?

    A The fumes from a barbecue made the players feel ill   *B The smoke restricted the batsmen's vision*   *C The ball landed in the frying pan and was unusable*   *D The fielding team left the field for a snack*

Answers on page 176

UN-STRAIGHT ARMS

1 Which bowler was no-balled for throwing in the Boxing Day Test at Melbourne in 1995?
A Muttiah Muralitharan B Darren Gough C Courtney Walsh D Kumar Dharmasena

2 Which England bowler, whose action has often been questioned although he has never been called for throwing, was Man of the Match after taking eight wickets on his Test debut against South Africa at Trent Bridge in 2003?
A Kabir Ali B Richard Johnson C James Kirtley D Ed Giddins

3 Who was no-balled for throwing in the 1960 Lord's Test, in which he also took a hat-trick?
A Ian Meckiff B Geoff Griffin C Peter Loader D Harold Rhodes

4 Who was no-balled several times in his only over of the 1963-64 Brisbane Test, and never played again?
A Ian Quick B Ian Johnson C Ian Meckiff D Ian McDonald

5 Which bowler, once reputed to have whistled a beamer through W.G. Grace's beard, was the first man to be called for throwing in a Test, in 1897-98?
A Charlie Turner B Ernie Jones C Arthur Mold D Tom Richardson

6 Which Zimbabwean fast bowler was called for throwing during his Test debut against Pakistan at Harare in 1994-95?
A Charlie Lock B Bryan Strang C Henry Olonga D Dave Brain

7 And which Zimbabwean spinner was no-balled for throwing in a Test in 2000?
A Adam Huckle B Grant Flower C Ray Price D Trevor Gripper

8 Who was no-balled for playfully chucking the final delivery of the 1986 Trent Bridge Test against New Zealand?
A Graham Gooch B Richard Hadlee C Mike Gatting D David Gower

9 Which England spinner was no-balled for throwing in a Test in the West Indies in 1953-54, and later changed his action after apparently being shocked by film of it?
A Jim Laker B Tony Lock C Johnny Wardle D David Allen

10 Which West Indian bowler of the 1960s, who was often accused of throwing but was never no-balled in a Test, called his 1970 autobiography *Chucked Around*?
A Wes Hall B Roy Gilchrist C Charlie Griffith D Chester Watson

11 Which Sri Lankan spinner – later the groundsman at the Galle ground – had a bowling action that earned him the nickname "Spearchucker" from various touring sides?
A Asoka de Silva B Jayananda Warnaweera C Don Anurasiri D Somachandra de Silva

The Googly

During the Test at Christchurch in 1967-68 the Indian allrounder Abid Ali was infuriated that New Zealand's Gary Bartlett, who he felt was a blatant chucker, had not been no-balled. What happened next?

A He squared up to Bartlett and had to be hauled back by the umpires B He was banned for arguing with the umpires C He walked off the field and his innings was recorded as "retired out" D He impersonated Bartlett's bowling action – and was no-balled for throwing himself

Answers on page 176

THE 1983 WORLD CUP

1 Who won the third World Cup?

 A England **B** *India* **C** *Sri Lanka* **D** *West Indies*

2 Who captained the winners?

 A Sunil Gavaskar **B** *Viv Richards* **C** *Clive Lloyd* **D** *Kapil Dev*

3 Who was the Man of the Match in the final at Lord's?

 A Mohinder Amarnath **B** *Sunil Gavaskar* **C** *Kapil Dev* **D** *Dilip Vengsarkar*

4 Who top-scored in the final, with 38?

 A Kirti Azad **B** *Kris Srikkanth* **C** *Gus Logie* **D** *Jeff Dujon*

5 Who umpired his third World Cup final?

 A Tom Spencer **B** *Barrie Meyer* **C** *David Constant* **D** *Dickie Bird*

6 Who smashed 175 not out in a group game against Zimbabwe after his team were 17 for 5?

 A Gordon Greenidge **B** *Kapil Dev* **C** *Ian Botham* **D** *David Hookes*

7 Who scored 130 for England against Sri Lanka at Taunton?

 A Allan Lamb **B** *Graham Gooch* **C** *Mike Gatting* **D** *David Gower*

8 And who took 5 for 39 for England in that match?

 A Norman Cowans **B** *Ian Botham* **C** *Vic Marks* **D** *Derek Pringle*

9 Who scored 69 not out and took 4 for 42 as Zimbabwe beat Australia at Trent Bridge?

 A Andy Waller **B** *Ian Butchart* **C** *Vince Hogg* **D** *Duncan Fletcher*

10 Who inflicted West Indies' first World Cup defeat, in a group game?

 A Australia **B** *England* **C** *India* **D** *Pakistan*

11 Who scored 110 for Australia in their group match against India?

 A Graeme Wood **B** *Kepler Wessels* **C** *Trevor Chappell* **D** *Greg Chappell*

The Googly

Who took 6 for 39 for Australia against India in the 1983 World Cup, and later played for Somerset on the strength of his Wiltshire birthplace?

A Peter Roebuck **B** *Rodney Hogg* **C** *Ken MacLeay* **D** *Tom Hogan*

Answers on page 176

ENGLAND IN TESTS

1 Who scored the winning run for England against New Zealand in the 2004 Lord's Test, and promptly retired?

A Mike Atherton B Nasser Hussain C Graham Thorpe D Alec Stewart

2 Who was the first Englishman to play in 100 Test matches?

A Mike Atherton B Geoff Boycott C Colin Cowdrey D Ted Dexter

3 Which ground staged the first Test match played in England, in 1880?

A Lord's B The Oval C Bramall Lane, Sheffield D Old Trafford, Manchester

4 And who scored England's first Test century in that 1880 match?

A James Lillywhite B W.G. Grace C E.M. Grace D Allan Steel

5 Which bowler took 9 for 57 against South Africa at The Oval in 1994?

A Darren Gough B Phillip DeFreitas C Phil Tufnell D Devon Malcolm

6 Who captained England in 54 Test matches between 1993 and 2001?

A Mike Atherton B Alec Stewart C Graham Gooch D Nasser Hussain

7 Who scored 20 Test centuries for England, on 18 different grounds?

A Alec Stewart B Geoff Boycott C Ken Barrington D Len Hutton

8 Who was the first England wicket-keeper to make 200 Test dismissals?

A Alan Knott B Godfrey Evans C Bob Taylor D Alec Stewart

9 Which England player was out handled the ball in a Test in 1993?

A Robin Smith B Alec Stewart C Peter Such D Graham Gooch

10 And who was out obstructing the field in a Test in 1951?

A Len Hutton B Bill Edrich C Denis Compton D Reg Simpson

11 Who was the first English bowler to take 200 Test wickets?

A Alec Bedser B Sydney Barnes C Maurice Tate D Brian Statham

The Googly

What did England achieve at Sydney in 1894-95, and at Headingley in 1981, that no other team managed in the interim?

A They bowled Australia out for under 100 in both innings B All their batsmen reached double figures C They won after following on D Two different batsmen scored double-centuries in the match

Answers on page 176

THE ASHES 1989

1 Who captained England throughout the series?

A David Gower *B Mike Gatting* *C Mike Atherton* *D Graham Gooch*

2 Which Australian scored 839 runs in the series?

A Allan Border *B Mark Taylor* *C Steve Waugh* *D Dean Jones*

3 How many players did England use in the course of losing the six-match series 4-0?

A 17 *B 23* *C 29* *D 31*

4 Who took 41 wickets in the series, to add to the 42 he managed in 1981?

A Terry Alderman *B Geoff Lawson* *C Craig McDermott* *D Dennis Lillee*

5 Who scored 393 runs in the series before he was dismissed?

A Graham Gooch *B Tim Curtis* *C Steve Waugh* *D Dean Jones*

6 Who was England's chairman of selectors at the time, who blamed (among other things) Venus's alignment with Mars for England's misfortunes?

A Peter May *B Alec Bedser* *C Ray Illingworth* *D Ted Dexter*

7 Which bowler, who went on to take 177 Test wickets, made his debut in the third Test at Edgbaston?

A Angus Fraser *B Neil Foster* *C Chris Lewis* *D Devon Malcolm*

8 And which batsman, who went to score 7728 Test runs, made a duck on his debut at Trent Bridge?

A Alec Stewart *B Robin Smith* *C Mark Waugh* *D Mike Atherton*

9 Who scored the only double-century of the series, 219 at Trent Bridge?

A Mark Taylor *B David Boon* *C Allan Border* *D David Gower*

10 Which bowler, who later became Australia's chairman of selectors, played in five of the Tests?

A Geoff Lawson *B Bob Holland* *C Trevor Hohns* *D Peter Taylor*

11 Which player, who is Ricky Ponting's uncle, made his debut in the first Test, but didn't play again in the series?

A Craig McDermott *B Simon O'Donnell* *C Greg Campbell* *D Wayne Holdsworth*

The Googly

Who made his Test debut at The Oval in 1989, and was probably not terribly encouraged when he was apparently informed by Micky Stewart, England's coach, that he was their 17th-choice fast bowler?

A Alan Igglesden *B John Stephenson* *C Tim Munton* *D Martin McCague*

Answers on page 176

PLUCKED FROM OBSCURITY

1 Who was so unknown when called up for Australia in 1986-87 that it was widely assumed the selectors had chosen the wrong man?
A Shane Warne B Peter Taylor C Peter Sleep D Bob Holland

2 Who was spotted in the nets at Karachi in 1979-80, was selected to play and took seven wickets against Australia?
A Tauseef Ahmed B Iqbal Qasim C Akram Raza D Nadeem Ghauri

3 Who impressed Brian Lara in the nets and was selected for West Indies in 2003 after playing just one match for Barbados?
A Pedro Collins B Tino Best C Corey Collymore D Fidel Edwards

4 Which bowler, who eventually took 789 international wickets, was supposedly spotted by Imran Khan, who was watching a domestic match on TV in hospital at the time?
A Abdul Qadir B Wasim Akram C Waqar Younis D Mushtaq Ahmed

5 Who was called up from county cricket with Gloucestershire to play for Australia during the 1981 "Botham's Ashes" series?
A Graham Yallop B Graeme Beard C Mike Whitney D Trevor Chappell

6 Whose call-up as a replacement for England's 1968-69 tour of South Africa led to its being cancelled?
A Tony Greig B Basil D'Oliveira C Mike Denness D Ron Headley

7 And which injured player dropped out of the originally selected side in 1968-69, to set up the scenario?
A Roger Prideaux B Colin Milburn C Tom Cartwright D Ken Higgs

8 Which 41-year-old was called up to reinforce England's battered side in Australia in 1974-75, and the day after he arrived found himself batting in a Test against Lillee and Thomson?
A Tom Graveney B John Edrich C Colin Cowdrey D Brian Close

9 Who was summoned from the Birmingham League to play for Pakistan in a Test in 1982, and promptly pulled a muscle when he bowled?
A Jalaluddin B Sikander Bakht C Tahir Naqqash D Ehteshamuddin

10 Who spent the 1907-08 winter in Australia for health reasons, was called up by England after injuries to the touring team, and scored 119 on debut in the first Test?
A John Crawford B Len Braund C George Gunn D Jack Hobbs

11 Which legspinner was described by Keith Stackpole as "the luckiest man ever to play for Australia" after being called up for a Test in 1972-73, in which he bowled six erratic overs?
A Kerry O'Keeffe B Bob Holland C John Watkins D Terry Jenner

The Googly

Ken Burn from Tasmania was selected for Australia's 1890 tour of England as a wicket-keeper. What did he tell the management once the team was safely embarked on their voyage?
A He'd broken his fingers so often his doctor had ordered him to stop keeping wicket
B He was a wanted man in England C He'd never kept wicket before D He wasn't eligible for Australia as he was born in New Zealand

Answers on page 176

SRI LANKA IN TESTS

1 Who made his debut as a teenager in Sri Lanka's inaugural Test, and also played in their 100th?

   A Aravinda de Silva **B** *Arjuna Ranatunga* **C** *Sidath Wettimuny* **D** *Roy Dias*

2 When Sri Lanka made a record Test total of 952, which player scored 340?

   A Aravinda de Silva **B** *Roshan Mahanama* **C** *Sanath Jayasuriya* **D** *Mahela Jayawardene*

3 Who scored Sri Lanka's first Test century, in 1981-82, and the following year was their first batsman to carry his bat through a Test innings?

   A Roy Dias **B** *Sidath Wettimuny* **C** *Arjuna Ranatunga* **D** *Duleep Mendis*

4 Who took a hat-trick with the first three balls of the second over of the match against Zimbabwe at Harare in 1999-2000?

   A Muttiah Muralitharan **B** *Pramodya Wickremasinghe* **C** *Chaminda Vaas* **D** *Nuwan Zoysa*

5 Who signed off from Test cricket with 206 against Bangladesh in Colombo in July 2002?

   A Aravinda de Silva **B** *Arjuna Ranatunga* **C** *Hashan Tillakaratne* **D** *Roshan Mahanama*

6 Who took 9 for 65 against England at The Oval in 1998?

   A Suresh Perera **B** *Muttiah Muralitharan* **C** *Chaminda Vaas* **D** *Kumar Dharmasena*

7 Who scored 105 in each innings for Sri Lanka against India at Madras in 1982-83?

   A Sidath Wettimuny **B** *Arjuna Ranatunga* **C** *Ranjan Madugalle* **D** *Duleep Mendis*

8 Where have Sri Lanka played home Tests at a ground called the Asgiriya Stadium?

   A Galle **B** *Moratuwa* **C** *Kandy* **D** *Dambulla*

9 Which batsman, who passed 1000 Test runs during 2004, at an average over 50, scored all his first three Test centuries at the Sinhalese Sports Club?

   A Tillakaratne Dilshan **B** *Thilan Samaraweera* **C** *Russel Arnold* **D** *Mahela Jayawardene*

10 What was the surname of the brothers who opened the innings together in two Tests in New Zealand in 1982-83?

   A Ranatunga **B** *de Alwis* **C** *Wettimuny* **D** *de Silva*

11 Which wicket-keeper made nine dismissals in successive Tests against India in 1985-86?

   A Amal Silva **B** *Mahes Goonatilleke* **C** *Pubudu Dissanayake* **D** *Guy de Alwis*

The Googly

What unwanted Test record was Sri Lanka's Roger Wijesuriya relieved to hand over to Rawl Lewis of West Indies in 1998-99?

A The worst batting average **B** *The worst bowling average* **C** *The most successive ducks*
D *The worst dropped catch in Test history, according to Wisden*

Answers on page 176

MEDIA MEN

1 Who was the Australian media mogul who signed up many of the world's best players in 1977?

A Alan Bond B Rupert Murdoch C Robert Holmes a'Court D Kerry Packer

2 Who, in 2004, became the first man to have witnessed – as player, journalist or commentator – more than 500 Test matches?

A Henry Blofeld B Richie Benaud C Christopher Martin-Jenkins D Mike Selvey

3 Who was the influential cricket correspondent of the UK's *Daily Telegraph* from 1946 to 1975?

A John Arlott B Brian Johnston C Jim Swanton D Denis Compton

4 Which radio commentator is also the chief cricket correspondent of the London *Times*?

A Angus Fraser B Vic Marks C Christopher Martin-Jenkins D Derek Pringle

5 For which newspaper did John Arlott write for many years?

A The Times B The Daily Telegraph C The Guardian D The Daily Sketch

6 Which man, who died in 2003, was the genial presenter of BBC Test cricket for many years until his retirement in 1986?

A David Coleman B Barrington Dalby C Peter West D Frank Bough

7 Which member of the Channel 9 TV commentary team in Australia is a well-known pigeon fancier?

A Tony Greig B Bill Lawry C Ian Healy D Glenn McGrath

8 Who started as the BBC Radio commentary team's scorer in 1965, and has produced several statistical tomes?

A Arthur Wrigley B Bill Frindall C Angus "Statto" Loughran D Wendy Wimbush

9 Which fun-loving cake-chomping broadcaster was BBC Radio's first official cricket correspondent?

A Clement Freud B Brian Johnston C Colin Milburn D Don Mosey

10 Who left his job as Sky Television's cricket statistician to become the Australian Cricket Board's media manager?

A Simon Hughes B Brian Murgatroyd C Irving Rosenwater D David Frith

11 Which long-time cricket correspondent (and former *Wisden* editor) celebrated 50 years of writing for *The Times* in 2004?

A John Woodcock B Bill Deedes C Frank Keating D Graeme Wright

The Googly

When England only had ten fit men on the eve of the 1963-64 Bombay Test, which British journalist covering the tour was asked to stand by to play?

A Jim Swanton B Henry Blofeld C Ian Wooldridge D David Frith

Answers on page 176

THE ASHES 1990-91

1 Who was England's tour captain?

A Mike Gatting B Mike Atherton C Graham Gooch D David Gower

2 And who captained England in the first Test when the appointed captain was injured?

A Allan Lamb B Ian Botham C Alec Stewart D Robin Smith

3 Who took 13 wickets in the second Test, at Melbourne?

A Angus Fraser B Bruce Reid C Merv Hughes D Phillip DeFreitas

4 Which England spinner, who finished with 121 Test wickets, made his debut at Melbourne, but didn't take a wicket in that game?

A Ian Salisbury B Richard Illingworth C Peter Such D Phil Tufnell

5 Who made his debut in the fourth Test at Adelaide, and scored 138?

A Mark Waugh B Michael Slater C Graham Thorpe D Robin Smith

6 Who, apart from David Gower, took part in the Tiger Moth "fly-past" during England's tour match in Queensland that landed both players with substantial fines from the management?

A Hugh Morris B John Morris C Phil Tufnell D Ian Botham

7 Whose century at Sydney took 424 minutes, the slowest in Ashes cricket at the time?

A Mike Atherton B Allan Border C Alec Stewart D Greg Matthews

8 Who flew straight from an England A tour to play in the final Test, but was out first ball?

A David "Syd" Lawrence B Phil Newport C Kim Barnett D Mark Ramprakash

9 Which batsman was run out in both innings, for the second time in his career, in the fourth Test at Adelaide?

A Mike Atherton B David Gower C Dean Jones D Mark Taylor

10 Who took 8 for 97, the best analysis of a career that brought him 291 wickets, in the fifth Test at Perth?

A Terry Alderman B Geoff Lawson C Craig McDermott D Devon Malcolm

11 Which batsman scored 64 and 54 in the second Test at Melbourne, the two highest scores of a Test career than began almost 11 years before?

A Eddie Hemmings B Wayne Larkins C Geoff Cook D Dirk Wellham

The Googly

Which Queensland player, who later appeared for Holland in the World Cup, took two sharp catches as a substitute in the first Test at Brisbane in 1990-91, despite reportedly having been out all the previous night dancing?

A Steve Atkinson B Nolan Clarke C Peter Cantrell D Neil Statham

Answers on page 176

STRANGE BIRTHPLACES: ENGLAND

1   Which England one-day captain was born in Melbourne in Australia?

  A Alan Mullally B Craig White C Adam Hollioake D Jason Gallian

2   Which England Test captain was born in Milan in Italy?

  A Nigel Howard B Mike Atherton C Colin Cowdrey D Ted Dexter

3   And which one was born in Lima in Peru?

  A Gubby Allen B Freddie Brown C George Mann D David Sheppard

4   Which England captain was born in Ayr in Scotland?

  A Gregor MacGregor B Cyril Walters C Ken Cranston D Mike Denness

5   And which one was born in Swansea in Wales?

  A Tony Lewis B Tony Lock C Peter May D David Evans

6   Which England player was born in Papua New Guinea?

  A Neil Williams B David Larter C Geraint Jones D Raman Subba Row

7   And which one was born at Scotts Head in Dominica?

  A Wilf Slack B Roland Butcher C Norman Cowans D Phillip DeFreitas

8   Which one was born in Langebaanweg in South Africa?

  A Allan Lamb B Basil D'Oliveira C Ian Greig D Tony Greig

9   And which one in Lusaka, which is now the capital of Zambia?

  A Graeme Hick B Chris Smith C Neal Radford D Phil Edmonds

10 Which player turned commentator was born in Hong Kong?

  A Paul Allott B Mike Atherton C David Gower D Dermot Reeve

11 Which early England captain was born in Trinidad, the 18th child of a father who had been the island's Attorney-General?

  A Lord Harris B Lord Hawke C Pelham Warner D Archie MacLaren

The Googly

Who was born in one country, played for another, and was banned from a third for playing in a fourth?

A Tony Greig B Robin Jackman C Ian Chappell D John Traicos

Answers on page 177

DERBYSHIRE

1 Who scored 53 first-class centuries for Derbyshire between 1979 and 1998?

A Chris Adams *B Kim Barnett* *C John Wright* *D Peter Kirsten*

2 Regular county games were staged at which ground in Chesterfield until 1998?

A Spire Park *B Mortimer Park* *C King's Park* *D Queen's Park*

3 Which Australian was prevented by injury from captaining Derbyshire in 2004?

A Shane Watson *B Glenn McGrath* *C Michael Di Venuto* *D Shane Warne*

4 Which wicket-keeper made 1304 dismissals for Derbyshire between 1961 and 1984?

A Bob Taylor *B George Dawkes* *C Jim Parks* *D Bernie Maher*

5 Which Derbyshire player captained England against India at Madras in 1951-52?

A Guy Willatt *B Charlie Elliott* *C Donald Carr* *D Cliff Gladwin*

6 Who scored 168 for Gloucestershire against Derbyshire in 2001, and moved to Derby in 2002?

A James Bryant *B Steve Selwood* *C Stephen Stubbings* *D Dominic Hewson*

7 Who was Derbyshire's captain when they won the inaugural NatWest Trophy in 1981?

A Kim Barnett *B Barry Wood* *C John Harvey* *D Ashley Harvey-Walker*

8 Which South African captained Derbyshire between 1976 and 1978?

A Henry Fotheringham *B Eddie Barlow* *C Peter Kirsten* *D Jimmy Cook*

9 Which Derbyshire bowler took 143 first-class wickets at just 10.99 apiece in 1958?

A Cliff Gladwin *B Les Jackson* *C Bill Copson* *D Harold Rhodes*

10 Who scored a century in each innings on his Championship debut for Derbyshire in 2001?

A Hassan Adnan *B Chris Bassano* *C Andrew Gait* *D Nathan Dumelow*

11 Which was the first year Derbyshire won the County Championship?

A 1836 *B 1919* *C 1936* *D 1992*

The Googly

What did Ashley Harvey-Walker hand to Dickie Bird, the umpire, for safe keeping during Derbyshire's match against Lancashire at Buxton in 1975?

A His wallet *B His last will and testament* *C His false teeth* *D A lighted cigarette*

Answers on page 177

ONE BIG MOMENT

1 Who took 16 wickets on his Test debut in 1972, more than he managed in the rest of his Test career?
A Jeff Hammond B Bob Massie C David Colley D John Gleeson

2 Who scored 165 in the first Test of all, in 1876-77, but didn't pass 50 again in the rest of his Test career?
A Dave Gregory B Billy Murdoch C Charles Bannerman D Bransby Cooper

3 Who scored 104 not out for England on Test debut in 1958, but scored only 100 more runs in his other five Tests?
A Arthur Milton B John Mortimore C Willie Watson D Don Smith

4 Which England player, and later coach, scored 214 not out in a Test in 1974, but otherwise never passed 50 in Tests?
A Keith Fletcher B Barry Wood C Mike Denness D David Lloyd

5 Who once scored a century on debut for Australia at The Oval in 1981, but never passed 50 in his other five Tests?
A Martin Kent B Trevor Chappell C Robbie Kerr D Dirk Wellham

6 Which man, later the secretary of MCC, scored a century on Test debut – his maiden first-class hundred too – but won only two more caps?
A Ronny Aird B Billy Griffith C John Stephenson D Jack Bailey

7 Who took a wicket with his first ball in a Test, for India in Colombo in 1997-98, but finished that innings with 1 for 195 from 70 overs as Sri Lanka ran up a record total of 952 for 6?
A Nilesh Kulkarni B Murali Kartik C Harvinder Singh D Harbhajan Singh

8 Which Australian made his debut at The Oval in 1977, bowled almost unchanged to take 5 for 63 and later scored 46 ... and never played another Test?
A Alan Hurst B Graeme Porter C Mick Malone D Graeme Beard

9 Whose only Test century was an innings of 210 not out against Australia at Faisalabad in 1979-80?
A Taslim Arif B Qasim Omar C Azmat Rana D Basit Ali

10 Which Indian made 103 on his Test debut at Durban in 1992-93, but managed only three more fifties in his other ten Tests?
A Ajay Sharma B Praveen Amre C Ajay Jadeja D Woorkeri Raman

11 Which man, who later captained Middlesex, toured Australia in 1950-51 and took one solitary wicket in his Test career, at a cost of 281 runs?
A John Dewes B John Warr C Colin Drybrough D Peter Parfitt

The Googly
Which man, who was later embroiled in a sensational legal trial after accusing a priest of adultery, took the wicket of Archie MacLaren with his first ball in Test cricket, at Melbourne in 1894-95, but never played again?
A Arthur Coningham B Sam Morris C Rowley Pope D William "Digger" Robertson

Answers on page 177

GROUNDS IN AUSTRALIA

1 On which Test ground might you watch play from the Brewongle Stand?

A Adelaide B Melbourne C Perth D Sydney

2 Which ground staged a Test for the first time in 1970-71?

A Adelaide B Brisbane C Perth D Hobart

3 Which Test ground is properly called "Woolloongabba", after the suburb it's situated in?

A Adelaide B Brisbane C Perth D Sydney

4 In which city would you find the Bellerive Oval?

A Hobart B Brisbane C Canberra D Fremantle

5 Which Test ground stands on land reclaimed from the Swan River?

A Adelaide B Brisbane C Perth D Hobart

6 Where would you find the Manuka Oval?

A Alice Springs B Ballarat C Canberra D Darwin

7 Which Australian ground was the first to have a Test triple-century scored on it, in 1965-66?

A Adelaide B Brisbane C Melbourne D Sydney

8 On which ground were Tests in Brisbane played before they moved to the Gabba?

A Exhibition Ground B Brisbane Oval C Cazaly's Oval D Moreton Bay Oval

9 Who scored 223 and 226 in successive Tests in Brisbane in the 1930s, on different grounds?

A Alan Kippax B Bill Ponsford C Stan McCabe D Don Bradman

10 In which town would you find the Bradman Oval and the Bradman Museum?

A Adelaide B Bowral C Cootamundra D Deniliquin

11 On which Test ground might bowling start from the Vulture Street end?

A Adelaide B Brisbane C Melbourne D Sydney

The Googly

Harrup Park in Mackay, Queensland, has staged a solitary one-day international – India v Sri Lanka in the 1991-92 World Cup. How long did the match last?

A Two balls B 90 minutes C 29.3 overs D Three days

Answers on page 177

SCREEN TESTS

1 Which England legend was a longtime team captain on the BBC TV quiz *A Question of Sport*?

   A *Mike Brearley* **B** *Ian Botham* **C** *Bob Willis* **D** *David Gower*

2 Which England women's player was part of the Channel 4 commentary team in 2003?

   A *Sarah Potter* **B** *Sarah Botham* **C** *Clare Connor* **D** *Charlotte Edwards*

3 Which former England player was voted the King of the Jungle on a reality TV show in 2003?

   A *Phil Tufnell* **B** *Phillip DeFreitas* **C** *Ryan Sidebottom* **D** *John Morris*

4 Which episode in cricket history was the subject of a six-part Australian drama series in 1982?

   A *The Packer Affair* **B** *The Bodyline series* **C** *The birth of the Ashes*
   D *The D'Oliveira Affair*

5 Which England legend was a longtime team captain on the BBC TV quiz *They Think It's All Over*?

   A *Mike Atherton* **B** *Bob Willis* **C** *Geoff Boycott* **D** *David Gower*

6 Which grandson of an actor who played Dr Who made his England one-day debut in 2003?

   A *Ian Blackwell* **B** *Jim Troughton* **C** *Rikki Clarke* **D** *John Davison*

7 Which Indian film featuring cricket was nominated for an Oscar in 2002?

   A *Bend It Like Beckham* **B** *Bend It Like Kumble* **C** *The Beach* **D** *Lagaan*

8 Who were the cricket-loving pair in *The Lady Vanishes* (1938) who mocked up Clarrie Grimmett's fielding positions on a table in the train's restaurant car?

   A *Morecambe and Wise* **B** *Flanagan and Allen* **C** *Charters and Caldicott*
   D *Abbott and Costello*

9 Which British film of 2003 featured the struggle of a young boy trying to learn how to play cricket?

   A *Wondrous Oblivion* **B** *The Lord's Prayer* **C** *Love, Actually* **D** *Leg Before Wicket*

10 Which former England captain acted in over 100 Hollywood movies, including *Rebecca*, *The Prisoner of Zenda* and *The Four Feathers*?

   A *Archie MacLaren* **B** *Aubrey Smith* **C** *Charles Fry* **D** *John Douglas*

11 Who made a guest appearance in an episode of *Dad's Army*, and was encouraged by the ARP warden to bowl bouncers at Captain Mainwaring?

   A *Alec Bedser* **B** *John Snow* **C** *Fred Trueman* **D** *Wes Hall*

The Googly
Which fast bowler had a cameo in the Australian soap *Neighbours*, and also presented the Aussie version of *Gladiators*?

A *Merv Hughes* **B** *Mike Whitney* **C** *Geoff Lawson* **D** *Dennis Lillee*

Answers on page 177

ESSEX

1 Who scored 94 hundreds – and more than 30,000 runs – for Essex between 1973 and 1997?

A Keith Fletcher B Graham Gooch C Nasser Hussain D Ken McEwan

2 In which town have Essex played occasional home matches at Valentine's Park?

A Ilford B Colchester C Clacton D Leyton

3 Which Zimbabwe Test player signed for Essex in 2002?

A Heath Streak B Henry Olonga C Scott Brant D Andy Flower

4 Which long-serving Essex player rejoiced in the nickname "Tonker"?

A Bill Lawry B Trevor Bailey C Brian Taylor D Mike Bear

5 Which Essex player was the first man to score two hundreds in the same Test for England?

A Jack O'Connor B Jack Russell C Johnny Douglas D Charlie McGahey

6 In which year did Essex win the County Championship for the first time?

A 1959 B 1969 C 1979 D 1989

7 Who took 100 first-class wickets in a season for Essex four times between 1978 and 1984?

A Neil Foster B Norbert Phillip C John Lever D Ray East

8 On which ground did the Australians score a record 721 runs in a day against Essex in 1948?

A Chelmsford B Colchester C Southend D Westcliff

9 Who scored 343 not out for Essex against Derbyshire at Chesterfield in 1904, but finished on the losing side?

A Percy Perrin B Jack O'Connor C Charlie McGahey D Jack Russell

10 Which former Essex captain won an Olympic boxing gold medal in 1908?

A Charles Kortright B Jack O'Connor C Francis Fane D Johnny Douglas

11 And which Essex spinner of the 1970s was also an Olympic fencer?

A David Acfield B Robin Hobbs C John Childs D Ray East

The Googly

Essex's Peter Smith, in 1946-47, was the last player to do what in a Test for England until Graham Gooch in 1975?

A To bag a pair on debut B To wear a moustache C To be out handled the ball
D To oversleep and miss the start of play

Answers on page 177

BRIAN LARA

1 On which Caribbean island was Lara born?

   A Antigua *B Barbados* *C Trinidad* *D Tobago*

2 On which ground did he score 400 not out in 2004?

   A St John's, Antigua *B Bridgetown, Barbados* *C Kingston, Jamaica* *D Port-of-Spain, Trinidad*

3 Which England batsman played in that game and the one in which Lara scored 375?

   A Mike Atherton *B Graham Thorpe* *C Nasser Hussain* *D Marcus Trescothick*

4 And which umpire was on duty for both those innings?

   A Venkat *B Steve Bucknor* *C Darrell Hair* *D David Shepherd*

5 Against which county did Lara score his 501 not out?

   A Essex *B Durham* *C Yorkshire* *D Somerset*

6 With whom did Lara share a county-record fifth-wicket stand of 322 during his 501 not out?

   A Dominic Ostler *B Trevor Penney* *C Keith Piper* *D Dermot Reeve*

7 Lara named his daughter after the city in which he scored his first Test century, 277 against Australia in 1992-93. What's her name?

   A Adelaide *B Melbourne* *C Sydney* *D Darwin*

8 Lara reached 10,000 Test runs at Old Trafford in 2004 – what happened the ball after he got there?

   A He was caught at slip *B He declared* *C He hit a six to celebrate* *D He broke a finger*

9 Against which team did Lara score 688 runs in six innings in 2001-02, at an average of 114 with three centuries, only for West Indies to lose all three Tests?

   A Australia *B England* *C India* *D Sri Lanka*

10 By 2003 Lara had scored two centuries in the World Cup, both against the same team – which one?

   A England *B Kenya* *C Pakistan* *D South Africa*

11 Who was West Indies' captain for Lara's Test debut, at Lahore in 1990-91?

   A Viv Richards *B Richie Richardson* *C Courtney Walsh* *D Desmond Haynes*

The Googly

Who played against Brian Lara when he scored his 501 not out, and was West Indies' 12th man when he scored his 375?

A Winston Benjamin *B Gareth Breese* *C Anderson Cummins* *D Phil Simmons*

Answers on page 177

THE ASHES 1993

1 Who captained England in the first four Tests of the series?

A Alec Stewart B Mike Atherton C Graham Gooch D Mike Gatting

2 Who made his debut in the first Test, and scored 152 in the second?

A Michael Slater B Matthew Hayden C Mark Taylor D Graeme Hick

3 Who was bowled by Shane Warne's first ball in Ashes Tests, at Old Trafford?

A Graham Gooch B Mike Atherton C Mike Gatting D Robin Smith

4 Who made his debut for England in the first Test at Old Trafford, and took 6 for 67?

A Andy Caddick B Mark Ilott C Phil Tufnell D Peter Such

5 Who scored the only double-century of the series, in the fourth Test at Headingley?

A Steve Waugh B David Boon C Graham Gooch D Allan Border

6 Who narrowly missed becoming Australia's fourth centurion in the Lord's Test, when he was bowled through his legs for 99?

A Mark Waugh B Allan Border C Steve Waugh D Ian Healy

7 And which Englishman was run out for 99 in the same Test – and never did score a century at Lord's?

A Mike Atherton B Graeme Hick C Chris Lewis D Robin Smith

8 Which Irish-born, Australian-raised player made his England debut in the third Test at Trent Bridge?

A Andy Caddick B Mark Ilott C Martin McCague D Martin Bicknell

9 And which Englishman scored a century on his debut in that same Test?

A Mark Lathwell B Graham Thorpe C Nasser Hussain D Alec Stewart

10 Who returned to Test cricket after serious injury problems, and took eight wickets as England won the final match at The Oval?

A Angus Fraser B Alan Igglesden C Neil Foster D Phil Tufnell

11 Who, when he was stumped at Lord's, was the first person given out by the third (TV-watching) umpire in a Test in England?

A Graeme Hick B Robin Smith C Chris Lewis D Alec Stewart

The Googly

What do Andy Caddick of England and Australia's Brendon Julian, who made their debuts together in the first Test at Old Trafford in 1993, have in common?

A They married sisters B They share the same birthday C They both had fathers who were Test umpires D They were both born in New Zealand

Answers on page 177

CARRYING THE BAT

1 Which West Indian was the first man to carry his bat through a complete innings three times in Tests?

   A Gordon Greenidge B Jeff Stollmeyer C Conrad Hunte D Desmond Haynes

2 Who carried his bat in a famous innings of 154 for England against West Indies at Headingley in 1991?

   A Mike Atherton B Alec Stewart C Graham Gooch D Graeme Fowler

3 Which South African carried his bat in both innings, scoring a century both times, for Somerset against Nottinghamshire at Trent Bridge in 1989?

   A Peter Kirsten B Adrian Kuiper C Jimmy Cook D Kepler Wessels

4 Who carried his bat for 99 not out in an Ashes Test at Perth in 1978-79?

   A Graeme Wood B Geoff Boycott C Mike Brearley D Rick Darling

5 Who was only 22 when he carried his bat for 43 in a Test at Lord's in 1969?

   A Roy Fredericks B Glenn Turner C Sunil Gavaskar D Dennis Amiss

6 Who carried his bat for 191 against England at Trent Bridge in 1957, and opened the bowling in both innings too?

   A John Reid B Garry Sobers C Vinoo Mankad D Frank Worrell

7 Who carried his bat for the second time in his career in the Adelaide Test of the acrimonious 1932-33 Bodyline series?

   A Jack Hobbs B Bill Woodfull C Bill Ponsford D Herbert Sutcliffe

8 Who was the first man to carry his bat while scoring a Test double-century, at Lord's in 1938?

   A Charles Barnett B Bill Brown C Cyril Washbrook D Jack Fingleton

9 Who carried his bat twice in Tests within six months between August 1950 and February '51?

   A Allan Rae B Len Hutton C Jeff Stollmeyer D Reg Simpson

10 Which South African was the first to carry his bat in a Test, at Cape Town in 1888-89?

   A Jack Sinclair B Bernard Tancred C Louis Tancred D Owen Dunell

11 Which Leicestershire batsman carried his bat 17 times in first-class cricket (equalling W.G. Grace's record), including twice in the same game in 1911?

   A Albert Knight B Les Berry C Cyril Wood D John King

The Googly

What unusual feat did Desmond Haynes achieve for West Indies against New Zealand at Dunedin in 1979-80?

A Carried his bat in first innings, out first ball in the second B He also scored a not-out century in the second innings C Lowest score (29) by a man carrying his bat D He opened but was the last man out in both innings

Answers on page 177

SURREY

1   Which well-known politician was Surrey's president in 2002?

    A *Alec Douglas-Home* B *John Major* C *Kenneth Clarke* D *Ken Livingstone*

2   Who scored 268 for Surrey against Glamorgan in a one-day match at The Oval in 2002?

    A *Alistair Brown* B *Adam Hollioake* C *Graham Thorpe* D *Mark Ramprakash*

3   Which Surrey player captained England on the 1932-33 Bodyline tour of Australia?

    A *Percy Fender* B *Jack Hobbs* C *Pelham Warner* D *Douglas Jardine*

4   Who scored over 43,000 runs – and 144 hundreds – for Surrey between 1905 and 1934?

    A *Bobby Abel* B *Jack Hobbs* C *Tom Hayward* D *Andy Sandham*

5   Who hit 279 not out for Surrey against Nottinghamshire at Whitgift School in 2003?

    A *Alistair Brown* B *Mark Butcher* C *Mark Ramprakash* D *Graham Thorpe*

6   Which Surrey player hit 325 (and 50) in what turned out to be his last Test, in West Indies in 1929-30?

    A *Jack Hobbs* B *Errol Holmes* C *Tip Foster* D *Andy Sandham*

7   Who captained Surrey for five years in the 1950s, and won the Championship each year?

    A *Alec Bedser* B *Peter May* C *Stuart Surridge* D *Micky Stewart*

8   Where do Surrey play home matches at a ground called Woodbridge Road?

    A *Guildford* B *Byfleet* C *Croydon* D *Kingston-upon-Thames*

9   Which Surrey player captained England for the only time at Sydney in 1974-75?

    A *Graham Roope* B *Ken Barrington* C *John Edrich* D *Micky Stewart*

10 Which Surrey player succeeded Godfrey Evans as England's wicket-keeper when he retired in 1959?

    A *Arnold Long* B *Arthur McIntyre* C *Roy Swetman* D *Geoff Millman*

11 Who took seven wickets in 11 balls for Surrey against Sussex at Eastbourne in 1972?

    A *Geoff Arnold* B *Robin Jackman* C *Intikhab Alam* D *Pat Pocock*

The Googly

For the 1972 Oval Test against Australia, England had two sometime Surrey players as substitute fielders who, a dozen years later, were opposing captains in a Test series. Who were they?

A *Alec Stewart and Javed Miandad* B *Ian Greig and Imran Khan*
C *Bob Willis and Geoff Howarth* D *Bob Willis and Intikhab Alam*

Answers on page 178

THE 1987 WORLD CUP

1 Who won the fourth World Cup, the first one played outside England?

A Australia *B England* *C India* *D Pakistan*

2 In which city was the final played?

A Lahore *B Karachi* *C Calcutta* *D Delhi*

3 Who captained the winners?

A Allan Border *B Mike Gatting* *C Kim Hughes* *D David Gower*

4 Who was the Man of the Match in the final?

A Bill Athey *B David Boon* *C Tim Robinson* *D Dean Jones*

5 Who swept his way to a century for England in the semi-final?

A Tim Robinson *B Chris Broad* *C Mike Gatting* *D Graham Gooch*

6 Which bowler, who took 5 for 44 in the semi-final, was promoted to No. 4 as a pinch-hitter in the final?

A Phil Edmonds *B Simon O'Donnell* *C Craig McDermott* *D John Emburey*

7 Who scored 181 for West Indies against Sri Lanka at Karachi?

A Richie Richardson *B Carlisle Best* *C Carl Hooper* *D Viv Richards*

8 Who took the first hat-trick in a World Cup, for India against New Zealand at Nagpur?

A Kapil Dev *B Manoj Prabhakar* *C Chetan Sharma* *D Maninder Singh*

9 Which man, who had only captained New Zealand in one Test before the tournament, led them in this World Cup?

A John Wright *B Jeff Crowe* *C Martin Crowe* *D Lee Germon*

10 Who scored 58 for England in the final?

A Bill Athey *B Neil Fairbrother* *C Mike Gatting* *D Paul Downton*

11 Which wicket-keeper caught Mike Gatting's top-edged reverse-sweep in the final?

A Wayne Phillips *B Tim Zoehrer* *C Ian Healy* *D Greg Dyer*

The Googly

Which 20-year-old played his only two one-day internationals for Australia during the 1987 World Cup, and had played his last first-class match before he was 23?

A Shane George *B Glenn Trimble* *C Andrew Zesers* *D Robbie Kerr*

Answers on page 178

GROUNDS IN NEW ZEALAND

1 In which city is the Eden Park ground?

   A Auckland B Wellington C Christchurch D Hamilton

2 And in which city is the Carisbrook ground?

   A Hamilton B Queenstown C Wellington D Dunedin

3 Where might you watch the play from the Hadlee Stand?

   A Auckland B Dunedin C Christchurch D Wellington

4 On which ground was the first Test triple-century scored on New Zealand soil, in 1932-33?

   A Auckland B Dunedin C Christchurch D Wellington

5 And on which ground was Martin Crowe once dismissed for 299 in a Test?

   A Auckland B Dunedin C Christchurch D Wellington

6 Where is Pukekura Park, the picturesque ground with the natural grass terraces?

   A Alexandra B Lincoln C New Plymouth D Wanganui

7 And where is McLean Park, which became the 50th ground used for Test cricket early in 1979?

   A Napier B Hamilton C Gisborne D Dunedin

8 Where is the ground originally known as Seddon Park, though it has been renamed after various sponsors since 1990?

   A Hamilton B Invercargill C Queenstown D Wanganui

9 Where is Owen Delany Park, which staged its first one-day international in 1998-99?

   A Alexandra B Taupo C Gisborne D Dannevirke

10 Where is the ground now known as Bert Sutcliffe Oval, which staged the women's World Cup final in 2000?

   A Lincoln B Wellington C Palmerston North D Dunedin

11 Aorangi Park – not the one at Wimbledon – staged two first-class matches in 1998. Where is it?

   A Alexandra B Timaru C Gisborne D Oamaru

The Googly

What is unusual about the location of the Basin Reserve ground in Wellington?

A It lies below sea level B It forms a giant traffic roundabout C It is surrounded by water D It straddles the Tropic of Capricorn

Answers on page 178

SHORT BUT SWEET

1 Who became a folk hero, and won the BBC Sports Personality of the Year award in 1975, for his gritty performances against Australia, but played only five more Tests?
A Peter Willey B Barry Wood C Chris Balderstone D David Steele

2 Which England bowler took 12 wickets in his four Tests at an average of just 20, and was banned after his retirement in 2003?
A Dean Headley B Ed Giddins C Chris Lewis D Tim Munton

3 Which great batsman played only four Tests for South Africa, in 1969-70, and scored 508 runs at 72.57?
A Mike Procter B Barry Richards C Graeme Pollock D Eddie Barlow

4 Who made 66 on his Test debut for England in 1988, but won only three more caps, and also scored 80 in his first one-day international … and never played another one?
A Andy Lloyd B Kim Barnett C Tim Curtis D Martyn Moxon

5 Who made 107 on Test debut for England in 1969, but won only seven more caps – since then he's umpired more than twice as many Tests as he played?
A Peter Willey B Jack Birkenshaw C John Hampshire D Ken Palmer

6 Who played 65 one-day internationals for India, and scored a century in a World Cup match – but never passed 50 in any of his other matches?
A Ajit Agarkar B Kirti Azad C Chetan Sharma D Yashpal Sharma

7 Who captained South Africa in four Tests, won the toss all four times, and won all four matches against Australia by wide margins?
A Ali Bacher B Eddie Barlow C Colin Bland D Graeme Pollock

8 Who made 164 on debut for Australia in 1928-29, but died of tuberculosis four years later?
A Archie Jackson B Stan McCabe C Karl Schneider D Stan Squires

9 Who played only five Tests for England against Australia, in 1961, but scored centuries in the first and last of them?
A Arthur Milton B Bob Barber C Raman Subba Row D Don Kenyon

10 Who played only five Tests, all in England in 1964, but helped Australia win the Ashes and dismissed Geoff Boycott in his first three Test innings?
A Rex Sellers B Ron Gaunt C Grahame Corling D Dave Renneberg

11 Who scored a century in each innings for Pakistan in 1998-99, in only his second Test, but won only four more caps?
A Ali Naqvi B Basit Ali C Wajahatullah Wasti D Azam Khan

The Googly

Who made his official one-day international debut in 1991-92, aged 42, some 20 years after being selected for a tour that didn't happen – but was dropped as his country's captain after three matches and never played again?
A Graeme Pollock B Norman Gifford C Clive Rice D Duncan Fletcher

Answers on page 178

HAT-TRICKS

1 Who took a hat-trick for England against West Indies in Barbados early in 2004?

   A Andrew Flintoff B Stephen Harmison C Ashley Giles D Matthew Hoggard

2 Who took a hat-trick for Australia against England at Melbourne in 1994-95?

   A Shane Warne B Glenn McGrath C Merv Hughes D Damien Fleming

3 Who took India's first Test hat-trick, against Australia at Calcutta in 2000-01?

   A Anil Kumble B Harbhajan Singh C Ajit Agarkar D Zaheer Khan

4 Who took a one-day hat-trick for England against Pakistan at The Oval in 2003?

   A James Anderson B Ashley Giles C Andrew Flintoff D Richard Johnson

5 Who took a hat-trick with the first three balls of a World Cup match in 2003?

   A Wasim Akram B Brett Lee C Chaminda Vaas D Glenn McGrath

6 Who took two hat-tricks in the same Test, in 1912?

   A Jimmy Matthews B Sydney Barnes C Charles Kelleway D Gilbert Jessop

7 Who took Zimbabwe's first Test hat-trick, against Bangladesh at Harare in 2003-04?

   A Andy Blignaut B Heath Streak C Eddo Brandes D Ray Price

8 Who took the first hat-trick in a one-day international, for Pakistan against Australia at Hyderabad in 1982-83?

   A Imran Khan B Jalaluddin C Tauseef Ahmed D Sikander Bakht

9 Which Indian bowler, who ended up with 236 Test wickets, took a hat-trick on his first-class debut in 1989-90?

   A Salil Ankola B Venkatapathy Raju C Javagal Srinath D Venkatesh Prasad

10 Who was the first West Indian to take a Test hat-trick, against Pakistan at Lahore in 1958-59?

   A Alf Valentine B Roy Gilchrist C Sonny Ramadhin D Wes Hall

11 Which Yorkshireman, who played 15 Tests in Australia but none at home, took a Test hat-trick at Melbourne in 1882-83?

   A Fred Morley B Willie Bates C Johnny Briggs D Billy Barnes

The Googly

What was remarkable about the future King George VI's hat-trick on the slopes of Windsor Castle in the early 1900s?

A It was made up of an earl, a marquess, and a visiting Prussian nobleman
B The victims were instructed to get out by a senior courtier C It included three kings
D The victims were Boer prisoners of war working on the royal estate

Answers on page 178

WHAT'S IN A NAME?

1 Which English county in 2004 fielded players called Mustard and Onions?

   A Derbyshire B Durham C Lancashire D Middlesex

2 Which county did John Hampshire captain in 1979 and 1980?

   A Derbyshire B Leicestershire C Nottinghamshire D Yorkshire

3 Which county regularly fielded a Butcher and a Baker together (but no Candlestick-Maker) in the 1970s?

   A Essex B Nottinghamshire C Somerset D Surrey

4 Who gave himself the third forename "Dylan" in homage to his favourite singer?

   A Allan Lamb B Bob Willis C Christopher Cowdrey D Jeff Dujon

5 Which county often had a Buss bowling at both ends in the 1960s?

   A Hampshire B Sussex C Warwickshire D Worcestershire

6 Three unrelated players with which surname have kept wicket for West Indies since 1963?

   A Jacobs B Murray C Findlay D Dujon

7 For which English county did Julius Caesar play?

   A Kent B Middlesex C Surrey D Sussex

8 Three unrelated players with which surname opened the batting for West Indies in the 1970s?

   A Fredericks B Greenidge C Haynes D Williams

9 For which English county did William Shakespeare play?

   A Leicestershire B Northamptonshire C Warwickshire D Worcestershire

10 Which New Zealand Test player of the 1990s was nicknamed "Senator"?

   A James Carter B Robert Kennedy C Kerry Walmsley D Bert Vance

11 For which English county did George Bernard Shaw play?

   A Glamorgan B Gloucestershire C Hampshire D Warwickshire

The Googly

Who had himself tattooed with the number 356, indicating that he was the 356th person to play for Australia, and then found out it should have been 357?

A Mark Waugh B Greg Blewett C Michael Slater D Shane Warne

Answers on page 178

MIXED BAG

1 Who scored 1710 Test runs in 1976, a new record for a calendar year?

   A Gordon Greenidge **B** *Viv Richards* **C** *Greg Chappell* **D** *Dennis Amiss*

2 And who took 85 Test wickets during 1981, another new record?

   A Terry Alderman **B** *Bob Willis* **C** *Ian Botham* **D** *Dennis Lillee*

3 Which country, in 2003, won a match in the World Cup at last, after losing their first ten?

   A Holland **B** *Bangladesh* **C** *Canada* **D** *Namibia*

4 Who played her first Test for England in 1960, and her last in 1979?

   A Mary Duggan **B** *Enid Bakewell* **C** *Carole Hodges* **D** *Rachael Heyhoe-Flint*

5 Who is the only player to score centuries in his first two Tests, and his last two Tests as well?

   A Mohammad Azharuddin **B** *Bill Ponsford* **C** *Alvin Kallicharran* **D** *Don Bradman*

6 Who captained New Zealand on his Test debut in 1995-96?

   A Nathan Astle **B** *Roger Twose* **C** *Lee Germon* **D** *Stephen Fleming*

7 Which Australian was bowled by the only ball he faced during their 1975 tour of England?

   A Alan Hurst **B** *Jeff Thomson* **C** *Jim Higgs* **D** *Richie Robinson*

8 Who was signed to join his brother at an English county for 2005, yet wasn't classified as an overseas player despite being his country's most-capped cricketer?

   A Ray Price **B** *Grant Flower* **C** *Mark Waugh* **D** *Gary Kirsten*

9 Which Australian played for Kent, his fourth different English county, during 2004?

   A Ian Harvey **B** *Michael Bevan* **C** *Greg Blewett* **D** *Andrew Symonds*

10 Which England player of the 1980s scored 201, 2 and 69 in his last three Test innings?

   A Graeme Fowler **B** *Chris Broad* **C** *Chris Tavare* **D** *Tim Robinson*

11 Who uniquely scored 2000 first-class runs in England in 1965, without making a century?

   A Ron Nicholls **B** *Ken Barrington* **C** *Mike Buss* **D** *David Green*

The Googly

Who, batting for Pakistan against West Indies at Karachi in 1990-91, helped break a partnership record established 33 years previously by his father and his uncle?

   A Mudassar Nazar **B** *Shoaib Mohammad* **C** *Majid Khan* **D** *Sadiq Mohammad*

Answers on page 178

GEOFFREY BOYCOTT

1 Against which country, on his home ground at Headingley in 1977, did Boycott become the first batsman to score his 100th first-class century in a Test match?

A Australia *B India* *C Pakistan* *D West Indies*

2 Who, in 1980-81, bowled an over at Boycott (and bowled him with the sixth ball) which is thought by eye-witnesses to be the fastest ever delivered?

A Andy Roberts *B Michael Holding* *C Colin Croft* *D Malcolm Marshall*

3 For which Yorkshire club did Boycott play as a youth, alongside Dickie Bird and the TV chat-show host Michael Parkinson?

A Bradford *B Bingley* *C Barnsley* *D Harrogate*

4 Boycott first played for Yorkshire in 1962 – in which year did he make his Test debut for England?

A 1963 *B 1964* *C 1965* *D 1966*

5 Who was Boycott's unexpected opening partner in his first Test?

A Bob Barber *B Fred Titmus* *C Fred Trueman* *D Ted Dexter*

6 In 1967, against whom did Boycott score 246 not out, his highest Test score, and then get dropped for "selfish batting"?

A Australia *B India* *C New Zealand* *D Pakistan*

7 Who were on the receiving end of Boycott's 146 for Yorkshire in the 1965 one-day Gillette Cup final?

A Kent *B Lancashire* *C Surrey* *D Sussex*

8 Who's the only man to score more than Boycott's 103 centuries for Yorkshire?

A Len Hutton *B Herbert Sutcliffe* *C Wilfred Rhodes* *D David Denton*

9 For which South African provincial side did Boycott score 107 against Rhodesia in 1971-72?

A Border *B Orange Free State* *C Northern Transvaal* *D Natal*

10 What was unusual about Boycott's bowling in the 1979 World Cup final?

A He bowled underarm *B He bowled with his cap on back to front* *C He had never bowled for England before* *D He bowled with his helmet on, as Viv Richards was hitting very powerfully*

11 Against which county did Boycott have his best record in Championship matches – 3303 runs at 76.81, with 15 centuries?

A Derbyshire *B Lancashire* *C Nottinghamshire* *D Worcestershire*

The Googly

Who was the non-striker when Boycott reached his 100th first-class century in 1977 – and was also at the other end when John Edrich scored his 100th hundred the same year?

A Alan Butcher *B Pat Pocock* *C Robin Jackman* *D Graham Roope*

Answers on page 178

MORE HAT-TRICKS

1 Who took a record seven hat-tricks in first-class cricket, six of them for Kent?

A Derek Underwood B Colin Blythe C Tich Freeman D Doug Wright

2 Who took four hat-tricks for Gloucestershire in the 1970s, two of them all made up of lbws?

A David Allen B Mike Procter C John Mortimore D Jack Davey

3 Who took four wickets in four balls and a hat-trick in the same innings of his own benefit match in 1907?

A Albert Trott B Sydney Barnes C Frank Foster D Wilfred Rhodes

4 Who took a one-day hat-trick for England against India at Trent Bridge in September 2004?

A Alex Wharf B Stephen Harmison C James Anderson D Darren Gough

5 Who took three hat-tricks for Kent in 1996, two of them in successive matches?

A Martin McCague B Mark Ealham C Matthew Fleming D Dean Headley

6 Who took two hat-tricks in Tests, and two more in one-day internationals?

A Hugh Trumble B Saqlain Mushtaq C Wasim Akram D Shane Warne

7 Which England batsman – and occasional bowler – took a hat-trick for Somerset in 1995?

A Mark Lathwell B Marcus Trescothick C Chris Tavare D Dermot Reeve

8 Who managed a rare wicket-keeper's hat-trick, off different bowlers, for Gloucestershire at The Oval in 1986?

A Andy Stovold B Andy Brassington C Jack Russell D Mark Alleyne

9 Who took six hat-tricks for Gloucestershire, including two in the same game in 1924?

A Cec Parkin B Tom Goddard C Charlie Parker D Walter Hammond

10 Who scored a hundred and took four wickets in four balls for Hampshire against the 1996 Indian tourists?

A Shaun Udal B Kevan James C Liam Botham D Dimitri Mascarenhas

11 Whose first three wickets in first-class cricket came in the form of a hat-trick for Sussex against Surrey in 1978?

A Paul Phillipson B John Spencer C Tony Pigott D Giles Cheatle

The Googly

What was unusual about Tony Lock's hat-trick for Leicestershire against Hampshire at Portsmouth in 1967?

*A It was on his debut for Leicestershire B It was the first Sunday hat-trick in England
C The three victims were all stumped D All three batsmen had made hundreds*

Answers on page 178

THE ASHES 1994-95

1 Who captained Australia in the series?

   A Allan Border B Steve Waugh C Mark Taylor D David Boon

2 Who took 8 for 71, and 11 wickets in all, in the first Test at Brisbane?

   A Shane Warne B Phil Tufnell C Craig McDermott D Darren Gough

3 Who set the tone for the series by smashing the first ball of the first Test for four, on his way to 176?

   A Mike Atherton B Graham Gooch C Mark Taylor D Michael Slater

4 Who was England's wicket-keeper throughout the series?

   A Alec Stewart B Jack Russell C Warren Hegg D Steven Rhodes

5 Who had reached 98 not out when Mike Atherton declared in the third Test at Sydney?

   A Graham Thorpe B Graham Gooch C Graeme Hick D John Crawley

6 Who scored 51 and took 6 for 49 for England in the third Test at Sydney?

   A Phillip DeFreitas B Martin McCague C Craig White D Darren Gough

7 Why was Devon Malcolm forced to miss the first Test at Brisbane?

   A He broke a finger in fielding practice B He got sunstroke on a day off at Surfers Paradise C He had chicken-pox D He sprained his ankle while surfing on the Gold Coast

8 Who scored a century on debut in the fourth Test at Adelaide?

   A Mark Waugh B Greg Blewett C Matthew Hayden D Justin Langer

9 Graham Gooch and which other veteran announced their retirements from Test cricket on the eve of the final Test?

   A Allan Lamb B Allan Border C David Boon D Mike Gatting

10 Who was left stranded on 99 not out in the final Test at Perth after the last three tailenders were run out?

   A Mike Atherton B Steve Waugh C Mark Waugh D Graham Thorpe

11 Who was called up from club cricket in Melbourne to play for England in the fourth Test at Adelaide, and took six wickets?

   A Angus Fraser B Mark Ramprakash C Chris Lewis D Craig White

The Googly

In 1994-95 Australia's annual World Series one-day tournament, usually a three-team event, was expanded to include which other side, which overcame England and Zimbabwe to reach the finals?

A The Australian Academy B New South Wales (the Australian one-day champions) C The Rest of the World D Australia "A"

Answers on page 179

GLAMORGAN

1. Who scored over 34,000 runs for Glamorgan between 1957 and 1983, but never won an official Test cap?

   A Alan Jones B Eifion Jones C Tony Lewis D Roger Davis

2. And who took 2174 wickets for Glamorgan (1950-72) and never won a Test cap either?

   A Len Muncer B Ossie Wheatley C Johnny Clay D Don Shepherd

3. Who captained Glamorgan to the County Championship in 1997?

   A Tony Cottey B Hugh Morris C Matthew Maynard D Steve James

4. Which Glamorgan player made his England Test debut at Lord's in 2002?

   A Robert Croft B Geraint Jones C Simon Jones D Steve James

5. Which Glamorgan captain won nine Test caps for England, and two rugby caps for Wales, before being killed in the Second World War?

   A Maurice Turnbull B Ken Farnes C Vivian Jenkins D Wilf Wooller

6. Which Glamorgan batsman, part of the 2002 National League-winning squad, was born on the island of Bermuda?

   A Adrian Dale B David Hemp C Matthew Maynard D Michael Powell

7. In which year did Glamorgan win the County Championship for the first time?

   A 1921 B 1948 C 1958 D 1969

8. Which Glamorgan player captained England on his Test debut in 1972-73?

   A Jeff Jones B Alan Jones C Tony Lewis D Peter Walker

9. In which town have Glamorgan played occasional home games at Ynysangharad Park?

   A Abergavenny B Pontypridd C Ebbw Vale D Llanelli

10. Who scored 309 not out for Glamorgan against Sussex at Colwyn Bay in 2000?

    A Matthew Elliott B Steve James C David Hemp D Adrian Dale

11. Which Pakistan Test player captained Glamorgan between 1973 and 1976?

    A Javed Miandad B Majid Khan C Sadiq Mohammad D Mushtaq Mohammad

The Googly

To which of their home grounds do Glamorgan's players usually travel by aeroplane?

A Aberystwyth B Harlech C Colwyn Bay D Abergavenny

Answers on page 179

THE WAUGHS

1 Who is the oldest of the Waugh brothers?

A Mark *B Steve* *C Danny* *D Dean*

2 Steve Waugh didn't score a century until his 27th Test – where was that breakthrough innings, in 1989?

A Headingley, Leeds *B Lord's* *C The Oval* *D Sydney*

3 What is Steve Waugh's middle name?

A Raymond *B Roderick* *C Rodger* *D Richardson*

4 Who did Mark Waugh replace in the team when he made his Test debut in 1990-91?

A Allan Border *B David Boon* *C Steve Waugh* *D Dean Jones*

5 For which English county did Steve Waugh play in 1987 and 1988?

A Essex *B Leicestershire* *C Somerset* *D Sussex*

6 And for which one did he play briefly in 2002?

A Hampshire *B Kent* *C Northamptonshire* *D Worcestershire*

7 Whose aggregate record for Test catches did Mark Waugh surpass at Lord's in 2001?

A Allan Border *B Ian Botham* *C Bobby Simpson* *D Mark Taylor*

8 Oddly, Mark Waugh's highest one-day score (173) was higher than his Test-best (153 not out) – against which country did he make that one-day best?

A England *B Holland* *C India* *D West Indies*

9 In 2003 Steve Waugh became the second batsman to score Test centuries against the maximum nine possible opponents – who was the first?

A Matthew Hayden *B Brian Lara* *C Gary Kirsten* *D Sachin Tendulkar*

10 Against which side did the Waugh twins share an unbroken world-record partnership of 464 for New South Wales in 1990-91?

A England XI *B Queensland* *C Victoria* *D Western Australia*

11 Where did Steve Waugh score his only Test double-century – a round 200 against West Indies in 1994-95?

A St John's, Antigua *B Bridgetown, Barbados* *C Kingston, Jamaica*
D Port-of-Spain, Trinidad

The Googly

Which country other than Australia did Mark and Steve Waugh both represent?

A Abu Dhabi *B Fiji* *C Ireland* *D Scotland*

Answers on page 179

FIELDING RECORDS (NOT WICKET-KEEPING)

1 Who is the only non-wicket-keeper to take 1000 catches in first-class cricket?

    A W.G. Grace *B Frank Woolley* *C Tony Lock* *D Micky Stewart*

2 Who was the first person to take seven catches in a Test, beating a record held jointly by his grandfather?

    A Paul Sheahan *B Mudassar Nazar* *C Greg Chappell* *D Dean Headley*

3 Who ran out three Australians in the 1975 World Cup final?

    A Vanburn Holder *B Keith Boyce* *C Clive Lloyd* *D Viv Richards*

4 Who, in 1939, became the first fielder to take 100 Test catches?

    A Walter Hammond *B Jack Hobbs* *C Frank Woolley* *D Don Bradman*

5 And who, in 1993, became the first to take 150 Test catches?

    A Allan Border *B Mark Waugh* *C Mark Taylor* *D Ian Botham*

6 Who was the first person to take 150 catches in one-day internationals?

    A Mohammad Azharuddin *B Viv Richards* *C Greg Chappell* *D Javed Miandad*

7 Which famous fielder was the first to take five catches in a one-day international, in 1993-94?

    A Graeme Hick *B Jonty Rhodes* *C Clive Lloyd* *D Derek Randall*

8 Who seemed to be stuck on 99 Test catches when he retired in 1967-68, but returned ten years later and held 11 more?

    A Mike Smith *B Bob Simpson* *C Colin Cowdrey* *D Nawab of Pataudi junior*

9 Whose 15 outfield catches in a Test series, set in 1920-21, was still a record 80 years later?

    A Frank Woolley *B Stork Hendry* *C Jack Gregory* *D Jack Hobbs*

10 Who took his 100th catch in his 100th Test in 1988-89, one game after scoring his 100th first-class century?

    A Allan Border *B Ian Botham* *C Viv Richards* *D Graham Gooch*

11 Who took 10 catches in a county match in 1928, and also scored a century in both innings?

    A Philip Mead *B Walter Hammond* *C Herbert Sutcliffe* *D Maurice Leyland*

The Googly

Which future England batsman and coach took a record seven outfield catches in an innings in a county match in 1957?

    A Ray Illingworth *B Micky Stewart* *C Keith Fletcher* *D Ken Barrington*

Answers on page 179

WEST INDIES IN TESTS

1 What were the surnames of the Three Ws?

A *Weekes, Wishart and Walcott* **B** *Weekes, Worrell and Walcott*
C *Williams, Wishart and Weekes* **D** *Williams, Worrell and Walcott*

2 Which is the only country on the South American mainland to stage Tests?

A *Grenada* **B** *Surinam* **C** *Guyana* **D** *Dominica*

3 Who scored a century on Test debut against South Africa at Cape Town in 2003-04?

A *Devon Smith* **B** *Sylvester Joseph* **C** *Dwayne Bravo* **D** *Dwayne Smith*

4 When Garry Sobers broke the then Test record with 365 not out, against Pakistan at Kingston in 1957-58, who scored 260 in the same innings?

A *Everton Weekes* **B** *Basil Butcher* **C** *Conrad Hunte* **D** *Rohan Kanhai*

5 Who took three wickets in four balls, then completed a hat-trick in the next Test, against Australia in 1960-61?

A *Wes Hall* **B** *Lance Gibbs* **C** *Chester Watson* **D** *Charlie Griffith*

6 Who captained West Indies in 74 Tests between 1974-75 and 1984-85?

A *Clive Lloyd* **B** *Viv Richards* **C** *Rohan Kanhai* **D** *Michael Holding*

7 Which wicket-keeper became, in 1992-93, the first West Indian Test cricketer from Grenada?

A *David Williams* **B** *David Murray* **C** *Junior Murray* **D** *Deryck Murray*

8 And which one became, in 1994-95, the first West Indian Test cricketer to have been born in London?

A *Jimmy Adams* **B** *Courtney Browne* **C** *Ridley Jacobs* **D** *David Williams*

9 Who hit 258 in his final Test innings, in 1968-69?

A *Seymour Nurse* **B** *Rohan Kanhai* **C** *Joey Carew* **D** *Basil Butcher*

10 Who took the first eight wickets to fall on his Test debut for West Indies in 1950?

A *Alf Valentine* **B** *Sonny Ramadhin* **C** *Collie Smith* **D** *Lance Pierre*

11 Who scored 250 for West Indies against India at Kanpur in 1978-79?

A *Alvin Kallicharran* **B** *Faoud Bacchus* **C** *Herbert Chang* **D** *Basil "Shotgun" Williams*

The Googly

The West Indian batsman Lawrence Rowe suffered from which unusual medical condition?

A *He had five fingers and a thumb on each hand* **B** *He was allergic to grass*
C *One arm was three inches longer than the other* **D** *Cold weather made his knees lock up*

Answers on page 179

THE ASHES 1997

1 Who scored 207 in the first Test, after England had bowled Australia out for 118?

  A Mike Atherton B Nasser Hussain C Graham Thorpe D Graeme Hick

2 Which pair of brothers made their Test debut together in the fifth Test at Trent Bridge?

  *A Adam and Ben Hollioake B Steve and Mark Waugh C Mike and Neil Smith
  D Shane and Brett Lee*

3 Which batsman ended a run of 21 innings without a half-century by scoring 129 in the first Test at Edgbaston?

  A Steve Waugh B Michael Bevan C Ian Healy D Mark Taylor

4 And who scored his third hundred against England, in his third Test against them, in the same innings?

  A Matthew Elliott B Michael Bevan C Greg Blewett D Mark Waugh

5 Which Surrey player made his debut in the first Test at Edgbaston?

  A Alex Tudor B Mark Butcher C Graham Thorpe D Alistair Brown

6 Who took 8 for 38 as England were shot out for 77 at Lord's?

  A Paul Reiffel B Michael Kasprowicz C Shane Warne D Glenn McGrath

7 Which player, whose father and grandfather also played Test cricket, made his debut in the third Test at Old Trafford?

  A Adam Hollioake B Brendon Julian C Graham Lloyd D Dean Headley

8 Who was out for 199 in the fourth Test at Headingley?

  A Steve Waugh B Matthew Hayden C Matthew Elliott D Mark Waugh

9 Who made 127 at Headingley, in his first innings in Ashes Tests?

  A Ricky Ponting B Mark Ramprakash C Graham Thorpe D Matthew Hayden

10 Which Gloucestershire bowler won his only England cap at Headingley, but failed to take a wicket?

  A Mark Alleyne B Mike Smith C Jon Lewis D Martyn Ball

11 And who was called up from Gloucestershire and played his only Test for Australia at The Oval?

  A Andrew Symonds B Ian Harvey C Shaun Young D Mike Whitney

The Googly

During the 1997 series Ben Hollioake became, at 19 years 269 days, the youngest person to play a Test for England since which 18-year-old back in 1949?

A Fred Trueman B Brian Statham C Brian Close D Denis Compton

Answers on page 179

LORD'S CRICKET GROUND

1 Who is the ground named after?

   A Thomas Lord B Lord Sheffield C Cyril Lord D Lord Ponsonby-Fane and Lord Winchilsea

2 What is the end opposite the pavilion called?

   A Clock Tower End B Wellington Road End C Nursery End D Hoi Polloi End

3 Who broke the record for the highest individual score at Lord's in 1990?

   A Graham Gooch B Mark Ramprakash C Robin Smith D Mohammad Azharuddin

4 What's the affectionate nickname given to the futuristic media centre opposite the pavilion?

   A Apollo 11 B The Tripod C The Space Shuttle D The Gherkin

5 What is the usual description of the brightly-coloured MCC members' tie?

   A Orange and lemon B Blood and thunder C Egg and bacon D Egg and chips

6 Which innovation in 2004 led Lord's to be sold out for a county game for the first time (other than a final) since 1953?

   A The first Twenty20 Cup match there B A lunchtime pop concert C All the tickets were free D Spectators were allowed onto the outfield during intervals

7 When was the first match played at the current Lord's Ground?

   A 1787 B 1814 C 1877 D 1921

8 Which future England captain, who later had a stand named after him at Lord's, took 10 for 40 in a county match there in 1929?

   A Gubby Allen B Bill Edrich C Gerald Mound D Pelham Warner

9 And which Middlesex favourite, who scored 208 in the 1947 Lord's Test, also has a stand named after him there?

   A George Mann B Bill Edrich C Denis Compton D Dick Tavern

10 Who, in 1939, was the first man to score two hundreds in the same Lord's Test?

   A Walter Hammond B Don Bradman C George Headley D Len Hutton

11 The ground at Lord's slopes some seven feet from the Grand Stand down to the Mound Stand. How did Sir Pelham Warner describe the size of the slope?

   A About the size of a tall man in a top hat B A fathom or so C 21 hands D Three stumps high

The Googly

What happened to David Steele when he went out to bat on his Test debut in 1975, the first time he had used the home dressing-room at Lord's rather than the visitors' one?

A He got lost and had to climb over the pavilion railings B He ended up in the road behind the pavilion C When he was out he absent-mindedly returned to the wrong room, and was jeered by the Aussies D He went down too many stairs and ended up in the basement toilets

Answers on page 179

GLOUCESTERSHIRE

1 Who broke W.G. Grace's 128-year-old record score for Gloucestershire with an innings of 341 in 2004?

A Mark Alleyne **B** Alex Gidman **C** Craig Spearman **D** Jonty Rhodes

2 Which Gloucestershire player captained England in the famous Timeless Test against South Africa at Durban in 1938-39?

A Walter Hammond **B** Charles Barnett **C** Beverley Lyon **D** Tom Graveney

3 In which town do Gloucestershire play home games at a ground called Archdeacon Meadow?

A Moreton-in-Marsh **B** Bristol **C** Cheltenham **D** Gloucester

4 Which South African topped Gloucestershire's batting averages in 2003?

A Jacques Kallis **B** Jonty Rhodes **C** Craig Spearman **D** Daryll Cullinan

5 Which Gloucestershire bowler took 122 Test wickets for England between 1959 and 1966?

A David Allen **B** John Mortimore **C** David Larter **D** David Smith

6 Jack Russell made his Test debut against Sri Lanka at Lord's in 1988 – along with which of his then county colleagues?

A Mark Alleyne **B** Kim Barnett **C** David "Syd" Lawrence **D** Phil Newport

7 Who, between 1976 and 1981, four times scored a double and a single century in the same match for Gloucestershire, and was not out in all eight innings?

A Zaheer Abbas **B** Andy Stovold **C** Sadiq Mohammad **D** Mike Procter

8 Which touring bowler took all ten wickets for 66 against Gloucestershire in 1921, and later called his autobiography *10 for 66 and All That*?

A Arthur Mailey **B** Bill O'Reilly **C** Clarrie Grimmett **D** Ted McDonald

9 The appointment of which amateur player as captain in 1961 led to Tom Graveney's departure from Gloucestershire?

A Tony Brown **B** Sir Derrick Bailey **C** Ken Graveney **D** Tom Pugh

10 Who scored 108 on his first-class debut for Gloucestershire in 1965?

A Mike Bissex **B** David Green **C** David Shepherd **D** Jim Foat

11 Which turn-of-the-century Gloucestershire great was known as "The Croucher", and has a stand named after him at Bristol?

A Gilbert Jessop **B** W.G. Grace **C** Len Mound **D** Charlie Parker

The Googly

Which Cornishman, who later became a Test umpire, scored more than 22,000 runs for Gloucestershire?

A Mike "Pasty" Harris **B** Charles Barnett **C** Jack Crapp **D** David Shepherd

Answers on page 179

NICKNAMES

1 Which England player was nicknamed "Fiery Fred"?

    A Fred Titmus *B Fred Trueman* *C Freddie Gough-Calthorpe* *D Freddie Flintoff*

2 And which one was nicknamed "Beefy"?

    A Colin Cowdrey *B Ian Botham* *C Brian Close* *D Colin Milburn*

3 Which West Indian bowler was known as "Big Bird"?

    A Curtly Ambrose *B Joel Garner* *C Colin Croft* *D Malcolm Marshall*

4 Which England player – later their coach – was nicknamed "Bumble"?

    A Micky Stewart *B Keith Fletcher* *C Duncan Fletcher* *D David Lloyd*

5 Which West Indian was known, early in his career, as "Big Cat"?

    A Andy Roberts *B Keith Boyce* *C Clive Lloyd* *D Courtney Walsh*

6 Which Australian is known as "Pigeon"?

    A Justin Langer *B Paul Reiffel* *C Glenn McGrath* *D Jason Gillespie*

7 Which England opener of the 1980s was nicknamed "Foxy"?

    A Wayne Larkins *B Chris Smith* *C Graeme Fowler* *D Chris Tavare*

8 Which Australian captain was known as "The Big Ship"?

    A Warwick Armstrong *B Richie Benaud* *C Ian Chappell* *D Dave Gregory*

9 Which New Zealand captain was nicknamed "Hogan"?

    A John Reid *B Ken Logan* *C Martin Crowe* *D Graham Dowling*

10 And which one was nicknamed "The Playing Mantis"?

    A Ken Rutherford *B John Bracewell* *C Jeremy Coney* *D Geoff Howarth*

11 Which Australian was known as "Phanto", because of his liking for the comic-book character The Phantom?

    A Lindsay Hassett *B Bill Lawry* *C Greg Chappell* *D Don Bradman*

The Googly

Which Australian was usually known as "Junior", but was lumbered with various other nicknames through his career, notably "Audi", after a spell of four consecutive ducks (he did manage to score in his next innings, to avoid the threatened nickname "Olympic")?

    A Mark Taylor *B Mark Waugh* *C Steve Waugh* *D Dean Jones*

Answers on page 179

KENT

1 Which Kent bowler took 304 wickets in 1928, and 298 in 1933?

   A Doug Wright *B Frank Woolley* *C Colin Blythe* *D Tich Freeman*

2 Who played five first-class matches for Kent in 2003 and took 33 wickets?

   A Martin Saggers *B Muttiah Muralitharan* *C Stuart MacGill* *D Amjad Khan*

3 Who captained Kent from 1957 to 1971?

   A Brian Luckhurst *B Alan Knott* *C Colin Cowdrey* *D Mike Denness*

4 Which Kent player appeared in 11 one-day internationals in the 1990s, but no Tests?

   A Mark Ealham *B Min Patel* *C David Fulton* *D Matthew Fleming*

5 Which Kent batsman played one Test for England, in 1986, and later became an umpire?

   A Dick Richardson *B Mark Benson* *C Chris Tavare* *D Chris Cowdrey*

6 Who scored almost 48,000 runs for Kent – with 122 hundreds – between 1906 and 1938?

   A Frank Woolley *B Les Ames* *C Arthur Fagg* *D Percy Chapman*

7 Who scored 112 and won the Gold Award in the 1995 Benson & Hedges Cup final, even though Kent lost it?

   A Aravinda de Silva *B Trevor Ward* *C Vince Wells* *D Graham Cowdrey*

8 In which town have Kent played home games at a ground called Hesketh Park?

   A Folkestone *B Gravesend* *C Tunbridge Wells* *D Dartford*

9 Who hit a double-century in each innings for Kent against Essex at Colchester in 1938?

   A Arthur Fagg *B Bryan Valentine* *C Les Ames* *D Wally Hardinge*

10 Which Kent wicket-keeper took eight catches in an innings and scored a century against Middlesex at Lord's in 1991?

   A Alan Knott *B Stuart Waterton* *C Steve Marsh* *D Paul Downton*

11 Which Kent batsman was the only Englishman to play first-class cricket before the First World War and after the Second?

   A Bill Ashdown *B Les Ames* *C Percy Chapman* *D Frank Woolley*

The Googly

What misfortune befell Colin Cowdrey as he listened on his car radio as his son Christopher took a wicket in his first over in Tests in 1984-85?

A He was given a parking ticket *B He drove the wrong way down a one-way street*
C He reversed into Mike Denness's car *D He missed his exit on the motorway and had to drive an extra 52 miles*

Answers on page 180

FAST STARTERS

1 Who scored 1000 first-class runs before the end of May 1988?

A Graeme Hick *B Jimmy Cook* *C Tim Curtis* *D Graham Gooch*

2 Who was the first batsman to score 1000 in May, in 1895?

A C.B. Fry *B W.G. Grace* *C K.S. Ranjitsinhji* *D F.S. Jackson*

3 Which touring player scored 1000 runs before the end of May 1973?

A Glenn Turner *B Roy Fredericks* *C Gordon Greenidge* *D Keith Stackpole*

4 Who scored 1000 runs before the end of May in 1930 – and did it again in 1938?

A Herbert Sutcliffe *B Bill Ponsford* *C Patsy Hendren* *D Don Bradman*

5 Who scored 1010 runs, all of them at Lord's, before the end of June 1938?

A Jack Robertson *B Bill Edrich* *C Patsy Hendren* *D Denis Compton*

6 Who scored 1115 runs in his first first-class season, for Cambridge University and Lancashire in 1987?

A Mike Atherton *B Mark Crawley* *C John Crawley* *D Jason Gallian*

7 Who scored 1000 runs, took 100 wickets, and played for England in his first first-class season, 1949?

A Bob Appleyard *B Brian Close* *C Ken Cranston* *D Trevor Bailey*

8 Who took 101 wickets in 1963, his first season of first-class cricket?

A John Snow *B David Brown* *C Pat Pocock* *D Derek Underwood*

9 Which future West Indian Test player scored centuries in his first three first-class innings, starting in 1956-57?

A Joe Solomon *B Basil Butcher* *C Collie Smith* *D Seymour Nurse*

10 Which Lancastrian scored 1000 runs in May 1928?

A Harry Makepeace *B Eddie Paynter* *C Charlie Hallows* *D Ernest Tyldesley*

11 Who scored 1000 runs in both June and August 1949?

A Len Hutton *B Reg Simpson* *C Cyril Washbrook* *D Denis Compton*

The Googly

Which Australian scored centuries in his first first-class matches in South Africa, West Indies, India and Pakistan?

A Allan Border *B Bob Simpson* *C Ricky Ponting* *D Don Bradman*

Answers on page 180

THE ASHES 1998-99

1 Who captained Australia throughout the series?

   A Steve Waugh **B** *Ricky Ponting* **C** *Mark Taylor* **D** *Ian Healy*

2 And who was England's captain?

   A *Mike Atherton* **B** *Alec Stewart* **C** *Nasser Hussain* **D** *Mark Butcher*

3 Why did Shane Warne miss the first four Tests of the series?

   A *He was banned* **B** *He was out of form* **C** *He was recovering after a shoulder operation*
   D *He had broken a finger*

4 Which Australian-raised bowler took 5 for 105 in the first Test ... for England?

   A *Alan Mullally* **B** *Andy Caddick* **C** *Martin McCague* **D** *Craig White*

5 Which spinner took 27 wickets in the series?

   A *Shane Warne* **B** *Colin Miller* **C** *Stuart MacGill* **D** *Robert Croft*

6 Who made his debut in the second Test at Perth, and dismissed both Waugh twins?

   A *Alex Tudor* **B** *Dean Headley* **C** *Robert Croft* **D** *Craig White*

7 Who scored his only century against Australia in the fourth Test at Melbourne?

   A *Alec Stewart* **B** *Graeme Hick* **C** *Mark Ramprakash* **D** *Mike Atherton*

8 Who took a hat-trick in the final Test at Sydney?

   A *Stuart MacGill* **B** *Colin Miller* **C** *Dominic Cork* **D** *Darren Gough*

9 Who kept wicket for England in the fourth and fifth Tests?

   A *Alec Stewart* **B** *Paul Nixon* **C** *Jack Russell* **D** *Warren Hegg*

10 Who took 6 for 60 as England pulled off a narrow victory in the fourth Test at Melbourne?

   A *Angus Fraser* **B** *Peter Such* **C** *Dominic Cork* **D** *Dean Headley*

11 Which Western Australian bowler made his Test debut in that match at Melbourne?

   A *Jo Angel* **B** *Brad Hogg* **C** *Matthew Nicholson* **D** *Paul Wilson*

The Googly

Which Australian scored his fourth and last Test hundred in the first Test at Brisbane – but
never scored a century outside a Test, despite playing 112 other first-class matches?

A *Paul Reiffel* **B** *Ian Healy* **C** *Brendon Julian* **D** *Greg Matthews*

Answers on page 180

MARVELLOUS MIDDLE NAMES: ENGLAND

1 Which England captain's middle name is Ivon?

A Stanley Jackson **B** *Buns Thornton* **C** *Freddie Brown* **D** *David Gower*

2 And which has the middle names John Knight?

A David Sheppard **B** *Mike Smith* **C** *Freddie Calthorpe* **D** *Norman Yardley*

3 Which England captain's middle names were Oswald Browning?

A Gubby Allen **B** *Freddie Brown* **C** *Cyril Walters* **D** *Johnny Douglas*

4 And whose middle names were Barker Howard?

A Mark Nicholas **B** *Shrimp Leveson Gower* **C** *Greville Stevens* **D** *Peter May*

5 Which England player's middle name is Sewards?

A Len Hutton **B** *Herbert Sutcliffe* **C** *Sam Staples* **D** *Fred Trueman*

6 And whose middle name is Verity?

A Alec Bedser **B** *Don Smith* **C** *Nick Knight* **D** *Hedley Verity*

7 Which England player has the middle names Grant Billson?

A Jack MacBryan **B** *Winston Place* **C** *Nick Cook* **D** *Arthur Gilligan*

8 And which has the middle names Simon Hunter?

A Ed Giddins **B** *Phil Tufnell* **C** *George Simpson-Hayward* **D** *Denis Compton*

9 Which England batsman's middle name is Thornton?

A Andy Lloyd **B** *Bob Barber* **C** *Clive Radley* **D** *John Dewes*

10 What was W.G. Grace's middle name?

A Gilbert **B** *George* **C** *Gerald* **D** *Gladstone*

11 Which bowler, who played one Test for England in 1994, has the middle name Emmanuel?

A Simon Brown **B** *Joey Benjamin* **C** *John Stephenson* **D** *Mike Smith*

The Googly

What were the real forenames names of the England captain (and Olympic middleweight champion) "Johnny Won't Hit Today" Douglas?

A John Walter Harry Troughton **B** *John William Henry Tyler*
C John Wisden Harbledown Thomas **D** *John Wesley Harper Taylor*

Answers on page 180

THE 1992 WORLD CUP

1   Who won the fifth World Cup, the first to include floodlit matches?

   A New Zealand B England C South Africa D Pakistan

2   In which city was the final played?

   A Auckland B Melbourne C Sydney D Perth

3   Who captained the winners?

   A Imran Khan B Javed Miandad C Graham Gooch D Ian Botham

4   Who was the Man of the Match in the final?

   A Imran Khan B Javed Miandad C Allan Lamb D Wasim Akram

5   Who was the tournament's leading runscorer, with 456 from nine games?

   A Andrew Hudson B Javed Miandad C Martin Crowe D Sachin Tendulkar

6   Who beat Australia in the first match of the tournament?

   A India B New Zealand C Pakistan D West Indies

7   And who did South Africa beat at Sydney, in their first World Cup match?

   A Australia B England C Sri Lanka D Zimbabwe

8   Who captained West Indies in the tournament?

   A Viv Richards B Richie Richardson C Carl Hooper D Malcolm Marshall

9   Which offspinner, in an innovative move, often opened the bowling for New Zealand?

   A Gavin Larsen B Rod Latham C Chris Harris D Dipak Patel

10 Australia didn't qualify for the semi-finals, but which of their batsmen scored two centuries?

   A Geoff Marsh B David Boon C Mark Waugh D Dean Jones

11 Who scored 110 for West Indies in their group game against Sri Lanka at Berri?

   A Clayton Lambert B Brian Lara C Carl Hooper D Phil Simmons

The Googly

The bowler who sent down the most wides (42) and no-balls (18) during the 1992 World Cup also ended up taking the most wickets (18) – who was it?

A Allan Donald B Ian Botham C Wasim Akram D Danny Morrison

Answers on page 180

MORE STRANGE BIRTHPLACES

1 Which great Australian legspinner was born in New Zealand on Christmas Day?

A *Shane Warne* B *Bill O'Reilly* C *Clarrie Grimmett* D *Richie Benaud*

2 Which great West Indian batsman was born in Panama?

A *Viv Richards* B *Garry Sobers* C *Rohan Kanhai* D *George Headley*

3 Which New Zealand batsman, who scored 214 on his Test debut in 1999-2000, was born in Australia's Northern Territory?

A *Mark Richardson* B *Scott Styris* C *Lou Vincent* D *Mathew Sinclair*

4 Which famous Zimbabwean player was actually born in Zambia?

A *Andy Flower* B *Henry Olonga* C *Heath Streak* D *Dave Houghton*

5 Which New Zealand player of the 1990s was a native of Devon in England?

A *Roger Twose* B *Lee Germon* C *Chris Pringle* D *Justin Vaughan*

6 Which England player was born in Cape Town in 1931, although he originally said it was in 1934?

A *Roger Prideaux* B *Basil D'Oliveira* C *Tony Greig* D *Raman Subba Row*

7 Which South African Test player – the first man to take four wickets in four balls twice in first-class cricket – was born in India and died in England?

A *Aubrey Faulkner* B *Reggie Schwarz* C *Bob Crisp* D *Dave Nourse*

8 Which Indian allrounder and one-day specialist was born in Trinidad?

A *Ajay Jadeja* B *Robin Singh* C *Chetan Sharma* D *Manoj Prabhakar*

9 Which player, whose debut Test was also India's first, was the first Test player born in Malaya?

A *Lala Amarnath* B *Amar Singh* C *Lall Singh* D *Mahomed Nissar*

10 In which country was the 1960s Indian allrounder Salim Durani born?

A *Afghanistan* B *Burma* C *Canada* D *Turkey*

11 Shakeel Ahmed, who played once for Pakistan in 1998-99, was the first Test cricketer born in which country?

A *Abu Dhabi* B *Kuwait* C *Nepal* D *Dubai*

The Googly

Who played Test cricket for two different countries but was born in neither of them?

A *Kepler Wessels* B *Gavin Hamilton* C *John Traicos* D *The Nawab of Pataudi senior*

Answers on page 180

SOUTH AFRICA IN TESTS

1 Who was the first South African to play in 100 Test matches?

    A Graeme Pollock **B** *Jonty Rhodes* **C** *Hansie Cronje* **D** *Gary Kirsten*

2 Who, against Australia in 1969-70, captained South Africa to a 4-0 clean sweep in their last official Test series for 22 years?

    A Ali Bacher **B** *Eddie Barlow* **C** *Mike Procter* **D** *Barry Richards*

3 Who scored 222 not out on his Test debut, against Bangladesh at Chittagong in 2003?

    A Martin van Jaarsveld **B** *Jacques Rudolph* **C** *Neil McKenzie* **D** *Graeme Smith*

4 Who took 170 wickets for South Africa between 1949-50 and 1960?

    A Neil Adcock **B** *Trevor Goddard* **C** *Hugh Tayfield* **D** *Peter Heine*

5 Who captained South Africa in their first Test after their readmission to international cricket in 1991-92?

    A Clive Rice **B** *Hansie Cronje* **C** *Jimmy Cook* **D** *Kepler Wessels*

6 Which spinner, who made his Test debut in 1995-96, had a bowling action described as "like a frog in a blender"?

    A Paul Adams **B** *Nicky Boje* **C** *Claude Henderson* **D** *Clive Eksteen*

7 Which South African wicket-keeper took more than 100 Test catches before he made his first stumping?

    A Dave Richardson **B** *Mark Boucher* **C** *Dennis Lindsay* **D** *John Waite*

8 Which South African player of the 1960s was famous for his scintillating cover fielding?

    A Ali Bacher **B** *Colin Bland* **C** *Tony Pithey* **D** *Graeme Pollock*

9 Who scored 163 on debut in South Africa's "comeback" Test against West Indies at Bridgetown in 1991-92?

    A Andrew Hudson **B** *Mark Rushmere* **C** *Kepler Wessels* **D** *Peter Kirsten*

10 Who followed his father into the Test side, and captained South Africa in England in 1951?

    A Eric Rowan **B** *Lindsay Tuckett* **C** *Alan Melville* **D** *Dudley Nourse*

11 In which South African city was there once a Test ground called Lord's?

    A East London **B** *Bloemfontein* **C** *Johannesburg* **D** *Durban*

The Googly

Who scored 102 against Australia at Port Elizabeth in March 1970, South Africa's last century in an official Test for more than 22 years?

A Ali Bacher **B** *Barry Richards* **C** *Lee Irvine* **D** *Graeme Pollock*

Answers on page 180

ONE-DAY INTERNATIONAL BATTING RECORDS

1 Who was the first batsman to score 10,000 runs in one-day internationals (ODIs)?

A *Mohammad Azharuddin* B *Steve Waugh* C *Mark Waugh* D *Sachin Tendulkar*

2 Who scored 189 not out, much of it in a last-wicket stand of 106, in an ODI at Old Trafford in 1984?

A *Ian Botham* B *Viv Richards* C *Martin Crowe* D *Dean Jones*

3 And who surpassed that record with an ODI innings of 194 in 1996-97?

A *Aamer Sohail* B *Saeed Anwar* C *Sanath Jayasuriya* D *Aravinda de Silva*

4 Who hit a century in 37 balls, the fastest at the time, in his first ODI innings, in 1996-97?

A *Sanath Jayasuriya* B *Shahid Afridi* C *Yousuf Youhana* D *Herschelle Gibbs*

5 Who scored the first century in an ODI – and the second, too?

A *Ian Chappell* B *Dennis Amiss* C *Keith Fletcher* D *Keith Stackpole*

6 Who was the first man to score three successive ODI hundreds, against India in 1982-83?

A *Zaheer Abbas* B *Kepler Wessels* C *Desmond Haynes* D *Javed Miandad*

7 Who hit 11 sixes and 11 fours in scoring 134 in an ODI in Singapore in 1995-96?

A *Aravinda de Silva* B *Mark Greatbatch* C *Chris Cairns* D *Sanath Jayasuriya*

8 Who scored ODI hundreds on successive days in England in 2003?

A *Graeme Smith* B *Marcus Trescothick* C *Jacques Kallis* D *Nasser Hussain*

9 Who was the first Englishman to carry his bat through an all-out ODI innings, scoring 125 not out against Pakistan at Trent Bridge in 1996?

A *Alec Stewart* B *Nick Knight* C *Alistair Brown* D *Mike Atherton*

10 Who scored half-centuries in nine consecutive ODI innings in the late 1980s?

A *Viv Richards* B *Desmond Haynes* C *Javed Miandad* D *Dean Jones*

11 Who was 39 years 51 days old when he scored his only ODI century, in 1979-80?

A *Mike Brearley* B *Geoff Boycott* C *Sunil Gavaskar* D *Mushtaq Mohammad*

The Googly

Who managed to bat through all 60 overs of India's first World Cup innings in 1975 at Lord's, scoring only 36 not out from 174 balls in the process, and provoking one disgruntled spectator to march out to the middle and dump his packed lunch at the batsman's feet in protest?

A *Dilip Sardesai* B *Brijesh Patel* C *Sunil Gavaskar* D *Gundappa Viswanath*

Answers on page 180

LANCASHIRE

1 Who took 1816 wickets for Lancashire, at an average of 15.12, between 1950 and 1968?

A Roy Tattersall **B** *Brian Statham* **C** *Ken Higgs* **D** *Dick Pollard*

2 Who scored 1820 runs at 91.00 for Lancashire in the 2003 County Championship?

A Andy Flintoff **B** *Stuart Law* **C** *Carl Hooper* **D** *Mal Loye*

3 Which player, who joined Lancashire from Leicestershire in 2003, won a Blue for boxing as well as cricket while at Oxford University?

A Iain Sutcliffe **B** *Mark Chilton* **C** *Alec Swann* **D** *Mal Loye*

4 Which Lancashire player smashed 26 runs in an over in near-darkness in the 1971 Gillette Cup semi-final?

A Farokh Engineer **B** *Jack Simmons* **C** *Clive Lloyd* **D** *David Hughes*

5 Who scored a century in each innings for Lancashire against Warwickshire at Southport in 1982, with the aid of a runner almost throughout?

A Barry Wood **B** *Graeme Fowler* **C** *Gehan Mendis* **D** *David Lloyd*

6 Which Lancashire spinner was among the first batch of players given an ECB central contract in 2000?

A Gary Keedy **B** *Gareth Batty* **C** *Chris Schofield* **D** *Mike Watkinson*

7 Who scored a century in 27 balls in contrived circumstances for Lancashire in 1993?

A Steve O'Shaughnessy **B** *Neil Fairbrother* **C** *Glen Chapple* **D** *Ian Austin*

8 In which town have Lancashire played home games at a ground called Stanley Park?

A Liverpool **B** *Southport* **C** *Blackpool* **D** *Lytham*

9 Which Lancashire player was voted Young Cricketer of the Year in 1975?

A Andrew Kennedy **B** *Graeme Fowler* **C** *John Abrahams* **D** *Neil Fairbrother*

10 Who captained Lancashire from 1926 to 1928, in which time they won the Championship each year?

A Tommy Higson **B** *Harry Makepeace* **C** *Leonard Green* **D** *Peter Eckersley*

11 Which great Australian fast bowler became one of county cricket's first overseas players when he joined Lancashire in 1924?

A Jack Gregory **B** *Tibby Cotter* **C** *Alan Fairfax* **D** *Ted McDonald*

The Googly

Which Test player is the grandfather of Kyle Hogg, the allrounder who made his debut for Lancashire in 2001?

A Rodney Hogg of Australia **B** *Peter Heine of South Africa* **C** *Bert Sutcliffe of New Zealand* **D** *Sonny Ramadhin of West Indies*

Answers on page 180

SACHIN TENDULKAR

1 How old was Tendulkar when he made his Test debut in November 1989?

A 14 **B** *15* **C** *16* **D** *17*

2 Against which country did he make that Test debut?

A Australia **B** *England* **C** *New Zealand* **D** *Pakistan*

3 With which future Test team-mate did Tendulkar once share a stand of 664 in a school game?

A Ajit Agarkar **B** *Vinod Kambli* **C** *V.V.S. Laxman* **D** *Rahul Dravid*

4 Where did Tendulkar score his first Test century, aged 17, in August 1990?

A Asgiriya Stadium, Kandy **B** *Old Trafford, Manchester* **C** *The Oval*
D *Trent Bridge, Nottingham*

5 With whom did Tendulkar share a record stand of 331 in a one-day international against New Zealand at Hyderabad in 2001-02?

A Ajay Jadeja **B** *Sourav Ganguly* **C** *Virender Sehwag* **D** *Rahul Dravid*

6 What is Tendulkar's middle name?

A Ramesh **B** *Rajesh* **C** *Raman* **D** *Rakesh*

7 Against which country did Tendulkar score 152 in the 2003 World Cup?

A Pakistan **B** *Bangladesh* **C** *Kenya* **D** *Namibia*

8 Tendulkar scored 217, his first Test double-century, at Ahmedabad in 1999-2000 – who was it against?

A Australia **B** *New Zealand* **C** *West Indies* **D** *Zimbabwe*

9 Against whom did Tendulkar improve his highest Test score to 241 not out in January 2004?

A Australia **B** *New Zealand* **C** *West Indies* **D** *Zimbabwe*

10 Who was Tendulkar's captain in his first Test match?

A Mohammad Azharuddin **B** *Kapil Dev* **C** *Sunil Gavaskar* **D** *Kris Srikkanth*

11 Tendulkar was the third player to score 1000 runs in the World Cup. Who was the first?

A Allan Border **B** *Viv Richards* **C** *Gordon Greenidge* **D** *Javed Miandad*

The Googly

Which Australian was quoted in *Wisden* 2003 as saying of Sachin Tendulkar: "You take Bradman away and he is next up, I reckon"?

A Don Bradman **B** *Mark Taylor* **C** *Rick McCosker* **D** *Steve Waugh*

Answers on page 181

THE 1996 WORLD CUP

1 Who won the sixth World Cup?

   A Australia *B India* *C Sri Lanka* *D West Indies*

2 In which city was the final played?

   A Calcutta *B Karachi* *C Lahore* *D Mumbai*

3 Who captained the winners?

   A Mark Taylor *B Arjuna Ranatunga* *C Steve Waugh* *D Sanath Jayasuriya*

4 Who was the Man of the Match in the final?

   A Aravinda de Silva *B Arjuna Ranatunga* *C Mark Taylor* *D Damien Fleming*

5 Which non-Test-playing country upset West Indies on Leap Year Day?

   A Holland *B Bangladesh* *C Kenya* *D Denmark*

6 Which Sri Lankan, later named the Player of the Tournament, blasted 82 from only 44 balls in the quarter-final against England?

   A Romesh Kaluwitharana *B Sanath Jayasuriya* *C Asanka Gurusinha* *D Aravinda de Silva*

7 Which specialist batsman scored just two runs in five innings in the tournament?

   A Keith Arthurton *B Graeme Hick* *C Craig Spearman* *D Daryll Cullinan*

8 Gary Kirsten broke the World Cup record with 188 not out against which country?

   A Holland *B Zimbabwe* *C Kenya* *D United Arab Emirates*

9 Who scored three centuries – and 463 runs – in the tournament?

   A Sachin Tendulkar *B Aravinda de Silva* *C Hansie Cronje* *D Mark Waugh*

10 Who was the 47-year-old Dutch opener, the oldest player in the tournament, who had scored 159 for Barbados against Mike Denness's touring team 22 years previously?

   A Flavian Aponso *B Bas Zuiderent* *C Peter Cantrell* *D Nolan Clarke*

11 Who scored 101 against England in the first match of the tournament, but collected just 10 runs from his other five innings?

   A Nathan Astle *B Jonty Rhodes* *C Chris Cairns* *D Daryll Cullinan*

The Googly

What was the result of the Calcutta semi-final in the 1996 World Cup?

A Australia won by one run *B Sri Lanka won by ten wickets*
C Sri Lanka won by default after the crowd rioted *D Australia won by 111 runs*

Answers on page 181

INITIALLY SPEAKING

1 Which man, who played over 100 Tests, had the appropriate initials "MCC"?

    A Martin Crowe B Chris Cairns C Colin Cowdrey D Hansie Cronje

2 Which recent Test player has five initials – and only four letters in his surname?

    A Andrew Hall B Shane Bond C Chaminda Vaas D Martin Love

3 Which England captain of the 1960s had the initials MJK?

    A Mike Brearley B Mike Smith C Micky Stewart D John Edrich

4 Which prolific Sri Lankan batsman has the initials PADS?

    A Aravinda de Silva B Kumar Sangakkara C Sanath Jayasuriya D Pubudu Dissanayake

5 Which England favourite of the 1960s and '70s had the initials APE?

    A Allan Lamb B Phil Edmonds C Alan Knott D Tony Greig

6 Which man, who once took 12 wickets in a Test at the SCG, has the initials SCG?

    A Sydney Barnes B Stuart MacGill C Shaun Pollock D Shane Warne

7 Which England captain had the initials PBH?

    A Peter Parfitt B Pelham Warner C "Tip" Foster D Peter May

8 And which had the initials GOB?

    A George Mann B Gubby Allen C Geoff Boycott D Graham Gooch

9 Which recent West Indian batsman had the initials RICH?

    A Robert Haynes B Roland Holder C Roger Harper D Ryan Hinds

10 Which old South African allrounder had the initials ABC?

    A Ali Bacher B "Buck" Llewellyn C "Chud" Langton D Athol Rowan

11 Which dapper South African batsman of the 1950s had the initials CARD?

    A Chris Duckworth B Charles Dixon C Colin Dyer D Richard Dumbrill

The Googly

What fate befell M.E.Z. "Ebbu" Ghazali of Pakistan in the third Test against England at Old Trafford in 1954?

A He was no-balled for throwing B He collected Test cricket's fastest pair of ducks
C He fell down the pavilion steps as he was going out to bat and had to retire hurt
D He dropped catches off three consecutive balls

Answers on page 181

NEW ZEALAND IN TESTS

1 Who took 431 Test wickets, even though he never played in a five-match series?

   A Danny Morrison *B Richard Hadlee* *C Chris Cairns* *D Lance Cairns*

2 Which wicket-keeper hit 173, batting at No. 9, against India at Auckland in 1989-90?

   A Ian Smith *B Tony Blain* *C Warren Lees* *D Adam Parore*

3 Which New Zealander, later their coach, just completed the Test double, scoring 1001 runs and taking 102 wickets in his career?

   A Bevan Congdon *B Bob Cunis* *C John Bracewell* *D Jeremy Coney*

4 Who captained both the 1958 and 1965 New Zealand touring teams to England?

   A John Reid *B Eric Petrie* *C Dick Motz* *D Graham Dowling*

5 Which player, who once broke his leg in a freak accident with a baggage trolley at an airport, scored his only Test century for New Zealand at Lord's in 1990?

   A Jeff Crowe *B Trevor Franklin* *C Shane Thomson* *D Dipak Patel*

6 Where do New Zealand play home Tests at a ground called Carisbrook?

   A Auckland *B Hamilton* *C Christchurch* *D Dunedin*

7 Who scored two double-centuries in the series against West Indies in 1971-72?

   A Glenn Turner *B Mark Burgess* *C Bevan Congdon* *D Vic Pollard*

8 Who batted 101 minutes without scoring a run against South Africa at Auckland in 1998-99?

   A Geoff Allott *B Blair Pocock* *C Roger Twose* *D Danny Morrison*

9 Who scored 107 on Test debut for New Zealand against West Indies at St George's in 2002?

   A Mark Richardson *B Lou Vincent* *C Scott Styris* *D Hamish Marshall*

10 Who took a hat-trick on Test debut for New Zealand against Pakistan at Lahore in 1976-77?

   A John Morrison *B Peter Petherick* *C Gary Troup* *D David O'Sullivan*

11 Who was the first New Zealander to take 100 Test wickets?

   A Tony MacGibbon *B Bruce Taylor* *C Dick Collinge* *D Dick Motz*

The Googly

Bert Sutcliffe was one of New Zealand's first great batsmen – but what was unusual about his 42-Test career?

A He never made a duck *B He never played a Test outside New Zealand*
C He averaged 50, but never scored a century *D He never finished on the winning side*

Answers on page 181

WHO SAID THAT?

1 Who famously reduced the BBC radio commentary box to hysterics after observing that Ian Botham "didn't quite manage to get his leg over" when he trod on his stumps in a 1991 Test?

A Jonathan Agnew B Bill Frindall C Henry Blofeld D Vic Marks

2 Who said, of Botham, that "he can't bowl a hoop downhill"?

A Alec Bedser B Viv Richards C Ian Chappell D Fred Trueman

3 Which New Zealander said that Graeme Hick was "just a flat-track bully"?

A Glenn Turner B John Bracewell C Martin Crowe D Ian Smith

4 Who described his 254 at Lord's in 1930 as "in my judgment, technically the best innings of my life"?

A Walter Hammond B Don Bradman C Len Hutton D Jack Hobbs

5 Who said, after beating Brian Lara's bat, "I don't suppose I can call you a lucky bleeder when you've got 347"?

A Angus Fraser B Andy Caddick C Stephen Harmison D Simon Jones

6 Which Australian commentator once observed: "The other advantage England have got when Phil Tufnell is bowling is that he isn't fielding"?

A Keith Stackpole B Richie Benaud C Ian Chappell D Bill Lawry

7 Which controversial politician once said, "Cricket civilises people and creates good gentlemen. I want everyone to play cricket. I want ours to be a nation of gentlemen"?

A Margaret Thatcher B Nelson Mandela C Robert Mugabe D John Howard

8 Who wrote "Lord's is the Valhalla of cricketers"?

A Sunil Gavaskar B Ian Botham C Neville Cardus D John Arlott

9 Which American rock star said: "I want to play cricket – it doesn't seem to matter if you win or lose"?

A Alice Cooper B Bruce Springsteen C Meat Loaf D Paul Simon

10 Who wrote "I felt like a boy who had killed a dove," after bowling his hero Victor Trumper in a club match?

A Arthur Mailey B Bill O'Reilly C Clarrie Grimmett D Don Bradman

11 Which football manager said, "Cricket is the only game that you can actually put on weight when playing"?

A Don Revie B Bill Shankly C Brian Clough D Tommy Docherty

The Googly

Which American comedian, after watching two hours' cricket at Lord's, asked politely "But when does it start?"

A Kelsey Grammer B Bob Hope C Eddie Murphy D Groucho Marx

Answers on page 181

PAKISTAN'S MOHAMMAD BROTHERS

1 Who is the oldest of the Test-playing Mohammad brothers?

   A Hanif B Mushtaq C Sadiq D Wazir

2 And who was the youngest?

   A Hanif B Mushtaq C Sadiq D Wazir

3 For which English county did Mushtaq play?

   A Northamptonshire B Nottinghamshire C Surrey D Warwickshire

4 And for which county did Sadiq play?

   A Glamorgan B Gloucestershire C Hampshire D Leicestershire

5 Which other Pakistan Test player was a long-time county colleague of Sadiq's?

   A Imran Khan B Javed Miandad C Sarfraz Nawaz D Zaheer Abbas

6 What's the name of Hanif's son, who scored 2705 Test runs for Pakistan?

   A Hanif junior B Aamer C Shoaib D Israr

7 What was the name of the fifth Mohammad brother, who was 12th man in a Test but never actually played in one?

   A Raees B Wasim C Qasim D Qamar

8 Which of the brothers made his Test debut at 15, and scored a Test century at 17?

   A Hanif B Mushtaq C Sadiq D Wazir

9 Hanif opened the batting in Pakistan's inaugural Test against India in 1952-53 with which unrelated Mohammad?

   A Maqsood B Waqar C Nazar D Farooq

10 And which unrelated Mohammad bowled Pakistan's first ball in Test cricket in that match?

   A Khan B Fazal C Hussain D Haseeb

11 In which town, now in India, were all the brothers born?

   A Jaipur B Jullundur C Junagadh D Johore

The Googly

Hanif (in his last Test) and Sadiq (in his first) opened the batting, and Mushtaq also played, against which team at Karachi in 1969-70?

A Australia B England C India D New Zealand

Answers on page 181

ENGLAND'S ONE-CAP WONDERS

1 Which Surrey batsman, whose son became an England regular, played his only Test against India at The Oval in 1979?
A Alan Butcher B Micky Stewart C Bill Smith D Roger Knight

2 Which Sussex player made his debut against West Indies in 1995, aged 33, and was dismissed first ball by Curtly Ambrose?
A Chris Adams B Colin Wells C Alan Wells D Tony Cottey

3 Who was hit on the head by Malcolm Marshall in front of his home crowd at Edgbaston in 1984, retired hurt for 10, and never batted for England again?
A Andy Moles B Andy Lloyd C Neil Smith D Dermot Reeve

4 Which Sussex batsman, who later moved to Durham, won his only Test cap against Australia at The Oval in 1981?
A Wayne Larkins B Ian Gould C Paul Parker D Gehan Mendis

5 Which Kent opener, who later became an umpire, won his only England cap against India at Edgbaston in 1986?
A Neil Taylor B Mark Benson C Laurie Potter D David Fulton

6 Which Somerset allrounder, who later became a Test umpire, was called up from a coaching stint to win his only Test cap in South Africa in 1964-65?
A Tom Cartwright B Graham Burgess C Ken Palmer D Roy Palmer

7 Which bowler played his only Test against India at The Oval in 1990, and scored 38 as nightwatchman?
A Alan Igglesden B Neil Williams C Tony Pigott D Min Patel

8 And which one played his only Test at The Oval four years later, took 4 for 42 in the first innings, but never featured again?
A Ed Giddins B Joey Benjamin C Martin McCague D Martin Saggers

9 Which Surrey batsman played his only Test against Australia at Headingley in 1921, and collapsed and died at the wicket in a wartime match at Lord's 21 years later?
A Alfred Evans B Donald Knight C Harry Peach D Andy Ducat

10 Which Lancashire player scored 80 on his England debut in 1939, but never came into contention again after the war, although he did umpire two Tests in the 1960s?
A Norman Oldfield B Eddie Paynter C Ken Cranston D Leonard Green

11 Which legspinner took time off from his day job as a teacher at Dulwich College to take 11 wickets in the 1933 Oval Test against West Indies, but never played again?
A Tommy Mitchell B Bomber Wells C Charles "Father" Marriott D Tich Freeman

The Googly

Who made his debut for England against Australia at The Oval in 1989, when he opened with his county colleague Graham Gooch in both innings (and outscored him both times), but never played again – and later started a club for England's One-Cap Wonders?
A Alan Wells B Paul Grayson C John Stephenson D Brian Hardie

Answers on page 181

LEICESTERSHIRE

1 Who scored the first first-class triple-century for Leicestershire, in 2003?

A Darren Stevens B Brad Hogg C Brad Hodge D Darren Maddy

2 Who captained Leicestershire to their first County Championship title, in 1975?

A Tony Lock B Ray Illingworth C Roger Tolchard D Brian Davison

3 Which Indian Test batsman played for Leicestershire in 2003?

A Sachin Tendulkar B V.V.S. Laxman C Virender Sehwag D Rahul Dravid

4 Which Leicestershire bowler, who won three Test caps in the 1980s, later became the BBC's cricket correspondent?

A Jonathan Agnew B Les Taylor C Nick Cook D Vic Marks

5 Which Leicestershire player took a hat-trick in the 1974 Benson & Hedges Cup final?

A Norman McVicker B Ken Higgs C Paddy Clift D Ray Illingworth

6 At which school did Leicestershire stage a home Championship match in 2004?

A Loughborough Grammar B Uppingham School C Oundle School D Oakham School

7 Which Leicestershire player lost 18 of his 32 Tests as England's captain?

A Ray Illingworth B Peter Willey C Tony Lock D David Gower

8 Which wicket-keeper returned to Leicestershire in 2003, after three seasons with Kent?

A Geraint Jones B Paul Nixon C Phil Whitticase D Vince Wells

9 Which Leicestershire batsman won his only Test cap for England in Australia in 1986-87?

A James Whitaker B Nigel Briers C Brian Davison D Barry Dudleston

10 Which opener carried his bat 17 times for Leicestershire, including twice in the same match in 1911?

A Albert Knight B John King C Les Berry D Cyril Wood

11 Which bowler took 10 for 18 for Leicestershire against Glamorgan at Pontypridd in 1929?

A Ewart Astill B Alex Skelding C George Geary D Jack Walsh

The Googly

What unique double did Leicestershire's Chris Balderstone manage on September 15, 1975?

A He played Championship cricket and league football on the same day
B He completed two centuries on the same day C He scored a century and passed his umpiring exam D He took a hat-trick and later hit the winning six

Answers on page 181

THE CHAPPELLS

1 Which of the Chappell brothers captained Australia in the first World Cup, in 1975?

A Ian B Glen C Greg D Trevor

2 On which ground did Trevor Chappell bowl his infamous underarm ball in a one-day international in 1980-81?

A Auckland B Brisbane C Melbourne D Sydney

3 What feat did Greg achieve in his first Test as captain, in 1975-76?

A He took a record five catches in an innings B He scored a century in each innings
C He took a record seven catches in the match D He scored 247 not out, his highest Test score

4 Which Test side did Trevor coach for a year from March 2001?

A Australia B Bangladesh C Sri Lanka D Zimbabwe

5 Which former Test captain was the Chappells' grandfather?

A Arthur Morris B Ted Chappell C Vic Richardson D Don Bradman

6 Greg scored 108 on his Test debut in 1970-71 – on which ground?

A Adelaide B Brisbane C Perth D Sydney

7 And on which ground did he score 182 in his final Test, in 1983-84?

A Adelaide B Brisbane C Perth D Sydney

8 For which English county side did Greg score the first Sunday League century, in 1969?

A Kent B Lancashire C Middlesex D Somerset

9 Where did Ian and Greg Chappell both score two centuries in the same Test in 1973-74?

A Melbourne B Sydney C Wellington D Dunedin

10 Who was Ian Chappell's captain when he made his Test debut in 1964-65?

A Richie Benaud B Bill Lawry C Bob Simpson D Brian Booth

11 At which sport other than cricket did Ian represent South Australia?

A Australian Rules football B Baseball C Stoolball D Tennis

The Googly

Greg Chappell captained Australia in both the Melbourne (1976-77) and Lord's (1980) Centenary Tests. Who were the other two Australians who played in both those games?

A Ray Bright and Rod Marsh B Rod Marsh and Dennis Lillee
C Dennis Lillee and Jeff Thomson D Jeff Thomson and Ray Bright

Answers on page 181

THE ASHES 2001

1 Who captained England in the second and third Tests when Nasser Hussain was unfit?

  A Alec Stewart B Marcus Trescothick C Mike Atherton D Mark Butcher

2 And who captained Australia at Headingley, when Steve Waugh was unfit?

  A Adam Gilchrist B Ricky Ponting C Shane Warne D Justin Langer

3 Who cracked 173 not out to help England win that Headingley match?

  A Marcus Trescothick B Mark Butcher C Graham Thorpe D Michael Vaughan

4 Who scored 152 in the first Test at Edgbaston, with five sixes and 22 runs off one over?

  A Adam Gilchrist B Marcus Trescothick C Matthew Hayden D Michael Slater

5 Which player, who was born in Pakistan, made his debut for England in the first Test?

  A Kabir Ali B Usman Afzaal C Owais Shah D Alamgir Sheriyar

6 Which Australian made his debut in the fourth Test at Headingley?

  A Ashley Noffke B Martin Love C Simon Katich D Nathan Bracken

7 Who, in the final Test at The Oval, scored his first Test century in England, ten years after his debut?

  A John Crawley B Mark Ramprakash C Craig White D Nick Knight

8 Which Australian took 32 wickets in the series, as many as England's top two wicket-takers put together?

  A Shane Warne B Glenn McGrath C Jason Gillespie D Brett Lee

9 Who made his debut for England in the final Test at The Oval, which wasn't his home ground at the time but became so later?

  A Ian Ward B Ed Giddins C Jimmy Ormond D Ian Salisbury

10 Who scored a century at The Oval before being hit on the head and retiring hurt?

  A Steve Waugh B Mark Waugh C Mark Ramprakash D Justin Langer

11 Who collected his 20th Test duck at Trent Bridge, a record for England at the time?

  A Mike Atherton B Phil Tufnell C Andy Caddick D Darren Gough

The Googly

Greg Blewett, who surprisingly missed out on selection for the tour, played county cricket for Nottinghamshire in 2001 instead. What distracted him when he was dismissed during their match against Durham at the end of May?

A A spectator next to the sightscreen preparing to streak B The radio commentary from the Test match C The umpire yelped after being stung by a wasp and he thought it was a no-ball D Three ducks waddling behind the bowler's arm

Answers on page 182

MORE MIDDLE NAMES

1 What was Don Bradman's middle name?

  A Geoffrey B Gerald C George D Gregory

2 Which recent Australian player has the middle name Gwyl?

  A Adam Gilchrist B Michael Bevan C Michael Slater D Dirk Wellham

3 Which Indian player's given forenames were Mulvantrai Himmatlal, although he was hardly ever known by those names?

  A Vijay Merchant B Vinoo Mankad C Nari Contractor D Farokh Engineer

4 Which South African player's given forenames were Horace Brakenridge, although he was usually known by a nickname?

  A Tiger Lance B Hansie Cronje C Jock Cameron D Tufty Mann

5 Which Zimbabwean bowler has the middle name Zvikomberero?

  A Mluleki Nkala B Blessing Mahwire C Everton Matambanadzo D Pommie Mbangwa

6 Which man, who scored Test centuries for two countries, has the middle name Christoffel?

  A Sammy Guillen B Billy Murdoch C Frank Mitchell D Kepler Wessels

7 Which Australian bowler of the 1960s had the middle names James Napier?

  A Tom Veivers B Neil Hawke C Grahame Corling D Graham McKenzie

8 Which Pakistan Test player has the middle name Albert?

  A Antao D'Souza B Wallis Mathias C Hafeez Kardar D Duncan Sharpe

9 How was the Australian batsman whose given forenames were Clayvel Lindsay better known?

  A Slasher Mackay B Bob Cowper C Jack Badcock D Stan McCabe

10 Which England wicket-keeper's given names were Clifton James, although he was universally known as Jack?

  A Russell B Richards C Brennan D Duckworth

11 Which New Zealand bowler has the middle name Logo?

  A Kerry Walmsley B Murphy Su'a C Chris Cairns D Daniel Vettori

The Googly

Which (male) New Zealand Test player has the middle name Mary?

  A Dayle Hadlee B Bryan Young C Chris Kuggeleijn D Daryl Tuffey

Answers on page 182

INDIA v AUSTRALIA 2000-01

1 Who captained India in the series?

   A Sachin Tendulkar **B** *Sourav Ganguly* **C** *Nayan Mongia* **D** *Rahul Dravid*

2 What trophy is at stake when India play Australia?

   A Border-Gavaskar Trophy **B** *Kapil Cup* **C** *Vizianagram Trophy* **D** *Sachin-Steve Trophy*

3 Who made 122 in the first Test, but bagged a king pair in the second and was out for 1 and 1 in the third?

   A Matthew Hayden **B** *Adam Gilchrist* **C** *Justin Langer* **D** *Ricky Ponting*

4 Who scored 180 in India's epic fightback at Kolkata?

   A Sachin Tendulkar **B** *Virender Sehwag* **C** *V.V.S. Laxman* **D** *Rahul Dravid*

5 Australia established a new record for consecutive victories in the first Test – how many?

   A 12 **B** *14* **C** *16* **D** *19*

6 Who, in the first Test, bagged a pair to collect his seventh successive duck against Australia?

   A Ajit Agarkar **B** *Harbhajan Singh* **C** *Anil Kumble* **D** *Javagal Srinath*

7 Who took 32 wickets in the series, 29 more than any other Indian bowler managed?

   A Anil Kumble **B** *Harbhajan Singh* **C** *Zaheer Khan* **D** *Javagal Srinath*

8 India won the second Test at Kolkata after following on – how many times had this happened previously in Test history?

   A Once **B** *Twice* **C** *Three times* **D** *Five times*

9 Who kept wicket on his debut for India in the third Test at Chennai?

   A Ajay Ratra **B** *Vijay Dahiya* **C** *Deep Dasgupta* **D** *Samir Dighe*

10 Who hit six sixes in his 203 in the Chennai Test?

   A Virender Sehwag **B** *Sourav Ganguly* **C** *Sachin Tendulkar* **D** *Matthew Hayden*

11 Who was out handled the ball in the third Test?

   A Steve Waugh **B** *Harbhajan Singh* **C** *Mark Waugh* **D** *Sadagoppan Ramesh*

The Googly

Which man, who was on the winning side the last time a team won a Test match after following on, was umpiring when it happened again at Kolkata?

A Venkat **B** *John Hampshire* **C** *Peter Willey* **D** *Vanburn Holder*

Answers on page 182

MARVELLOUS MIDDLE NAMES: WEST INDIES

1 Which West Indian Test player has the middle name St Aubrun?

A Frank Worrell *B Basil Butcher* *C Collie Smith* *D Garry Sobers*

2 Which one has the middle names Charlie Griffith, after a former West Indian pace legend?

A Sylvester Clarke *B Kenny Benjamin* *C Franklyn Stephenson* *D Ezra Moseley*

3 And which has the middle names Everton Hunte, after two other former players?

A Andy Roberts *B David Murray* *C Colin Croft* *D Junior Murray*

4 Whose middle names are Elconn Lynwall?

A Curtly Ambrose *B Patterson Thompson* *C Courtney Walsh* *D Irving Shillingford*

5 Which player, who finished on the winning side in all ten of his Test matches, had the middle names Ashworth Elderfield?

A Sylvester Clarke *B Eldine Baptiste* *C Ezra Moseley* *D Derick Parry*

6 Which player, who made his one-day debut in 2004, has the middle names Julius Garvey?

A Ian Bradshaw *B Dwayne Smith* *C Dwayne Bravo* *D Darren Sammy*

7 And which member of the 2004 touring side in England has the middle name La Bertram?

A Chris Gayle *B Tino Best* *C Fidel Edwards* *D Devon Smith*

8 Which West Indian captain's middle names were Mortimer Maglinne?

A Karl Nunes *B Frank Worrell* *C Nelson Betancourt* *D Teddy Hoad*

9 And whose middle names were Copeland Murray?

A Gerry Alexander *B Bruce Pairaudeau* *C Charlie Griffith* *D Denis Atkinson*

10 Which 1960s batsman had the middle names Dudley Ashley St John?

A Joey Carew *B Basil Butcher* *C Seymour Nurse* *D Easton McMorris*

11 How was the 1950s Jamaican allrounder O'Neil Gordon Smith better known?

A Cammie Smith *B Collie Smith* *C Gordie Smith* *D Slogger Smith*

The Googly

Which West Indian Test player's middle names are Alexei McNamara, after Soviet and American politicians (he also has a sister called Golda)?

A Milton Small *B Balfour Patterson* *C Carlisle Best* *D Nixon McLean*

Answers on page 182

RICHIE BENAUD

1 For which Australian state did Benaud play?

A New South Wales *B Queensland* *C South Australia* *D Victoria*

2 Against which team did Benaud slam a Test century in only 78 minutes in 1954-55?

A England *B New Zealand* *C South Africa* *D West Indies*

3 Benaud was the first allrounder to complete which "double" in Tests?

A 1000 runs/100 wickets *B 2000 runs/200 wickets* *C 2000 runs/100 wickets*
D 3000 runs/200 wickets

4 Which opening batsman made his debut in the same Test as Benaud, and went on to play 46 more times for Australia?

A Arthur Morris *B Bobby Simpson* *C Colin McDonald* *D Jim Burke*

5 Who did Benaud succeed as Australia's Test captain in 1958-59?

A Lindsay Hassett *B Neil Harvey* *C Ian Craig* *D Ian Johnson*

6 Who was Benaud's rival captain in that 1958-59 Ashes series?

A Peter May *B Freddie Brown* *C Colin Cowdrey* *D Ted Dexter*

7 Of which country's cricket association did Benaud become patron?

A Australia *B Belgium* *C Germany* *D France*

8 Who captained Australia at Lord's in 1961, when Benaud was unfit?

A Bob Simpson *B Barry Jarman* *C Neil Harvey* *D Bill Lawry*

9 What was the first name of Benaud's brother, who also played Test cricket?

A Alan *B Bruce* *C Gordon* *D John*

10 What was unusual about Richie's brother's maiden Test century?

A It didn't contain a boundary *B It came after he had been dropped from the next Test*
C It came in Richie's first Test as a commentator *D He was batting at No. 8, and all of his
runs were scored in a last-wicket partnership*

11 *Wisden* established in 2003 that Richie Benaud was about to become the first person to witness – as young spectator, player, journalist or broadcaster – how many Test matches?

A 250 *B 300* *C 500* *D 750*

The Googly
What remarkable feat did Benaud's father, Lou, achieve in a two-day match in 1923-24?

A He scored a quadruple-century *B He captained a side containing only younger Benauds*
C He took all 20 wickets in a two-innings game *D He scored a century in each innings, and
attended Richie's birth in between*

Answers on page 182

KEEPING IT IN THE FAMILY

1 Who played 128 Tests but never captained his country, although he played under his brother's leadership almost 50 times?
A Grant Flower **B** *Mark Waugh* **C** *Greg Chappell* **D** *Sadiq Mohammad*

2 Which England cricketer had a father and a grandfather who played Tests for a different country?
A Graeme Hick **B** *Ian Greig* **C** *Derek Pringle* **D** *Dean Headley*

3 Which scorer of 5444 Test runs had a brother who also captained New Zealand?
A Geoff Howarth **B** *John Parker* **C** *Martin Crowe* **D** *John Wright*

4 Which member of India's 1983 World Cup-winning team had a father and a brother who both scored centuries on Test debut?
A Mohinder Amarnath **B** *Sunil Gavaskar* **C** *Ashok Mankad* **D** *Yashpal Sharma*

5 Which pair of brothers made their England Test debuts together in 1997?
A John and Mark Crawley **B** *Chris and Robin Smith* **C** *Adam and Ben Hollioake*
D *John and Peter Lever*

6 Who carried his bat for Pakistan against India in 1982-83, 30 years after his father did so too?
A Mohsin Khan **B** *Shoaib Mohammad* **C** *Rameez Raja* **D** *Mudassar Nazar*

7 Which Yorkshire fast bowler played one Test in 1985, and had a son who also played for Yorkshire, and played one Test in 2001?
A Arnie Sidebottom **B** *Steve Oldham* **C** *Tony Hamilton* **D** *Paul Jarvis*

8 For which English county did Ben Hutton (grandson of Len) and Nick Compton (grandson of Denis) play together in 2004?
A Lancashire **B** *Middlesex* **C** *Surrey* **D** *Yorkshire*

9 Which England offspinner played in Tests with both Colin Cowdrey and his son Chris?
A Ray Illingworth **B** *Pat Pocock* **C** *Vic Marks* **D** *Fred Titmus*

10 Which England coach of the 1990s had a son who played in six one-day internationals for them?
A Ray Illingworth **B** *Keith Fletcher* **C** *Duncan Fletcher* **D** *David Lloyd*

11 Which pair of half-brothers opened the bowling for West Indies against England in 2003-04?
A Corey Collymore and Jermaine Lawson **B** *Tino Best and Pedro Collins*
C *Pedro Collins and Fidel Edwards* **D** *Tino Best and Ian Bradshaw*

The Googly

Who was widely blamed for costing England the match at Old Trafford in 1902, when he got out trying to hit the four that would have brought victory against Australia ... afterwards he tearfully informed anyone who cared to listen that he had a son at home who would make up for it (he did, taking a wicket with his first ball in Tests and finishing with 155 wickets in 39 matches)?
A Thomas Verity **B** *Walter Brearley* **C** *Fred Tate* **D** *Derek Larwood*

Answers on page 182

NORTHAMPTONSHIRE

1 Which Northants batsman scored 4656 runs in 79 Tests for England?

A Colin Milburn B Peter Willey C Allan Lamb D Wayne Larkins

2 Who scored 222 for Northants against Yorkshire in 2003 – and played for Yorkshire in 2004?

A Michael Hussey B Jeff Cook C Russell Warren D Phil Jaques

3 Which Northants player captained England in the 1950-51 Ashes series?

A Len Hutton B Freddie Brown C Dennis Brookes D Norman Yardley

4 And which Northants player was the sensation of the 1954-55 Ashes series in Australia?

A Keith Andrew B Jim McConnon C Frank Tyson D Bob Appleyard

5 Who scored a county-record 331 not out for Northants against Somerset at Taunton in 2003?

A Matthew Hayden B Michael Hussey C Simon Katich D Phil Jaques

6 Which Northants batsman was the surprise batting star of the 1975 Ashes series?

A Wayne Larkins B Peter Willey C Colin Milburn D David Steele

7 In which town have Northants staged home games at a ground called Wardown Park?

A Tring B Wantage C Luton D Wellingborough

8 Who scored the first triple-century for Northants, against his old county Surrey in 1958?

A Raman Subba Row B Dennis Brookes C Jim Watts D Roger Prideaux

9 Which county bowled Northants out for 12 – equalling the lowest score in first-class history – in 1907?

A Nottinghamshire B Yorkshire C Gloucestershire D Kent

10 Which tall Scottish-born Northants fast bowler toured Australia for the Ashes series of 1962-63 and 1965-66?

A Frank Tyson B David Larter C Fred Rumsey D Barry Knight

11 Who took all 10 for 127 for Northants against Kent at Tunbridge Wells in 1932?

A Vallance Jupp B Freddie Brown C Nobby Clark D Reg Partridge

The Googly

From mid-May 1935, Northants had a run of 99 consecutive County Championship matches without winning a single one. What happened in their 100th game?

A They tied with Yorkshire, the champions B They beat Leicestershire by an innings C They decided not to play against Surrey D They received a special award from MCC – but lost again

Answers on page 182

ENGLAND v WEST INDIES: THE WISDEN TROPHY 2000

1 Who was the West Indian captain, who made 98 in the first Test, which they won?

A Jimmy Adams B Brian Lara C Courtney Walsh D Richie Richardson

2 Which landmark, in terms of matches staged, did Lord's reach during the second Test?

A First ground to stage 50 Tests B First to stage 100 Tests C First to stage 200 Tests
D First to stage 250 internationals (one-dayers and Tests)

3 When West Indies were shot out for 54 at Lord's, their lowest score against England at the time, which bowler took 5 for 16?

A Graeme Hick B Craig White C Andy Caddick D Darren Gough

4 And which bowler, who later took a Test hat-trick against West Indies, made his debut at Lord's but didn't take a wicket?

A Ashley Giles B Matthew Hoggard C Stephen Harmison D Dominic Cork

5 Which England batsman made his debut in the third Test, at Old Trafford, and scored 66 and 38 not out?

A Marcus Trescothick B Mark Butcher C Craig White D Darren Maddy

6 Who scored a century at Old Trafford, in his 100th Test?

A Alec Stewart B Brian Lara C Carl Hooper D Mike Atherton

7 Who took four wickets in an over at Headingley as West Indies were bundled out for 61?

A Andy Caddick B Dominic Cork C Craig White D Darren Gough

8 And who took his 400th Test wicket in that match at Headingley?

A Curtly Ambrose B Andy Caddick C Courtney Walsh D Darren Gough

9 Who scored 83 and 108 to help clinch the series for England at The Oval?

A Mike Atherton B Michael Vaughan C Graham Thorpe D Nasser Hussain

10 Which West Indian spinner made his debut in the final Test at The Oval?

A Omari Banks B Mahendra Nagamootoo C Dave Mohammed D Dinanath Ramnarine

11 Who, in the first innings at The Oval, was the first bowler to dismiss Brian Lara first ball, after 120 Test innings?

A Andy Caddick B Dominic Cork C Craig White D Darren Gough

The Googly
Which man, who had been on the winning side in the 1969 Wisden Trophy series, umpired one of the Tests in this 2000 series?

A Peter Willey B Vanburn Holder C John Hampshire D John Holder

Answers on page 182

MIDDLESEX

1   Who took 2361 wickets for Middlesex between 1949 and 1982?

   A Jack Young B John Price C John Emburey D Fred Titmus

2   Which Middlesex player captained England in the 1979 World Cup final at Lord's?

   A Mike Selvey B Mike Brearley C Mike Gatting D John Emburey

3   Who scored a record 18 first-class centuries in 1947, 13 of them for Middlesex?

   A Jack Robertson B Bill Edrich C Denis Compton D Sid Brown

4   Which South African-born bowler was Middlesex's leading wicket-taker in 2003?

   A Sven Koenig B Tim Bloomfield C Chad Keegan D Jamie Dalrymple

5   Who stepped down as Middlesex's captain in 2002 to become the cricket correspondent for a British daily newspaper?

   A Mike Selvey B Derek Pringle C Angus Fraser D Phil Tufnell

6   Which Middlesex bowler took 5 for 28 on his England debut in 1975, and finished up with 125 Test wickets?

   A Phil Edmonds B Phil Tufnell C Norman Cowans D John Emburey

7   Where is the Walker Ground, where Middlesex have staged some home matches?

   A Uxbridge B Southgate C Richmond D Hampstead

8   Who scored over 40,000 runs for Middlesex, at an average of 48.81, between 1907 and 1937?

   A Jack Robertson B Jack Hearne C Denis Compton D Patsy Hendren

9   Who took 10 for 40 for Middlesex against Lancashire at Lord's in 1929?

   A Gubby Allen B Jim Sims C Jack Hearne D Jim Smith

10   What was the surname of the father and son who both captained Middlesex and England?

   A Brearley B Mann C Cowdrey D Hutton

11   Which Middlesex player was the manager of the infamous Bodyline tour of Australia?

   A Bill Edrich B Patsy Hendren C Gubby Allen D Pelham Warner

The Googly

Which future Prime Minister played a few matches for Middlesex in the 1930s?

A Anthony Eden B Alec Douglas-Home C Harold Wilson D James Callaghan

Answers on page 183

THE ASHES 2002-03

1 Who scored 633 runs in the series, the best by an Englishman in Australia for 32 years?

A Nasser Hussain **B** *Mark Butcher* **C** *Michael Vaughan* **D** *Marcus Trescothick*

2 Who took the first wicket of the series, but then damaged his knee so badly he had to return home?

A Andrew Flintoff **B** *Simon Jones* **C** *Richard Johnson* **D** *Darren Gough*

3 Who reached an epic century from the last ball of the second day of the Sydney Test?

A Michael Vaughan **B** *Ricky Ponting* **C** *Steve Waugh* **D** *Mark Butcher*

4 Who scored a hundred in each innings in the first Test at Brisbane?

A Justin Langer **B** *Damien Martyn* **C** *Ricky Ponting* **D** *Matthew Hayden*

5 Who kept wicket for England in the fourth Test at Melbourne?

A Alec Stewart **B** *Warren Hegg* **C** *Chris Read* **D** *James Foster*

6 Who took 7 for 94 as England finished the series with a win at Sydney?

A Andy Caddick **B** *Stephen Harmison* **C** *Matthew Hoggard* **D** *Darren Gough*

7 How many days' play did it take Australia to retain the Ashes?

A 11 **B** *13* **C** *15* **D** *17*

8 Who made his debut in the fourth Test at Melbourne after playing 129 first-class matches (an Australian record for a debutant) and scoring more than 10,000 runs?

A Andrew Symonds **B** *Michael Hussey* **C** *Martin Love* **D** *Darren Lehmann*

9 Who, at Melbourne, almost doubled his previous run-tally against Australia, making 85 after collecting only 86 runs in 11 previous completed innings?

A Alex Tudor **B** *Dominic Cork* **C** *Craig White* **D** *John Crawley*

10 Who dismissed his brother-in-law during the second Test at Adelaide?

A Ashley Giles **B** *Andrew Caddick* **C** *Craig White* **D** *Andy Bichel*

11 Who was called up as a replacement for the third Test at Perth after injuries to other players, and broke down injured himself after only four overs?

A Alex Tudor **B** *Dominic Cork* **C** *Chris Silverwood* **D** *Richard Johnson*

The Googly

According to *Wisden*, the Australians were so impressed with Michael Vaughan's batting in 2002-03 that they "paid him their highest compliment" – what was it?

A They gave him a baggy green Australian cap **B** *They stopped sledging him*
C They invited him in to the dressing-room for a drink **D** *They asked him to give a coaching class at the Australian Academy*

Answers on page 183

INDIA IN TESTS

1 Who was the first Indian to play in 100 Tests?

A Sachin Tendulkar *B Sunil Gavaskar* *C Kapil Dev* *D Dilip Vengsarkar*

2 Who was the first Indian to take 300 Test wickets?

A Anil Kumble *B Bishan Bedi* *C Kapil Dev* *D Bhagwat Chandrasekhar*

3 Who scored 770 runs in his very first Test series, in 1970-71?

A Dilip Sardesai *B Sachin Tendulkar* *C Gundappa Viswanath* *D Sunil Gavaskar*

4 Which 18-year-old spinner took 19 wickets in successive Tests against England in 1984-85, but claimed only eight more in his Test career?

A Arshad Ayub *B Narendra Hirwani* *C Laxman Sivaramakrishnan* *D Gopal Sharma*

5 Who captained India to their first series victories in England and the West Indies, both in 1971?

A Ajit Wadekar *B Farokh Engineer* *C Dilip Sardesai* *D Nawab of Pataudi junior*

6 Which wicket-keeper smashed a very fast century – with 94 before lunch – against West Indies at Bombay in 1966-67?

A K.S. Indrajitsinhji *B Budhi Kunderan* *C Farokh Engineer* *D Khokan Sen*

7 Who played 46 Tests for India despite virtually losing the sight in one eye in a car accident in England in 1961?

A Farokh Engineer *B Nawab of Pataudi junior* *C Salim Durani* *D Dilip Sardesai*

8 In which city have India played Tests at the Baribati Stadium?

A Ahmedabad *B Bangalore* *C Cuttack* *D Delhi*

9 Who scored a century on his Test debut against England at Old Trafford in 1959?

A Abbas Ali Baig *B Chandu Borde* *C Nari Contractor* *D Hanumant Singh*

10 Who took 6 for 103 in his first Test in 1979-80, and went on to become only the second bowler to take 100 Test wickets after making his debut when over 30 years of age?

A Shivlal Yadav *B Roger Binny* *C Karsan Ghavri* *D Dilip Doshi*

11 Which former Test wicket-keeper was Sunil Gavaskar's uncle?

A Naren Tamhane *B Budhi Kunderan* *C Madhav Mantri* *D Nana Joshi*

The Googly

What fate befell India in their second innings of the 1952 Headingley Test?

A They were all out for 26, the lowest Test total *B They were 0 for 4, the worst Test start* *C Five batsmen were absent or retired hurt* *D No-one reached double figures*

Answers on page 183

BODYLINE

1 Who was England's captain and the architect of the Bodyline strategy?

A Percy Fender **B** *Bob Wyatt* **C** *Harold Larwood* **D** *Douglas Jardine*

2 And who was Australia's captain in that 1932-33 series?

A Don Bradman **B** *Bill Ponsford* **C** *Bill Woodfull* **D** *Vic Richardson*

3 Who was the leading (and fastest) exponent of Bodyline bowling?

A Harold Larwood **B** *Bill Voce* **C** *Bill Bowes* **D** *Ken Farnes*

4 Which Australian suffered a fractured skull after being hit at Adelaide, ironically not by a Bodyline delivery?

A Don Bradman **B** *Bert Oldfield* **C** *Clarrie Grimmett* **D** *Jack Fingleton*

5 Why did Don Bradman miss the first Test?

A He was in dispute with the board about his newspaper contract
B He had broken a finger while practising against Bodyline bowling **C** *He was ill*
D He pulled a muscle playing soccer before the match

6 Who played a sensational innings of 187 not out against the Bodyline attack in the first Test?

A Alan Kippax **B** *Leo O'Brien* **C** *Stan McCabe* **D** *Vic Richardson*

7 Whose only wicket of the series came when he bowled Bradman first ball in the second Test?

A Maurice Tate **B** *Bill Voce* **C** *Bill Bowes* **D** *Harold Larwood*

8 Which member of the England team returned for the next Ashes series four years later, as captain?

A Gubby Allen **B** *Bob Wyatt* **C** *Cyril Walters* **D** *Douglas Jardine*

9 And which one made his second tour of Australia 18 years later, in 1950-51, as captain?

A Walter Robins **B** *Freddie Brown* **C** *Errol Holmes* **D** *Walter Hammond*

10 In the final Test, Larwood went in as nightwatchman and scored 98, before being caught by which man, who was 50 and easily the worst of the Australian fielders?

A Bill Ponsford **B** *Bert Ironmonger* **C** *Laurie Nash* **D** *Don Blackie*

11 Which journalist is credited with coining the term "Bodyline"?

A Neville Cardus **B** *Percy Beames* **C** *Hugh Buggy* **D** *Bruce Harris*

The Googly

Who limped off with an injured foot in the last Test of the Bodyline series, and never played for England again?

A Jack Hobbs **B** *Bill Voce* **C** *Harold Larwood* **D** *Douglas Jardine*

Answers on page 183

W.G. GRACE

1 What was Grace's profession?

   A Architect *B Headmaster* *C Solicitor* *D Doctor*

2 For which county side did Grace play from 1870 to 1899?

   A Middlesex *B Kent* *C Gloucestershire* *D Surrey*

3 What was the nickname of W.G.'s brother, E.M.?

   A The Unbowlable *B The Untouchable* *C The Coroner* *D The Demon*

4 How many of the Grace brothers played in the first Test in England, in 1880?

   A None *B One* *C Two* *D Three*

5 Which new first-class side did Grace start up in 1900, after leaving his old county?

   A Free Foresters *B London County* *C Somerset* *D W.G. Grace's XI*

6 On which ground did his new side play their home matches?

   A Lord's *B Queen's Club* *C Crystal Palace* *D King's School*

7 How old was Grace when he played his final Test match, in 1899?

   A 41 *B 45* *C 50* *D 54*

8 And which 21-year-old, who himself played Test cricket until he was 52, made his debut in Grace's last Test?

   A Wilfred Rhodes *B Jack Hobbs* *C George Gunn* *D Nigel Haig*

9 What then-unprecedented feat did Grace achieve early in the 1895 season, when he was 46?

   A He scored six successive centuries *B He scored his 200th hundred*
   C He scored 1000 runs in May *D He scored two centuries on the same day*

10 For which side did Grace score 74 in a first-class match on his 58th birthday, in 1906?

   A Gentlemen *B Players* *C MCC* *D I Zingari*

11 Grace was the first president of which sport's governing body in 1903?

   A Archery *B Bowls* *C Croquet* *D Darts*

The Googly

When, in a match against Surrey in 1878, a throw from the outfield lodged in W.G.'s shirt, what did he do?

A He hid the ball in his beard *B He claimed a foul and was awarded five runs by the umpire*
C He ran an extra three runs with the ball still stuck *D He shook it loose, and hit it to the boundary as it dropped*

Answers on page 183

ONE-CAP WONDERS FROM AROUND THE WORLD

1 Which prolific scorer for Queensland, Essex and Lancashire hit 54 not out on his Test debut – and never won another Test cap, although he did play in 54 one-day internationals?
A Andrew Symonds B Stuart Law C Jimmy Maher D Martin Love

2 Who bagged a pair on his Test debut for England, after starring for another country in the 1999 World Cup?
A Chris Adams B Gavin Hamilton C Craig Spearman D George Salmond

3 Who played a solitary Test for India, in 1998-99, to go alongside 136 one-day internationals?
A Atul Bedade B Hemang Badani C Robin Singh D Venkatesh Prasad

4 Who scored 112 in his first Test for West Indies, in 1947-48 – and never played again?
A Andy Ganteaume B Michael Frederick C George Carew D Roy Marshall

5 What surname is shared by three Indians who won one Test cap apiece?
A Apte B Banerjee C Chopra D Desai

6 Whose only Test for Zimbabwe, in 1994-95, was the last first-class match of a career which had started more than 14 years previously in Harare?
A Andy Waller B Iain Butchart C Andy Pycroft D Malcolm Jarvis

7 Which fast bowler, who played in South Africa's first Test back after readmission in 1991-92, died in mysterious circumstances in Durban in 2000, aged only 33?
A Omar Henry B Tertius Bosch C Craig Matthews D Meyrick Pringle

8 Which Barbados offspinner, who won one Test cap in 1971-72, took over as West Indies' manager in 2004?
A Tony Howard B Ricky Skerritt C Tony Cozier D Willie Rodriguez

9 Which Trinidadian, who had a more famous brother, scored 96 in his only innings, at The Oval in 1939 in the last Test before the Second World War?
A Norman Marshall B Victor Stollmeyer C Leslie Walcott D Kenneth Weekes

10 Which opener, in India in 1956-57, was the first player from Western Australia to win a Test cap?
A George Thoms B John Rutherford C Keith Carmody D Jim de Courcy

11 When Bill Lawry was dumped as captain and opener by Australia in 1970-71, which fellow Victorian – who was even older than Lawry – was brought in for his only Test?
A Les Joslin B Jeff Moss C Ken Eastwood D Rex Sellers

The Googly

Roy Park played one Test for Australia in 1920-21, and was bowled by the only ball he faced. What misfortune reportedly caused his wife, who was in the stands at the MCG at the time, to miss his entire Test career?
A A tall man in a hat stood up in front of her at the vital moment B She was answering a call of nature C She dropped her knitting, and he was out while she picked it up D The match was at the SCG

Answers on page 183

DEBUT HUNDREDS

1 Who scored a hundred on his Test debut for England in 2004?

A Andrew Strauss *B Geraint Jones* *C Paul Collingwood* *D Robert Key*

2 Who scored a century in each of his first three Tests, in 1984-85?

A Allan Lamb *B Mohammad Azharuddin* *C Chris Broad* *D Dean Jones*

3 Who scored 230 on his first-class debut, and 137 on his Test debut for India in 1969-70?

A Sunil Gavaskar *B Ashok Mankad* *C Gundappa Viswanath* *D Mohinder Amarnath*

4 Who was only 18 when he hit 210 not out on his first-class debut for Northants in 1996?

A Adrian Rollins *B Graeme Swann* *C Jeff Cook* *D David Sales*

5 Who scored 148 on his one-day debut for West Indies, in 1977-78, before he'd played a Test?

A Alvin Greenidge *B Basil Williams* *C Faoud Bacchus* *D Desmond Haynes*

6 Who scored a century on his debut for Pakistan against South Africa at Rawalpindi in 1997-98, but never passed 50 in his other four Tests?

A Azhar Mahmood *B Ali Naqvi* *C Taufeeq Umar* *D Wajahatullah Wasti*

7 Who scored a hundred in his first Test for Australia, and one in his second Test for South Africa?

A Frank Mitchell *B Kepler Wessels* *C Hansie Cronje* *D Mike Haysman*

8 Who scored a hundred on his debut for Leicestershire in 1986, and another on his Derbyshire debut in 1989, but couldn't quite complete the set when he moved to Somerset in 1995?

A Neil Burns *B Peter Bowler* *C Michael Burns* *D Piran Holloway*

9 Who scored 115 not out in his first official one-day international for Zimbabwe, in the 1992 World Cup?

A Andy Flower *B Ian Butchart* *C Alistair Campbell* *D Dave Houghton*

10 Which New Zealander scored his maiden first-class hundred on his Test debut, in 1964-65?

A Graham Vivian *B Bruce Taylor* *C Bevan Congdon* *D Glenn Turner*

11 Who scored 108 in his first Test innings, in 1970-71, and 182 in his last, in 1983-84?

A Sunil Gavaskar *B Rod Marsh* *C Greg Chappell* *D Gundappa Viswanath*

The Googly

Which Australian scored a century on his first-class debut, in 1937-38, and made an unbeaten hundred in his first match for an English county, more than 21 years later?

A Arthur Morris *B Bill Alley* *C Keith Miller* *D Bruce Dooland*

Answers on page 183

THE 1977 CENTENARY TEST

1 Who captained England in the Centenary Test at Melbourne?

  A Mike Brearley **B** *Tony Greig* **C** *Tony Lewis* **D** *Mike Denness*

2 And who captained Australia?

  A Bob Simpson **B** *Greg Chappell* **C** *Ian Chappell* **D** *Bill Lawry*

3 Who marked his Test debut by stroking Tony Greig for five successive fours?

  A Ian Davis **B** *Gary Cosier* **C** *Gary Gilmour* **D** *David Hookes*

4 Who took 6 for 26 as England were shot out for 95 in their first innings?

  A Jeff Thomson **B** *Max Walker* **C** *Gary Gilmour* **D** *Dennis Lillee*

5 Who was bowled off his jaw – which was badly broken – by a Bob Willis bouncer in the first innings?

  A Ian Davis **B** *Rick McCosker* **C** *Gary Cosier* **D** *Dennis Lillee*

6 Who opened Australia's second innings instead of the man with the broken jaw?

  A Gary Cosier **B** *Gary Gilmour* **C** *Kerry O'Keeffe* **D** *Max Walker*

7 Who, in the second innings, became the first Australian wicket-keeper to score a Test century against England?

  A Richie Robinson **B** *Rod Marsh* **C** *Kevin Wright* **D** *John Maclean*

8 Which batsman, who usually opened, moved down to No. 4 and scored 64 in England's second innings?

  A Dennis Amiss **B** *Bob Woolmer* **C** *Mike Brearley* **D** *Graham Barlow*

9 Who was out lbw to end the match, which finished in exactly the same result as the inaugural Test 100 years previously?

  A Alan Knott **B** *Bob Willis* **C** *Chris Old* **D** *Derek Underwood*

10 Who was the only England player who appeared in both this match and the Lord's Centenary Test of 1980?

  A John Lever **B** *Bob Willis* **C** *Chris Old* **D** *Derek Randall*

11 Which former Australian captain, at 87 one of the oldest of more than 200 former players who accepted invitations to the Centenary Test, sadly passed away less than a month after the match?

  A Alan Kippax **B** *Bill Woodfull* **C** *Herbie Collins* **D** *Jack Ryder*

The Googly

The Centenary Test was the brainchild of which Melbourne Cricket Club committeeman, who played one Test for Australia as a fast bowler, at The Oval in 1934?

  A Ted a'Beckett **B** *Hans Ebeling* **C** *Bernard Callinan* **D** *Donald Cordner*

Answers on page 183

AUSTRALIAN DOMESTIC CRICKET

1 Who donated the Sheffield Shield, the Australian inter-state trophy competed for between 1892-93 and 1998-99?

A Sheffield Wednesday Football Club B Lord Sheffield C Green Shield stamps
D Sheffield Steel

2 And which trophy replaced the Sheffield Shield in 1999-2000?

A Mercantile-Mutual Cup B Pura Cup C Packer Cup D Foxtel Trophy

3 Which team totalled 1107 in a Shield match in 1926-27?

A New South Wales B Queensland C Victoria D Western Australia

4 Which team won the Shield for a record 43rd time in 2002-03?

A New South Wales B South Australia C Victoria D Western Australia

5 Which state was admitted to the Shield in 1947-48, and won it at their first attempt?

A Northern Territory B Queensland C Tasmania D Western Australia

6 Which man, who played only one one-day international for Australia and no Tests, was the first to score 10,000 runs in the Sheffield Shield (or its replacement)?

A John Inverarity B Jamie Siddons C Jamie Cox D Sam Trimble

7 Who was the first man to take 500 Shield wickets?

A Ashley Mallett B Bill O'Reilly C Clarrie Grimmett D Dennis Lillee

8 Who played 31 Shield matches for South Australia and averaged 112 with the bat?

A David Hookes B Don Bradman C Greg Chappell D Ian Chappell

9 Who was Queensland's captain when they won the Shield for the first time, in 1994-95?

A Allan Border B Ian Healy C Stuart Law D Carl Rackemann

10 Which fast bowler took 10 for 36 in a Shield match in 1932-33?

A Hans Ebeling B Lisle Nagel C Laurie Nash D Tim Wall

11 Who scored 300 not out for Queensland against Victoria in 2003-04?

A Andrew Symonds B Jimmy Maher C Martin Love D Matthew Hayden

The Googly

What's the unusual scorecard entry in Wisden 1973 alongside Graeme Watson's name in the match between Western Australia and Queensland?

A Retired ill B Retired tired C Retired "out" D Retired in protest

Answers on page 184

SOMERSET

1 Who scored 322 for Somerset against Warwickshire at Taunton in 1985?

A Peter Roebuck B Ian Botham C Martin Crowe D Viv Richards

2 Who moved to Somerset in 1971, after 22 years with another county, and took over as captain in 1972?

A Brian Langford B Brian Close C Jim Parks D Derek Taylor

3 Who scored 247 not out for Somerset v Derbyshire at Taunton in 2003 – including 204 in 98 balls between lunch and tea?

A Peter Bowler B Ian Blackwell C Jamie Cox D Marcus Trescothick

4 Who scored more than 3000 runs for Somerset in 1961?

A Bill Alley B Peter Wight C Merv Kitchen D Roy Virgin

5 Who made a controversial declaration, which led to Somerset's disqualification, in a Benson & Hedges Cup match in 1979?

A Viv Richards B Brian Rose C Vic Marks D Peter Roebuck

6 Who uniquely bowled eight overs for no runs in a Sunday League match in 1969?

A Ken Palmer B Tom Cartwright C Fred Rumsey D Brian Langford

7 In which town have Somerset played home games at a ground called Clarence Park?

A Wells B Bath C Frome D Weston-super-Mare

8 Which Somerset player captained England in the first one-day internationals in England, against Australia in 1972?

A Tom Cartwright B Ian Botham C Brian Close D Vic Marks

9 Which batsman scored a century in 63 minutes on his first-class debut for Somerset in 1935?

A Wally Luckes B Reggie Ingle C Harold Gimblett D Ben Brocklehurst

10 Which Somerset player took a hat-trick against the Young Australia touring side in 1995?

A Steffan Jones B Dermot Reeve C Andy Caddick D Marcus Trescothick

11 Which member of the 1948 Australian "Invincibles" later played for Somerset?

A Ray Lindwall B Ron Hamence C Colin McCool D Keith Miller

The Googly

Both captains in the 1980 Headingley Test between England and West Indies – Ian Botham and Viv Richards – played for Somerset. But neither of them was Somerset's skipper at the time: which man, who was also playing in that Test, was their county captain?

A Peter Roebuck B Brian Close C Brian Rose D Vic Marks

Answers on page 184

THE 1999 WORLD CUP

1 Who won the seventh World Cup?

A Australia B New Zealand C Pakistan D South Africa

2 Who captained the winners?

A Mark Taylor B Steve Waugh C Inzamam-ul-Haq D Wasim Akram

3 Who was the Man of the Match in the final at Lord's?

A Abdul Razzaq B Shoaib Akhtar C Shane Warne D Darren Lehmann

4 Who was run out with the scores level in the pulsating Australia-South Africa semi-final?

A Allan Donald B Mark Boucher C Lance Klusener D Shaun Pollock

5 Who captained England in the tournament, but was sacked after they failed to qualify from the group stages?

A Adam Hollioake B Alec Stewart C Mike Atherton D Nasser Hussain

6 Which Scot scored more runs than any England player managed in the tournament?

A Mike Allingham B John Blain C Gavin Hamilton D George Salmond

7 Which Indian was the leading runscorer in the tournament with 461?

A Ajay Jadeja B Sourav Ganguly C Sachin Tendulkar D Rahul Dravid

8 Who took a hat-trick for Pakistan against Zimbabwe at The Oval?

A Abdul Razzaq B Saqlain Mushtaq C Shoaib Akhtar D Wasim Akram

9 Which New Zealander was joint leading wicket-taker in the tournament (with Shane Warne), with 20?

A Geoff Allott B Chris Harris C Chris Cairns D Daniel Vettori

10 Who took three wickets in the last over to give Zimbabwe victory over India at Trent Bridge?

A Adam Huckle B Heath Streak C Henry Olonga D Pommie Mbangwa

11 Who scored two centuries in the tournament, one of them in the semi-final?

A Saeed Anwar B Stephen Fleming C Gary Kirsten D Steve Waugh

The Googly

Who did Steve Waugh supposedly tell "You've just dropped the World Cup" after he dropped him at a vital stage of Australia's last group game in 1999?

A Adam Hollioake B Herschelle Gibbs C Hansie Cronje D Jonty Rhodes

Answers on page 184

MIND THE GAP

1 Who played two Tests for England in 1993, and two more ten years later?

   A Matthew Maynard **B** *Martin Bicknell* **C** *Steve James* **D** *Mark Ilott*

2 Which Pakistan batsman played two Tests in 1969-70, and two more 17 years later?

   A Aftab Baloch **B** *Aftab Gul* **C** *Shafiq Ahmed* **D** *Younis Ahmed*

3 Which Nottinghamshire favourite played for England in West Indies in 1929-30 aged 50, almost 18 years after his previous Test appearances?

   A Arthur Carr **B** *Wilfred Rhodes* **C** *Charlie Harris* **D** *George Gunn*

4 Who made nine Test centuries for England between 1984-85 and 1987, then scored his tenth (and last) more than seven years later?

   A Allan Lamb **B** *Chris Broad* **C** *Mike Gatting* **D** *David Gower*

5 Which New Zealander played three Tests in 1937, then three more in 1949, and played rugby for England in between?

   A Merv Wallace **B** *Eric Tindill* **C** *Curly Page* **D** *Martin Donnelly*

6 Which toothless umpire, one of the officials in the first World Cup final in 1975, stood in his first Test in England in 1954, then didn't do another one for 15 years?

   A Arthur Fagg **B** *Bill Alley* **C** *Jack Crapp* **D** *Tommy Spencer*

7 Which prolific Hampshire batsman toured Australia in 1911-12 – and again in 1928-29, when one well-wisher said he remembered his father touring before the Great War?

   A Lionel Tennyson **B** *George Brown* **C** *Philip Mead* **D** *Frank Woolley*

8 Who played his first Test for West Indies in 1934-35, and had to wait 13 years for another chance, whereupon he scored 107?

   A Andy Ganteaume **B** *Kenneth Weekes* **C** *George Carew* **D** *Victor Stollmeyer*

9 Which metronomic medium-pacer, who took 100 wickets in a season 20 times in England, played his third Test in 1951-52, and his fourth in 1963?

   A Jack Flavell **B** *Tom Cartwright* **C** *Len Coldwell* **D** *Derek Shackleton*

10 Which South African captain scored consecutive Test centuries more than eight years apart?

   A Alan Melville **B** *Bruce Mitchell* **C** *Clive van Ryneveld* **D** *Herbie Taylor*

11 Which much-feared county bowler played once for England in 1949, and once more 12 years later?

   A Harold Rhodes **B** *Peter Loader* **C** *Cliff Gladwin* **D** *Les Jackson*

The Googly

Why was there a 22-year gap between John Traicos's third Test appearance and his fourth?

   A He gave up first-class cricket for 20 years **B** *He played for South Africa and then Zimbabwe*
   C He was banned from playing **D** *He had a very bad case of the bowling "yips"*

Answers on page 184

JIM LAKER

1 In which county was Laker born?

   A Lancashire B Nottinghamshire C Surrey D Yorkshire

2 On which ground did Laker take 19 wickets in a Test against Australia in 1956?

   A Old Trafford, Manchester B The Oval C Trent Bridge, Nottingham D Headingley, Leeds

3 Who toiled away for one wicket while Laker took 19 in that 1956 Test?

   A Fred Trueman B Brian Statham C Tony Lock D Trevor Bailey

4 Who was the only batsman to escape Laker's clutches?

   A Ken Mackay B Jim Burke C Colin McDonald D Ray Lindwall

5 Who was "Lakered" twice on the second day of that match for a pair?

   A Keith Miller B Richie Benaud C Neil Harvey D Graeme Hole

6 Laker took ten wickets in an innings twice in that 1956 season – who were the opponents on the other occasion?

   A Australia (again) B Kent C Cambridge University D Middlesex

7 Which of Laker's county team-mates also took all ten in a match in 1956, against Kent?

   A Alec Bedser B Eric Bedser C Tony Lock D Peter Loader

8 Laker took 7 for 103 on his Test debut – against whom?

   A Australia B New Zealand C South Africa D West Indies

9 Who was the Glamorgan offspinner surprisingly preferred to Laker for the 1954-55 tour of Australia?

   A Gilbert Parkhouse B Emrys Davies C Jim McConnon D Don Shepherd

10 For which county did Laker make a brief comeback in the 1960s, after his initial retirement?

   A Essex B Middlesex C Surrey D Sussex

11 Which West Indian did Laker dismiss more than anyone else (11 times) among his 192 Test wickets?

   A Allan Rae B Alf Valentine C Clyde Walcott D Gerry Gomez

The Googly

Jim Laker rather ruined the Test Trial match in 1950, by taking advantage of a turning pitch at Bradford. What were Laker's figures as England bowled out "The Rest" for 27 on the first morning?

A 10 for 22 B 9 for 12 C 8 for 2 D 7 for 0

Answers on page 184

EVER-PRESENT

1 Who played a record 153 consecutive Tests between 1978-79 and 1993-94?

   A Allan Border *B Kapil Dev* *C Ian Healy* *D Dilip Vengsarkar*

2 Who captained England in 52 consecutive Tests between 1993 and 1997-98?

   A Mike Atherton *B Graham Gooch* *C Graham Thorpe* *D Nasser Hussain*

3 Who played 106 successive Tests for India between 1974-75 and 1986-87?

   A Gundappa Viswanath *B Bishan Bedi* *C Sunil Gavaskar* *D Dilip Vengsarkar*

4 Which South African-born allrounder's career comprised 58 successive Tests for England between 1972 and 1977, after which he moved to Australia?

   A Tony Greig *B Basil D'Oliveira* *C Chris Smith* *D Allan Lamb*

5 Who kept wicket for England in 65 consecutive Tests between 1970-71 and 1977?

   A Alan Knott *B Bob Taylor* *C Jim Parks* *D David Bairstow*

6 Which Indian played 66 successive Tests before missing one in 1984-85 for disciplinary reasons, played 65 more in a row, and then retired?

   A Syed Kirmani *B Kapil Dev* *C Gundappa Viswanath* *D Dilip Vengsarkar*

7 Whose Test career for New Zealand comprised 58 successive matches (1949-65), the last 34 as captain?

   A Tony MacGibbon *B Bert Sutcliffe* *C John Reid* *D Walter Hadlee*

8 Who played in Zimbabwe's first 56 Tests, from 1992-93 to 2001-02?

   A Andy Flower *B Grant Flower* *C Alistair Campbell* *D Guy Whittall*

9 Who played in 185 consecutive one-day internationals between 1989-90 and 1997-98?

   A Mohammad Azharuddin *B Brian Lara* *C Sachin Tendulkar* *D Richie Richardson*

10 Who played in Tests on six successive England tours of Australia, from 1954-55 to 1974-75?

   A Tony Lock *B Ken Barrington* *C Colin Cowdrey* *D Fred Titmus*

11 Who joined the English first-class umpires' panel in 1969, and was still on it 35 years later?

   A David Shepherd *B Dickie Bird* *C David Constant* *D Ken Palmer*

The Googly

Who played a record 423 consecutive County Championship matches from 1954 to 1969?

A Brian Taylor *B Jimmy Binks* *C Ken Suttle* *D Don Shepherd*

Answers on page 184

SUSSEX

1 Which famous Sussex player was the first man to score 3000 runs in a season, in 1899?

A Ted Killick B K.S. Ranjitsinhji C C.B. Fry D Fred Tate

2 Who captained Sussex to their first County Championship title, in 2003?

A Chris Adams B Richard Montgomerie C Tony Cottey D Murray Goodwin

3 Which Sussex player took 202 wickets in 49 Tests for England, starting in 1965?

A Tony Greig B John Snow C Ian Thomson D Ted Dexter

4 Who took 103 wickets for Sussex in their Championship year of 2003?

A Mushtaq Ahmed B Jason Lewry C James Kirtley D Robin Martin-Jenkins

5 Which Sussex player captained England on the 1962-63 Ashes tour of Australia?

A David Sheppard B Jim Parks C Mike Smith D Ted Dexter

6 In which town have Sussex played home games at a ground called The Saffrons?

A Arundel B Hastings C Lewes D Eastbourne

7 In which year did Sussex win the inaugural one-day Gillette Cup?

A 1960 B 1961 C 1963 D 1965

8 Who took 2211 wickets for Sussex, at 17.41 apiece, between 1912 and 1937?

A Arthur Gilligan B Bert Relf C Fred Tate D Maurice Tate

9 Which Sussex player of the 1970s later played Tests for two different countries?

A Javed Miandad B Kepler Wessels C John Traicos D Tony Greig

10 Who scored 34,152 runs for Sussex, with 76 hundreds, and also took 779 catches ... but never played for England?

A James Langridge B John Langridge C Charlie Oakes D Harry Parks

11 When Jim Laker took 19 wickets against Australia in the 1956 Old Trafford Test, which Sussex player held five catches off his bowling?

A Alan Oakman B Hubert Doggart C Ken Suttle D David Sheppard

The Googly

What did the Sussex fast bowler Tony Pigott put off after being called up to make his England Test debut in New Zealand in 1983-84?

A An operation on his back B His university exams C His wedding
D Flying home to attend the birth of his first child

Answers on page 184

HEADINGLEY '81

1 Who returned as England captain for this famous match?

 A Geoff Boycott B Ian Botham C Mike Brearley D Bob Willis

2 What, famously, were the betting odds that flashed up on the electronic scoreboard during the fourth day, when England were facing what seemed to be certain defeat?

 A 100-1 B 250-1 C 500-1 D 1000-1

3 Which Australian scored 102 in the first innings of the match?

 A Graham Yallop B Graeme Wood C Allan Border D John Dyson

4 Which wicket-keeper broke the aggregate record for Test dismissals during the match?

 A Alan Knott B Bob Taylor C Ian Healy D Rod Marsh

5 And which keeper broke the aggregate record for first-class dismissals during the match?

 A Alan Knott B Bob Taylor C Paul Downton D Rod Marsh

6 Who took 6 for 95 in Australia's first innings of 401?

 A Chris Old B Bob Willis C Ian Botham D Graham Dilley

7 Who top-scored for England with 50 in their disappointing first innings of 174?

 A Graham Gooch B Mike Gatting C David Gower D Ian Botham

8 After Ian Botham's heroics, who roared in to take 8 for 43 as England turned the tables?

 A Ian Botham B Bob Willis C Peter Willey D Graham Dilley

9 Which Australian was making his third and final Test appearance in this match?

 A Martin Kent B Graeme Beard C Trevor Chappell D Mike Whitney

10 Which of the England players was dropped for the next match, despite scoring 56?

 A Peter Willey B Bob Taylor C Chris Old D Graham Dilley

11 How many times before this had a team won a Test match after being forced to follow on?

 A Never B Once C Twice D Four times

The Googly

Ian Botham became only the second player to score a century and take five wickets in an innings in the same Ashes Test – who was the first to do it, back in the 1920s?

 A Warwick Armstrong B Jack Gregory C Wilfred Rhodes D Maurice Tate

Answers on page 185

ENGLAND v AUSTRALIA

1 Where was the first-ever Test match played, in March 1877?

   *A Lord's** B Melbourne** C Sydney** D The Oval*

2 What was the result of that game – and of the Centenary Test exactly 100 years later?

   *A Australia won by 45 runs** B England won by five wickets*
   *C Australia won by two wickets** D Drawn*

3 Who captained Australia in England in 1985, 1989 and 1993?

   *A Allan Border** B Kim Hughes** C Greg Chappell** D Mark Taylor*

4 Which wicket-keeper made 148 dismissals in Ashes Tests?

   *A Alan Knott** B Ian Healy** C Rod Marsh** D Godfrey Evans*

5 Who scored 839 runs in his first Ashes series, in 1989?

   *A Steve Waugh** B David Boon** C Mark Taylor** D Dean Jones*

6 Who was the first bowler to take 150 wickets in Ashes Tests?

   *A Terry Alderman** B Ian Botham** C Jim Laker** D Dennis Lillee*

7 Who scored a century on his Test debut for England, at Trent Bridge in 1993?

   *A Alec Stewart** B Mike Atherton** C Nasser Hussain** D Graham Thorpe*

8 Who captained England for the only time at Headingley in 1968, when Colin Cowdrey was injured?

   *A John Edrich** B Ken Barrington** C Tom Graveney** D Basil D'Oliveira*

9 And who captained Australia for the only time in the same game, as Bill Lawry was unfit?

   *A Graham McKenzie** B Barry Jarman** C Paul Sheahan** D Neil Hawke*

10 Who scored 3636 runs for England in Ashes Tests?

   *A Len Hutton** B Geoff Boycott** C Walter Hammond** D Jack Hobbs*

11 Which Australian made a record 52 appearances against England in Tests?

   *A Allan Border** B Syd Gregory** C Clem Hill** D Don Bradman*

The Googly

In the closing stages of the drawn final Test at The Oval in 1921, Australia's captain Warwick Armstrong picked up a newspaper that was blowing across the ground and started flicking through it. What did he say he was looking for?

*A He wanted to know who they were playing** B He had a bet on a horse in the 2.15 at Ascot*
*C He was checking out the theatre timings** D The previous day's scorecard*

Answers on page 185

GROUNDS IN THE WEST INDIES

1 Where is the Bourda Oval?

A Georgetown, Guyana *B Bridgetown, Barbados* *C Kingston, Jamaica*
D Port-of-Spain, Trinidad

2 Which Test ground features the Blue Mountains in the background?

A Georgetown, Guyana *B Bridgetown, Barbados* *C Kingston, Jamaica*
D Port-of-Spain, Trinidad

3 Which Test ground was formerly tended by inmates of the local prison?

A St John's, Antigua *B Berbice, Guyana* *C Arnos Vale, St Vincent* *D Gros Islet, St Lucia*

4 On which ground was Test cricket's first triple-century scored, in 1929-30?

A Georgetown, Guyana *B Bridgetown, Barbados* *C Kingston, Jamaica*
D Port-of-Spain, Trinidad

5 And on which ground was Test cricket's first quadruple-century scored, in 2003-04?

A St John's, Antigua *B Bridgetown, Barbados* *C Kingston, Jamaica* *D Gros Islet, St Lucia*

6 Where is the 2007 World Cup final scheduled to be played?

A Georgetown, Guyana *B Bridgetown, Barbados* *C Kingston, Jamaica*
D Port-of-Spain, Trinidad

7 On which ground was a Test match abandoned in 1997-98 after 56 minutes, as the pitch was too dangerous for play to continue?

A Georgetown, Guyana *B Bridgetown, Barbados* *C Kingston, Jamaica*
D Port-of-Spain, Trinidad

8 Which Caribbean island was the first to use two different grounds for official internationals?

A Antigua *B Barbados* *C Grenada* *D St Vincent*

9 On which Test ground might you sit in the Three Ws Stand or the Sir Garfield Sobers Pavilion?

A Georgetown, Guyana *B Bridgetown, Barbados* *C Kingston, Jamaica*
D Port-of-Spain, Trinidad

10 Which Test ground is below sea level and surrounded by an often-full moat?

A Georgetown, Guyana *B Bridgetown, Barbados* *C Kingston, Jamaica*
D Port-of-Spain, Trinidad

11 Which Test ground has an "Airport End" and is adjacent to its island's airport?

A Arnos Vale, St Vincent *B St John's, Antigua* *C Kingstown, St Vincent*
D Gros Islet, St Lucia

The Googly

Viv Richards predictably scored a century in the first Test in his native Antigua in 1980-81. But who scored the first Test century there, earlier in the same game?

A Geoff Boycott *B David Gower* *C Peter Willey* *D Desmond Haynes*

Answers on page 185

MIXED BAG 2

1 Who scored a century on his first-class debut for Bombay in 1988-89, aged only 15 years and 232 days?

   A Vinod Kambli **B** *Sachin Tendulkar* **C** *Sairaj Bahutule* **D** *Hemang Badani*

2 The Warwick Road End at Old Trafford was renamed after which Lancashire legend in 2003?

   A Roy Tattersall **B** *Brian Statham* **C** *Cyril Washbrook* **D** *Mike Atherton*

3 What was unusual about the bat Dennis Lillee used briefly in a Test at Perth in 1979-80?

   A It was double-sided **B** *It was made of aluminium*
   C It had a protective shield in front of the handle **D** *It had a rounded face*

4 Who smashed a record 20 sixes during a County Championship match in 1995?

   A Andrew Symonds **B** *Ian Botham* **C** *Andrew Flintoff* **D** *Dimitri Mascarenhas*

5 Who started a Test match as wicket-keeper, but took off the pads to bowl and claimed the first opposition wicket to fall?

   A Rod Marsh **B** *Alan Smith* **C** *Tatenda Taibu* **D** *Rahul Dravid*

6 Who won the gold medal for cricket in the 1998 Commonwealth Games in Kuala Lumpur?

   A Antigua & Barbuda **B** *Australia* **C** *Zimbabwe* **D** *South Africa*

7 Who captained Australia Under-19s against England in 1989-90, but made his Test debut for England in 1995?

   A Alan Mullally **B** *Jason Gallian* **C** *Craig White* **D** *Martin McCague*

8 Who, in 2003, scored his third County Championship triple-century for Northamptonshire?

   A Michael Hussey **B** *Russell Warren* **C** *Jeff Cook* **D** *David Sales*

9 Which former England opener collapsed and died at the crease in a friendly match in The Gambia in 1989?

   A Colin Milburn **B** *Andy Lloyd* **C** *Wilf Slack* **D** *John Jameson*

10 In which year was the last Gentlemen v Players match contested at Lord's?

   A 1939 **B** *1951* **C** *1962* **D** *1967*

11 Who played four Tests for India in the 1930s, but had a son and two nephews who captained Pakistan?

   A Mohammad Nissar **B** *Jahangir Khan* **C** *Amar Singh* **D** *Syed Nazir Ali*

The Googly

What was unusual about Doug Watson's century for KwaZulu-Natal against Boland at Durban in September 2003?

A It took him 96 minutes to get off the mark **B** *He batted left- and right-handed*
C It was spread over four days **D** *He was out for 98, but was awarded his century after the match finished, when the umpires realised they had signalled a six as a four*

Answers on page 185

A FUNNY WAY TO GO

1 Who was out handled the ball in the 1993 Ashes Test at Old Trafford?
A Mike Atherton **B** *Shane Warne* **C** *Merv Hughes* **D** *Graham Gooch*

2 And which man, who played in the above match, was himself out handled the ball in a Test eight years later?
A Steve Waugh **B** *Graham Thorpe* **C** *Nasser Hussain* **D** *Glenn McGrath*

3 Who was given out handled the ball *and* obstructing the field in one-day internationals?
A Moin Khan **B** *Mohinder Amarnath* **C** *Chris Lewis* **D** *David Gower*

4 Who was the first man given out obstructing the field in a Test match, at The Oval in 1951?
A Athol Rowan **B** *Eric Rowan* **C** *Len Hutton* **D** *Denis Compton*

5 And how was Russell Endean – the wicket-keeper in that 1951 match – out against England at Cape Town in 1956-57?
A Timed out **B** *Handled the ball* **C** *Hit the ball twice* **D** *Obstructing the field*

6 Which England player was out handled the ball in a Test at Bangalore in 2001-02?
A Marcus Trescothick **B** *Mark Butcher* **C** *Dominic Cork* **D** *Michael Vaughan*

7 Which Australian was given out handled the ball after picking up the ball and giving it back to the Pakistani bowler at Perth in 1978-79?
A Andrew Hilditch **B** *Graeme Wood* **C** *Peter Toohey* **D** *Graham Yallop*

8 After he twice ran out the non-striker Bill Brown while he was backing up too far in 1947-48, which Indian allrounder's name is still used in Australia for that sort of dismissal?
A Lala Amarnath **B** *Vinoo Mankad* **C** *Polly Umrigar* **D** *Ram Ramchand*

9 Who was bowled by a no-ball in a Test in Georgetown in 1990-91, was run out when he walked off thinking he was out, and not reprieved even when the Australian coach showed the umpires the laws in *Wisden*?
A Allan Border **B** *Mark Waugh* **C** *Greg Matthews* **D** *Dean Jones*

10 Who hooked Dennis Lillee out of the ground early on in the first World Cup final, but slipped, dislodged the bails, and was out hit wicket?
A Alvin Kallicharran **B** *Roy Fredericks* **C** *Gordon Greenidge* **D** *Desmond Haynes*

11 What was unusual about Keith Stackpole's catch to dismiss West Indies' Seymour Nurse in a Test at Melbourne in 1968-69?
A It bounced off the wicket-keeper's cap back to silly point **B** *It hit short leg on the head and ballooned 30 yards to square leg* **C** *He ran over the boundary while taking it but threw it up as he did so, to complete a legal catch* **D** *It was parried by the keeper and kicked upwards by first slip*

The Googly

What was the unusual entry in the scorebook alongside the England legspinner Ian Peebles's name in the last match of MCC's tour of South Africa in 1927-28?
A Absent shopping **B** *Absent, asleep* **C** *Absent, flown home* **D** *Absent bathing*

Answers on page 185

ENGLAND v SOUTH AFRICA

1 Who captained South Africa in England in 1994, having previously played for Australia?

    A Mike Procter *B Kepler Wessels* *C Hansie Cronje* *D Geoff Marsh*

2 Who scored two double-centuries in the 2003 series?

    A Andrew Flintoff *B Marcus Trescothick* *C Graeme Smith* *D Herschelle Gibbs*

3 Who dropped anchor for 185 not out – in 643 minutes – to save the 1995-96 Johannesburg Test?

    A Mike Atherton *B Gary Kirsten* *C Jack Russell* *D Kepler Wessels*

4 Who scored 753 runs for England in the 1947 Test series?

    A Len Hutton *B Bill Edrich* *C Denis Compton* *D Cyril Washbrook*

5 Who took 33 wickets for South Africa in the 1998 Test series in England?

    A Paul Adams *B Makhaya Ntini* *C Shaun Pollock* *D Allan Donald*

6 Who made 219 for England in the 2003 Oval Test?

    A Andrew Flintoff *B Graham Thorpe* *C Marcus Trescothick* *D Michael Vaughan*

7 Who scored his maiden Test century at Headingley in 1994, when he was nearly 40?

    A Dave Richardson *B Brian McMillan* *C Jimmy Cook* *D Peter Kirsten*

8 Who scored 1270 runs at 55.21 to top England's averages on tour in South Africa in 1956-57 – which included a miserable time in the Tests, where he managed only 153 runs in 10 innings?

    A Denis Compton *B Peter May* *C Colin Cowdrey* *D Doug Insole*

9 Who captained South Africa in England in 1965 – their last tour there for 29 years?

    A Trevor Goddard *B Jackie McGlew* *C Ali Bacher* *D Peter van der Merwe*

10 Which bowler made his Test debut at Trent Bridge in 1998 for South Africa, although he was actually born in Zimbabwe?

    A Neil Johnson *B Makhaya Ntini* *C Steve Elworthy* *D Monde Zondeki*

11 How many of the South African team from the 1960 Lord's Test played there in the 1965 Test against England?

    A None *B One* *C Ten* *D Eleven*

The Googly

Who played 20 Test matches for South Africa, but never appeared once against England, even though he toured there twice, in 1994 and 1998?

    A Adam Bacher *B Pat Symcox* *C Craig Matthews* *D Fanie de Villiers*

Answers on page 185

THE 2003 WORLD CUP

1 Who was the Man of the Match in the final, after scoring 140 not out for the winners?

A Andrew Symonds B Damien Martyn C Ricky Ponting D Matthew Hayden

2 Who were the two beaten semi-finalists?

A England and New Zealand B New Zealand and South Africa
C South Africa and Sri Lanka D Kenya and Sri Lanka

3 Who took a hat-trick for Australia?

A Glenn McGrath B Brett Lee C Shane Warne D Jason Gillespie

4 Which two umpires officiated in the final, for the third World Cup in a row?

A Aldridge and Hair B Bucknor and Shepherd C Bucknor and Taufel D Hair and Shepherd

5 Who scored over 200 more runs than anyone else in the tournament, finishing with 673?

A Sachin Tendulkar B Herschelle Gibbs C Matthew Hayden D Rahul Dravid

6 Who took 23 wickets in the tournament, a new record for any World Cup?

A Glenn McGrath B Zaheer Khan C Collins Obuya D Chaminda Vaas

7 Which Test-playing country did Canada beat?

A Zimbabwe B Bangladesh C New Zealand D Pakistan

8 And which Test-playing country bowled Canada out for 36?

A Australia B Bangladesh C Sri Lanka D West Indies

9 Which Namibian, who took 5 for 43 against England, played in the 2003 Rugby World Cup as well?

A Jan-Berrie Burger B Bjorn Kotze C Rudi van Vuuren D Burton van Rooi

10 Who took 7 for 20, and then scored an important 34, as Australia beat England in the group stages?

A Ian Harvey B Jason Gillespie C Brett Lee D Andy Bichel

11 Who were Zimbabwe playing when Andy Flower and Henry Olonga made their momentous black-armband protest against what they called "the death of democracy" in their country?

A Australia B Bangladesh C Canada D Namibia

The Googly

Who scored a World Cup century in 67 balls against West Indies in 2003, and the following year took 17 wickets in a first-class match?

A Lance Klusener B Andy Blignaut C Chris Cairns D John Davison

Answers on page 185

WARWICKSHIRE

1 Who scored a triple-century for Warwickshire at Lord's in 2004?

   A Nick Knight   *B Ian Bell*   *C Jim Troughton*   *D Mark Wagh*

2 Which Warwickshire player captained England in Australia in 1965-66?

   A Alan Smith   *B Mike Smith*   *C David Brown*   *D Dennis Amiss*

3 Who scored 35,146 runs – and 78 centuries – for Warwickshire between 1960 and 1987?

   A Dennis Amiss   *B Rohan Kanhai*   *C Mike Smith*   *D John Jameson*

4 Which Warwickshire player was England's vice-captain in the 1932-33 Bodyline Test series?

   A Freddie Brown   *B Bob Wyatt*   *C Dick Spooner*   *D George Paine*

5 Which Kenyan World Cup player made a few appearances for Warwickshire in 2003?

   A Maurice Odumbe   *B Steve Tikolo*   *C Collins Obuya*   *D Martin Suji*

6 Who captained Warwickshire from 1985 to 1987, after a long career with another county?

   A Dermot Reeve   *B Chris Old*   *C Eddie Hemmings*   *D Norman Gifford*

7 Where did Warwickshire play a Championship match for the first time in 2004?

   A Stratford-upon-Avon   *B Wolverhampton*   *C Coventry*   *D Warwick*

8 Who scored 173 on his first-class debut for Warwickshire in 1971, and later captained them?

   A Neal Abberley   *B John Whitehouse*   *C Alvin Kallicharran*   *D Dudley Owen-Thomas*

9 Who was Warwickshire's captain when they won the County Championship in 1951?

   A Eric Hollies   *B Jack Bannister*   *C Dick Spooner*   *D Tom Dollery*

10 Which Warwickshire player opened the batting for England in three of their matches at the 1996 World Cup?

   A Nick Knight   *B Neil Smith*   *C Dougie Brown*   *D Dermot Reeve*

11 Jack Bannister took all ten wickets in an innings for Warwickshire in 1959 – against whom?

   A Oxford University   *B Free Foresters*   *C Combined Services*   *D D.H. Robins' XI*

The Googly

Against Essex at Clacton in 1965 Alan Smith captained Warwickshire and kept wicket – but what else did he do during the match that was remarkable?

A He got married on the rest day   *B He took off his pads and bowled – and took a hat-trick* *C He went to the beach and swam two miles for charity after play each day*   *D He scored a century in each innings, both while batting as a nightwatchman*

Answers on page 185

TEST MATCH FIRSTS

1 Who was the first batsman to score 11,000 runs?

   A *Allan Border* B *Sunil Gavaskar* C *Javed Miandad* D *Steve Waugh*

2 Who was the first bowler to take 500 wickets?

   A *Muttiah Muralitharan* B *Shane Warne* C *Courtney Walsh* D *Wasim Akram*

3 Who was the first man to play in 100 Tests?

   A *Godfrey Evans* B *Garry Sobers* C *Colin Cowdrey* D *Len Hutton*

4 Who was the first batsman to score 10,000 runs?

   A *Allan Border* B *Steve Waugh* C *Sunil Gavaskar* D *Brian Lara*

5 Who was the first bowler to take 400 wickets?

   A *Richard Hadlee* B *Ian Botham* C *Curtly Ambrose* D *Kapil Dev*

6 Who was the first wicket-keeper to make 300 dismissals?

   A *Alan Knott* B *Ian Healy* C *Rod Marsh* D *Godfrey Evans*

7 Who was the first batsman to score 8000 runs?

   A *Ken Barrington* B *Geoff Boycott* C *Colin Cowdrey* D *Garry Sobers*

8 Who was the first bowler to take 300 wickets?

   A *Lance Gibbs* B *Brian Statham* C *Fred Trueman* D *Derek Underwood*

9 Who was the first fielder (not a wicket-keeper) to take 100 catches?

   A *Ian Botham* B *Bobby Simpson* C *Ian Chappell* D *Walter Hammond*

10 Who was the first batsman to score 6000 runs?

   A *Jack Hobbs* B *Don Bradman* C *Patsy Hendren* D *Walter Hammond*

11 Who was the first bowler to take 100 wickets?

   A *Charlie Turner* B *Johnny Briggs* C *George Lohmann* D *Fred Spofforth*

The Googly

Who was the first man to score 5000 runs, take 300 wickets, and take 100 catches in Tests?

A *Imran Khan* B *Richard Hadlee* C *Ian Botham* D *Kapil Dev*

Answers on page 186

PAKISTAN IN TESTS

1 Who became, in June 2000, the first Pakistani to take 400 Test wickets?

   A Wasim Akram B Waqar Younis C Mushtaq Ahmed D Saqlain Mushtaq

2 Who scored Pakistan's first Test triple-century, in 1957-58?

   A Hanif Mohammad B Mushtaq Mohammad C Sadiq Mohammad D Wazir Mohammad

3 Who took 40 wickets for Pakistan in the series against India in 1982-83?

   A Abdul Qadir B Imran Khan C Azeem Hafeez D Sarfraz Nawaz

4 Who was the first Pakistani wicket-keeper to record 200 Test dismissals?

   A Imtiaz Ahmed B Wasim Bari C Moin Khan D Rashid Latif

5 Who took Pakistan's first Test hat-trick, against Sri Lanka at Lahore in 1998-99, and repeated the feat in the next Test?

   A Abdul Razzaq B Wasim Akram C Waqar Younis D Saqlain Mushtaq

6 Who scored 274 against England, in only his second Test appearance, at Edgbaston in 1971?

   A Zaheer Abbas B Aftab Gul C Sadiq Mohammad D Aftab Baloch

7 Who was the first Pakistani to take 100 Test wickets?

   A Sarfraz Nawaz B Intikhab Alam C Imran Khan D Fazal Mahmood

8 Where have Pakistan played home Tests at a ground called the Iqbal Stadium?

   A Quetta B Faisalabad C Rawalpindi D Multan

9 Who scored Pakistan's first Test century, against India at Lucknow in 1952-53?

   A Imtiaz Ahmed B Waqar Hassan C Nazar Mohammad D Hanif Mohammad

10 Who scored two centuries on his Test debut against Bangladesh in August 2003?

   A Taufeeq Umar B Mohammad Hafeez C Younis Khan D Yasir Hameed

11 Which player appeared in all of Pakistan's first 39 Tests?

   A Abdul Hafeez Kardar B Hanif Mohammad C Imtiaz Ahmed D Fazal Mahmood

The Googly

When Shakoor Rana had his very public argument with England's captain Mike Gatting during the 1987-88 series in Pakistan, who was the other umpire?

A Haseeb Ahsan B Shakeel Khan C Mahboob Shah D Khizar Hayat

Answers on page 186

BOOKWORMS

1 Whose series of tour diaries briefly made him the best-selling author in Australia?

   A Shane Warne B Mark Waugh C Glenn McGrath D Steve Waugh

2 Who wrote *Phoenix from the Ashes*, a first-hand account of the amazing 1981 Ashes series?

   A Mike Brearley B Ian Botham C Geoff Boycott D Kim Hughes

3 Who defended the Bodyline tactics in his 1933 book *In Quest of the Ashes*?

   A Pelham Warner B Gubby Allen C Harold Larwood D Douglas Jardine

4 Who wrote *It Sort of Clicks*, a book about Ian Botham, but later fell out spectacularly with him?

   A Peter Roebuck B Vic Marks C Viv Richards D Don Mosey

5 Who called his 1998 autobiography *Anything But An Autobiography*?

   A Allan Border B Richie Benaud C Imran Khan D Mark Taylor

6 Which player's wife wrote two acclaimed behind-the-scenes accounts of England tours in the 1980s?

   A Susie Emburey B Elaine Gatting C Frances Edmonds D Kathy Botham

7 Whose book *Cricket Crisis* is generally accepted as the best first-hand account of the Bodyline series?

   A Bill Bowes B Bill Woodfull C Jack Fingleton D Don Bradman

8 Who wrote the award-winning 1997 book *A Lot of Hard Yakka*, an amusing look at his time on the county circuit?

   A Graeme Fowler B Steve James C Jonathan Agnew D Simon Hughes

9 Who was the Australian subject of Gideon Haigh's awardwinning 1999 biography *Mystery Spinner*?

   A Jack Iverson B Bert Ironmonger C Shane Warne D John Gleeson

10 Who followed a book comparing cricket and baseball with a successful diary of his 2003 season, during which he made his England Test debut?

   A Kabir Ali B Ed Smith C Anthony McGrath D James Kirtley

11 Who wrote accounts of the Ashes tours of 1953 and 1956, and another more than 30 years later in 1986-87?

   A John Arlott B Peter West C Jim Swanton D John Woodcock

The Googly

What is the subject of David Frith's 2001 book *Silence of the Heart*?

A Sledging B Incorrect umpiring decisions C Cricketers who committed suicide
D Cricketers and divorce

Answers on page 186

YORKSHIRE

1 Who took over as Yorkshire captain in 2004?

   A Matthew Wood B Michael Vaughan C Craig White D Darren Lehmann

2 Which Yorkshire fast bowler took 307 Test wickets for England?

   A Bob Appleyard B Fred Trueman C Chris Old D Darren Gough

3 Which Yorkshire fast bowler took a Test hat-trick in Barbados in 2004?

   A Matthew Hoggard B Craig White C Chris Silverwood D Darren Gough

4 Who was Yorkshire's first official overseas player, in 1992?

   A Richie Richardson B Sachin Tendulkar C Craig McDermott D Mohammad Azharuddin

5 Who scored 38,561 runs – and 112 hundreds – for Yorkshire between 1919 and 1945?

   A Len Hutton B Wilfred Rhodes C Herbert Sutcliffe D Percy Holmes

6 Who returned as Yorkshire's captain in 1982, when he was 50, and led them to the Sunday League title the following year?

   A Ray Illingworth B Geoff Boycott C Brian Close D Phil Sharpe

7 Who took 3608 wickets for Yorkshire, at an average of 16.00, between 1898 and 1930?

   A Hedley Verity B Schofield Haigh C Wilfred Rhodes D George Hirst

8 In which town have Yorkshire staged home games at a ground called Abbeydale Park?

   A Harrogate B Bradford C Sheffield D Middlesbrough

9 Which Yorkshireman captained England in Don Bradman's final Test in 1948?

   A Len Hutton B Don Brennan C Alec Coxon D Norman Yardley

10 Who took a Sunday League hat-trick for Yorkshire in 1982, aged just 17?

   A Arthur "Rocker" Robinson B Arnie Sidebottom C Paul Jarvis D Simon Dennis

11 Which Yorkshire player was out for 99 against New Zealand at Auckland in 1987-88 – and never did make a Test century?

   A Bill Athey B David Bairstow C Martyn Moxon D Richard Blakey

The Googly

Why were Geoffrey Keighley's appearances for Yorkshire (1947-51) unusual?

A He had an artificial limb B He was only ever available to play in August
C He was born in France, not in Yorkshire D He was a diehard Lancashire fan

Answers on page 186

WORLD CUP: GENERAL

1 Who was the only player to appear in the first six World Cups?

   A Viv Richards B Javed Miandad C Sunil Gavaskar D Desmond Haynes

2 And who was the only other player to appear in the first five?

   A Graham Gooch B Richard Hadlee C Dave Houghton D Imran Khan

3 Who was the first man to take 50 wickets in World Cup cricket?

   A Andy Roberts B Wasim Akram C Chris Cairns D Muttiah Muralitharan

4 Who played in three finals, the first in 1979, and lost all three?

   A Allan Border B Ian Botham C Greg Chappell D Graham Gooch

5 Apart from Steve Waugh, which Australian was in the Cup-winning squads in both 1987 and 1999?

   A Mark Waugh B David Boon C Tom Moody D Dean Jones

6 Who was in one country's squad in 1983 but didn't play, but did appear in the final for a different country nine years later?

   A Aamir Sohail B Waqar Younis C Graeme Hick D Dermot Reeve

7 Who scored the run that won the 1999 final, and took the catch that clinched the 2003 one?

   A Adam Gilchrist B Matthew Hayden C Ricky Ponting D Darren Lehmann

8 Which Sri Lankan won a winner's medal in 1996 after opening the bowling in four matches, including the final, but not managing to take a wicket?

   A Asanka Gurusinha B Pramodya Wickremasinghe C Chaminda Vaas
   D Ravindra Pushpakumara

9 Which one-day specialist played in the 1999 and 2003 finals, but didn't bat or bowl in either of them?

   A Andrew Symonds B Brad Hogg C Michael Bevan D Ian Harvey

10 Which unheralded member of a famous cricketing family made one appearance in the 1975 World Cup?

   A Rajinder Amarnath B Barry Hadlee C Trevor Chappell D Ron Headley

11 Which was the first ground outside England to stage a World Cup match, in 1983?

   A Edinburgh B Swansea C Cardiff D Dublin

The Googly

Which Kenyan player, who also played Davis Cup tennis, retired after the 1999 World Cup, but returned four years later – having played almost no cricket in the interim – and returned figures of 8.2-6-7-3 in the Super Six match against Australia?

A Aasif Karim B Steve Tikolo C Maurice Odumbe D Hitesh Modi

Answers on page 186

ENGLAND v WEST INDIES

1 For which trophy do England and West Indies compete?

A The Lawrence Trophy B The Wisden Trophy C Viv's Vase D The Frank Worrell Trophy

2 Who were known as "Those two little pals of mine"?

A Ramadhin and Valentine B Weekes and Walcott C Trueman and Statham
D Richards and Richardson

3 Who took 14 wickets in the match for West Indies at The Oval in 1976?

A Andy Roberts B Keith Boyce C Michael Holding D Wayne Daniel

4 Who captained England in 10 Tests against West Indies – and lost the lot?

A Ian Botham B Mike Gatting C Graham Gooch D David Gower

5 Who scored two double-centuries – and 829 runs in all – in the 1976 Test series?

A Dennis Amiss B David Steele C Viv Richards D Gordon Greenidge

6 What was the surname of the brothers who captained West Indies on successive tours of England, in 1933 and 1939?

A Stollmeyer B Grant C St Hill D Goddard

7 Who took a hat-trick for England at Headingley in 1957?

A Peter Loader B Tony Lock C Jim Laker D Fred Trueman

8 Who captained England for the only time in a Test at Headingley in 1988?

A John Emburey B Chris Broad C Chris Cowdrey D Derek Pringle

9 Who scored 325 for England at Kingston in 1929-30?

A Andy Sandham B Jack Hobbs C George Gunn D Patsy Hendren

10 Who took a wicket with his first ball in Test cricket, at Trent Bridge in 1991?

A Devon Malcolm B Steve Watkin C Richard Illingworth D Dermot Reeve

11 Who scored 107 on his Test debut for England at Lord's in 1969?

A Frank Hayes B Brian Luckhurst C Mike Denness D John Hampshire

The Googly

What was unusual about Lawrence Rowe's 302 for West Indies against England at Bridgetown in 1973-74?

A It was his first Test hundred B It was his first first-class century outside his native island
C It was West Indies' first Test triple-century D No other batsman scored more than 32

Answers on page 186

SLOW STARTERS 2

1 Who went wicketless on his debut in 1971, didn't play again for three years, but finished up with 362 Test wickets?

A Richard Hadlee B Bob Willis C Imran Khan D Dennis Lillee

2 Who managed only one run in his first six Test innings – but scored his sixth Test double-century during 2004?

A Marvan Atapattu B Ken Rutherford C Hashan Tillakaratne D V.V.S. Laxman

3 Who scored Test cricket's slowest century, in 557 minutes, at Lahore in 1977-78?

A Geoff Boycott B Mushtaq Mohammad C Mudassar Nazar D Haroon Rashid

4 Which famous stonewaller took 357 minutes to reach 50 in a Test at Brisbane in 1958-59?

A Jim Burke B Trevor Bailey C Colin Cowdrey D Colin McDonald

5 Which country took 26 years, and 45 matches, to record their first Test victory?

A India B New Zealand C South Africa D Zimbabwe

6 Whose 84 against England at Brisbane in 1970-71 didn't contain a single boundary?

A Ian Redpath B Bill Lawry C Ian Chappell D Kerry O'Keeffe

7 Who lasted a record 101 minutes without scoring a run before being out for 0 in a Test in 1998-99?

A Geoff Allott B Gary Kirsten C Danny Morrison D Mark Vermeulen

8 Who, in 1984, scored his only first-class hundred in his 618th innings?

A Bob Taylor B Dennis Lillee C Derek Underwood D Joel Garner

9 Who made his Test debut for England in 1899, batting No. 10, but a dozen years later was opening with Jack Hobbs, and scored 179 in an Ashes Test at Melbourne?

A George Hirst B George Gunn C Wilfred Rhodes D Archie MacLaren

10 Who scored Test cricket's slowest double-century, in 777 minutes, on his Test debut in 1986-87?

A Navjot Sidhu B Brendon Kuruppu C Shoaib Mohammad D Grant Flower

11 Which Indian once batted through an entire day of a Test and scored just 49 runs?

A Sunil Gavaskar B Navjot Sidhu C M.L. Jaisimha D Nari Contractor

The Googly

Who played his first one-day international in 1974, but didn't score a century until his 107th match, in 1987-88, and then played only one more before retiring?

A Graham Gooch B Ian Botham C Sunil Gavaskar D Greg Chappell

Answers on page 186

AFRICAN GROUNDS

1 Where was the 2003 World Cup final played?

   A Port Elizabeth B Johannesburg C Cape Town D Durban

2 Which was the first ground in South Africa to stage a Test, in 1889?

   A Port Elizabeth B Johannesburg C Cape Town D Durban

3 In which city has Test cricket been played at the Old and New Wanderers, and at Ellis Park?

   A Port Elizabeth B Johannesburg C Cape Town D Durban

4 In which town is Willowmoore Park, where Denis Compton once scored a triple-century in 181 minutes?

   A Pietermaritzburg B Benoni C Paarl D Durban

5 On which ground was the famous "Timeless Test" played out in 1938-39?

   A Port Elizabeth B Johannesburg C Cape Town D Durban

6 Where was the controversial 1999-2000 Test played in which Hansie Cronje forfeited South Africa's second innings, and lost?

   A Alexandra B Bloemfontein C Centurion D Durban

7 In which South African city is Buffalo Park?

   A Kimberley B Bloemfontein C East London D Paarl

8 Queen's Club now stages Test cricket in Bulawayo – but which other ground there has staged Tests too?

   A Bulawayo Oval B Bulawayo Athletic Club C Bulawayo Bullring D Rhodes Ground

9 Which ground in Kenya staged a match during the 2003 World Cup?

   A Aga Khan Ground B Simba Union Ground C Kenyatta Stadium D Nairobi Gymkhana

10 Which Australian spinner took a Test hat-trick at Cape Town in 1957-58?

   A Johnny Martin B Richie Benaud C Tom Veivers D Lindsay Kline

11 Where in South Africa is the North-West Stadium, which hosted its first Test in October 2002?

   A Kimberley B Bloemfontein C East London D Potchefstroom

The Googly

Who, in 1995-96, became the first Test centurion at Centurion Park in South Africa?

   A Andrew Hudson B Jonty Rhodes C Hansie Cronje D Graeme Hick

Answers on page 186

ONE-DAY INTERNATIONAL BOWLING RECORDS

1 Who was the first bowler to take 500 wickets in one-day internationals (ODIs)?

A Waqar Younis B Muttiah Muralitharan C Courtney Walsh D Wasim Akram

2 Who was the first bowler to take eight wickets in an ODI innings – 8 for 19 against Zimbabwe in 2001-02?

A Andy Bichel B Glenn McGrath C Chaminda Vaas D Nuwan Zoysa

3 Which West Indian took 6 for 22 on his ODI debut, against Zimbabwe in 2003-04?

A Fidel Edwards B Tino Best C Corey Collymore D Dwayne Bravo

4 Who took 7 for 37, the best ODI figures at the time and including a hat-trick, in an ODI in Sharjah in 1991-92?

A Aqib Javed B Kapil Dev C Javagal Srinath D Imran Khan

5 Who destroyed England with 6 for 23, the best ODI figures for India at the time, in the 2003 World Cup?

A Ashish Nehra B Javagal Srinath C Irfan Pathan D Zaheer Khan

6 Who was the first bowler to take seven wickets in a World Cup match, in 1983?

A Joel Garner B Richard Hadlee C Lance Cairns D Winston Davis

7 Who took 5 for 1 in an ODI in Sharjah in 1986-87?

A Craig McDermott B Bruce Reid C Courtney Walsh D Malcolm Marshall

8 Who took 141 wickets in 98 ODIs for West Indies, at a leading economy rate of only 3.09 runs per over?

A Joel Garner B Malcolm Marshall C Colin Croft D Michael Holding

9 Which Englishman took a wicket with his first ball in ODIs, in 2003?

A James Anderson B Gareth Batty C Rikki Clarke D Martin Saggers

10 And who had been the previous bowler to do this for England, at Old Trafford in 1972?

A Geoff Arnold B John Snow C Tony Greig D Derek Underwood

11 Who took 69 ODI wickets in 1997, beating his own record of 65 set the previous year?

A Shane Warne B Glenn McGrath C Wasim Akram D Saqlain Mushtaq

The Googly

Which Australian took the first wicket in an official one-day international in 1970-71 ... and never took another one?

A Alan "Froggy" Thomson B Ian Chappell C Graham McKenzie D Jeff Hammond

Answers on page 186

NOTTINGHAMSHIRE

1 Who hammered 254 not out for Nottinghamshire against Middlesex in 2002?

A Usman Afzaal B Kevin Pietersen C Chris Cairns D Darren Bicknell

2 Who did the 1000-run/100-wicket double for Nottinghamshire in 1988?

A Richard Hadlee B Franklyn Stephenson C Clive Rice D Eddie Hemmings

3 Which former captain of Young Australia took over as Nottinghamshire's skipper in 1998?

A Jason Gallian B Wayne Noon C Stuart MacGill D David Hussey

4 And which Australian Test player took 770 wickets for Nottinghamshire in the 1950s?

A George Tribe B Bruce Dooland C Jack Walsh D Vic Jackson

5 Who scored over 30,000 runs for Nottinghamshire, and played for England when he was 52?

A Joe Hardstaff B John Gunn C George Gunn D Arthur Shrewsbury

6 In which town have Notts played home matches at a ground called Central Avenue?

A Newark B Retford C Cleethorpes D Worksop

7 Which two Notts bowlers were the main purveyors of Bodyline bowling in 1932-33?

A Allen and Voce B Bowes and Voce C Larwood and Voce D Bowes and Larwood

8 Which Nottinghamshire player was Young Cricketer of the Year in 2000?

A Usman Afzaal B Paul Franks C Kevin Pietersen D Chris Read

9 Which Notts batsman scored 156 not out against Australia at Melbourne in 1950-51?

A Reg Simpson B Brian Bolus C Joe Hardstaff D Walter Keeton

10 Who equalled the county record with nine centuries for Nottinghamshire in 1990?

A Derek Randall B Chris Broad C Paul Johnson D Tim Robinson

11 Which famous cricketer played one match for Notts in 1959, scoring 102 not out and 62?

A Keith Miller B Richie Benaud C Frank Worrell D Don Bradman

The Googly

In 1939 Nottinghamshire's Walter Keeton scored 312 not out, a county record, in an away match against Middlesex. But why was that game played at The Oval?

A Lord's had been requisitioned for war recruitment B A plague of leatherjackets had rendered the Lord's square unplayable C Lord's was being used for the Eton v Harrow match D A London hotel strike meant the only accommodation was near The Oval

Answers on page 187

EDEN GARDENS, KOLKATA

1 In which year did Eden Gardens stage the World Cup final?

  A 1987 **B** *1992* **C** *1996* **D** *1999*

2 Who did India beat in a Test at Eden Gardens in 2000-01 after being forced to follow on?

  A Australia **B** *England* **C** *Pakistan* **D** *West Indies*

3 And who scored 281 for India in that match?

  A Sachin Tendulkar **B** *V.V.S. Laxman* **C** *Sourav Ganguly* **D** *Rahul Dravid*

4 And who took a hat-trick on his way to 13 wickets in that same game?

  A Anil Kumble **B** *Javagal Srinath* **C** *Harbhajan Singh* **D** *Zaheer Khan*

5 Who made his Test debut at Eden Gardens in 1996-97, and took 8 for 64, the best bowling figures there at the time?

  A Javagal Srinath **B** *Shaun Pollock* **C** *Lance Klusener* **D** *Venkatesh Prasad*

6 Who carried his bat for 188 not out in a Test at Kolkata in 1998-99?

  A Gary Kirsten **B** *Saeed Anwar* **C** *Matthew Hayden* **D** *Navjot Sidhu*

7 In which year did Eden Gardens stage its first Test match?

  A 1924 **B** *1934* **C** *1944* **D** *1954*

8 Whose 256 at Eden Gardens was the highest Test score there until 2001?

  A Polly Umrigar **B** *Rohan Kanhai* **C** *Nari Contractor* **D** *Garry Sobers*

9 Who were India's opponents in the 1996 World Cup semi-final at Eden Gardens, when an unruly crowd ended play prematurely?

  A Australia **B** *England* **C** *South Africa* **D** *Sri Lanka*

10 Whose 100 against New Zealand in 1955-56 was the only Test century by a Kolkata-born player at the ground in the 20th century?

  A Polly Umrigar **B** *Ram Ramchand* **C** *Pankaj Roy* **D** *Deepak Shodhan*

11 Whose 298 not out for Punjab against Bengal in 1988-89 broke the record for the highest individual first-class score at Eden Gardens?

  A Ajay Sharma **B** *Gursharan Singh* **C** *Vikram Rathour* **D** *Dhruv Pandove*

The Googly

Who scored the first Test century at Eden Gardens – and added the second in the second innings of the same game?

  A Lala Amarnath **B** *Bryan Valentine* **C** *Mushtaq Ali* **D** *Everton Weekes*

Answers on page 187

ENGLAND v NEW ZEALAND

1 In which year did England and New Zealand first play an official Test?
   A 1920 B 1930 C 1940 D 1950

2 And how many years did it take New Zealand to win a Test against England?
   A 12 B 24 C 36 D 48

3 Who scored 310 not out for England at Headingley in 1965?
   A Raman Subba Row B Ken Barrington C Colin Cowdrey D John Edrich

4 Who took a record 97 wickets in England-New Zealand Tests?
   A Andy Caddick B Ian Botham C Chris Cairns D Richard Hadlee

5 Which New Zealander was the leading runscorer on either side in the 2004 series in England, even though his team lost all three Tests?
   A Stephen Fleming B Mark Richardson C Chris Cairns D Brendon McCullum

6 Who reached his double-century in only 153 balls at Christchurch in 2001-02?
   A Nathan Astle B Marcus Trescothick C Craig McMillan D Andrew Flintoff

7 Who was stranded on 99 not out when England won the 1999 Edgbaston Test against New Zealand?
   A Aftab Habib B Alex Tudor C Mark Ramprakash D Graham Thorpe

8 Who scored a century in each innings for New Zealand at Auckland in 1977-78?
   A Glenn Turner B Mark Burgess C Jeremy Coney D Geoff Howarth

9 Who took a hat-trick – and four wickets in five balls – in his first Test, at Christchurch in 1929-30?
   A Maurice Allom B Tich Freeman C Tom Goddard D David Freeman

10 Who became England's youngest Test player, at 18 years 149 days, against New Zealand at Old Trafford in 1949?
   A Peter May B Brian Close C Colin Cowdrey D Denis Compton

11 Who took 34 wickets at only 7.47 apiece in the 1958 series against New Zealand?
   A Alec Bedser B Jim Laker C Tony Lock D Fred Trueman

The Googly
What happened to Richard Hadlee before the 1990 Lord's Test against England?

*A He was knighted B He was rushed to hospital with heart palpitations
C His taxi-driver took him to The Oval by mistake D His team-mates elected him captain to mark his last Test*

Answers on page 187

CRICKETER-FOOTBALLERS

1 Who scored a hat-trick in the 1966 World Cup final, but didn't score at all in his only first-class cricket match?

A Bobby Moore **B** *Bobby Charlton* **C** *Geoff Hurst* **D** *Martin Peters*

2 Which famous cricketer's last big football match was the 1950 FA Cup final, which his side Arsenal won 2-0?

A Walter Hammond **B** *Bill Edrich* **C** *Donald Carr* **D** *Denis Compton*

3 Which famous cricketer played in a World Cup qualifier for his native Antigua?

A Curtly Ambrose **B** *Eldine Baptiste* **C** *Viv Richards* **D** *Richie Richardson*

4 Who played for MCC against Germany at Lord's in 1992, was out for a single, and said "I always score one against the Germans"?

A Mark Viduka **B** *Gary Lineker* **C** *Geoff Hurst* **D** *Ian Wright*

5 Which international goalkeeper was disciplined by his football club Rangers after playing cricket for Scotland?

A Andy Goram **B** *Jim Leighton* **C** *Alan Rough* **D** *Stuart Kennedy*

6 Who was on the books of both Leicestershire and Leicester City in the 1970s?

A Ted Hemsley **B** *Chris Balderstone* **C** *Graham Cross* **D** *Keith Weller*

7 Which famous umpire also refereed a World Cup soccer qualifying match?

A Steve Bucknor **B** *Dickie Bird* **C** *Charlie Elliott* **D** *Darrell Hair*

8 Which England batsman of the '50s was a member of the 1950 soccer World Cup squad, although he didn't actually play?

A Arthur Milton **B** *Mike Smith* **C** *Hubert Doggart* **D** *Willie Watson*

9 Who was the only 2004 county cricketer who had played league football in England?

A Adam Hollioake **B** *Graeme Swann* **C** *Tony Cottey* **D** *Darren Thomas*

10 Who is the only person to captain England at both cricket and football?

A W.G. Grace **B** *Ian Botham* **C** *"Tip" Foster* **D** *Stanley Jackson*

11 Which member of England's Euro 2004 football squad had set run-scoring records for his Lancashire age-group teams before moving to the other Old Trafford?

A Ryan Giggs **B** *Phil Neville* **C** *Paul Scholes* **D** *Gary Neville*

The Googly

Walter Robins, who captained England in three of his 19 Tests, also played two Football League matches for Nottingham Forest. What was unusual about both of those games?

A They were both against Manchester United **B** *They were both played on Christmas Day* *C They were the first home games of two successive seasons* **D** *He played cricket at Trent Bridge both days before crossing the road to Forest's ground*

Answers on page 187

ENGLAND v INDIA

1 Who scored 333 and 123 against India at Lord's in 1990?

A Allan Lamb **B** *Robin Smith* **C** *Graham Gooch* **D** *David Gower*

2 Who scored a century and took 13 wickets in the Golden Jubilee Test at Bombay in 1979-80?

A Kapil Dev **B** *Ian Botham* **C** *Manoj Prabhakar* **D** *John Emburey*

3 Who scored 115, 148 and 217 in successive Test innings in England in 2002?

A Sachin Tendulkar **B** *Sourav Ganguly* **C** *V.V.S. Laxman* **D** *Rahul Dravid*

4 Who took 8 for 31 against India in only his third Test, at Old Trafford in 1952?

A Fred Trueman **B** *Brian Statham* **C** *Johnny Wardle* **D** *Frank Tyson*

5 Who scored 131 on his Test debut for India at Lord's in 1996?

A Sachin Tendulkar **B** *Sourav Ganguly* **C** *Vikram Rathour* **D** *Rahul Dravid*

6 Who took 7 for 46 (and ten wickets in the match) on his Test debut at Delhi in 1976-77?

A John Lever **B** *Peter Lever* **C** *Geoff Cope* **D** *Mike Selvey*

7 Who scored 214 not out, his only Test century, against India at Edgbaston in 1974?

A Barry Wood **B** *Brian Luckhurst* **C** *Phil Sharpe* **D** *David Lloyd*

8 In which year did England and India play their first official Test?

A 1901 **B** *1922* **C** *1932* **D** *1937*

9 And which Indian-born player captained England in that first match?

A Bob Wyatt **B** *Freddie Brown* **C** *Colin Cowdrey* **D** *Douglas Jardine*

10 Which player, making his Test debut, took five catches in an innings (and seven in the match) against England at Bangalore in 1976-77?

A Eknath Solkar **B** *Brijesh Patel* **C** *Yajurvindra Singh* **D** *Yashpal Sharma*

11 Which accurate Indian spinner bowled 32 overs for five runs – with 27 maidens – against England at Madras in 1963-64?

A Bapu Nadkarni **B** *Bishan Bedi* **C** *Jasu Patel* **D** *Salim Durani*

The Googly

In the 1990 Lord's Test Kapil Dev smote four successive sixes into the building works then occupying the Nursery End to save the follow-on for India. Who was the frustrated bowler?

A Phil Tufnell **B** *John Emburey* **C** *Eddie Hemmings* **D** *Vic Marks*

Answers on page 187

THE MELBOURNE CRICKET GROUND

1 Who played the first of his 168 Tests for Australia at Melbourne in 1985-86?

A Allan Border B David Boon C Steve Waugh D Ian Healy

2 Who smashed 195, with 25 fours and five sixes, in the Test on Boxing Day 2003?

A Matthew Hayden B Virender Sehwag C Sachin Tendulkar D Darren Lehmann

3 Who enlivened the Melbourne Centenary Test by scoring 174 for England?

A Tony Greig B Bob Woolmer C Dennis Amiss D Derek Randall

4 Who took two Test hat-tricks at the MCG, and later became secretary of the Melbourne Cricket Club?

A Fred Spofforth B Bill O'Reilly C Monty Noble D Hugh Trumble

5 In which year did the MCG stage the first Test match of them all?

A 1877 B 1880 C 1882 D 1886

6 Which Melbourne-born man hit 268 against Pakistan at the MCG in 1983-84?

A Graham Yallop B Wayne Phillips C Dav Whatmore D Dean Jones

7 What major event was centred on the MCG in 1956?

A Football World Cup B Australia's Declaration of Independence C Olympic Games D Empire Games

8 Which other venue in Melbourne has staged official one-day internationals?

A Kooyong B Junction Oval C Colonial Stadium D Melbourne Park

9 Whose 307 in 1965-66 was the first triple-century in a Test at the MCG?

A Bill Lawry B Bob Simpson C Bob Cowper D Ken Barrington

10 In which year was the World Cup final played at the MCG?

A 1975 B 1987 C 1992 D 1996

11 Which man, born in Melbourne, scored 109 on his Test debut at the MCG in 1975-76?

A Julien Wiener B Trevor Laughlin C Gary Cosier D Ian Redpath

The Googly

Which event attracted the highest single-day crowd attendance at the MCG?

A The Australian Rules grand final of 1934 B A Billy Graham crusade C A Madonna concert D The 1956 Olympic Games closing ceremony

Answers on page 187

THE ICC TROPHY

1 Who were the first winners of the ICC Trophy (the World Cup qualifying competition for non-Test nations) in 1979?

A Kenya B Sri Lanka C Canada D Zimbabwe

2 Who took 10 wickets for Denmark in that 1979 tournament, and later had a successful county career with Derbyshire?

A Adrian van Troost B Paul-Jan Bakker C Ole Mortensen D Soren Henriksen

3 Who qualified for the 1983 World Cup by winning the ICC Trophy in 1982?

A Kenya B Sri Lanka C Canada D Zimbabwe

4 Who played for Hong Kong in that 1982 tournament, and later played for England in the World Cup final?

A Adam Hollioake B Graeme Hick C Robin Smith D Dermot Reeve

5 The 1986 ICC Trophy final was played at Lord's for the first time. Who won it?

A Kenya B Bangladesh C Canada D Zimbabwe

6 Which former West Indies allrounder captained the United States in that 1986 tournament?

A Sew Shivnarine B Faoud Bacchus C Peter Lashley D David Holford

7 Where was the 1990 ICC Trophy, the first one held outside England, played?

A Holland B Bangladesh C Canada D Denmark

8 Which former Barbados player scored 523 runs for Holland in that tournament, including 154 against Israel?

A Emmerson Trotman B Robin Bynoe C Nolan Clarke D Flavian Aponso

9 Who beat the hosts Kenya to win the 1994 ICC Trophy final?

A Holland B Bangladesh C United States D United Arab Emirates

10 Who hit 147 for Kenya in the final of the 1997 ICC Trophy, which they lost to Bangladesh?

A Maurice Odumbe B Steve Tikolo C Ravindu Shah D Hitesh Modi

11 Who won the ICC Trophy for the first time in Canada in 2001?

A Namibia B Bangladesh C Canada D Holland

The Googly

Scotland qualified for the 1999 World Cup by beating which team in the third-place playoff at the 1997 ICC Trophy in Kuala Lumpur?

A Malaysia B Bangladesh C Canada D Ireland

Answers on page 187

AUTOBIOGRAPHIES

1 Which former umpire's autobiography, published in 1997, was a huge best-seller?

A Bill Alley *B Dickie Bird* *C Frank Chester* *D David Shepherd*

2 Whose best-selling 1994 book was subtitled "Don't Tell Kath"?

A Shane Warne *B Ian Botham* *C Graham Gooch* *D Allan Lamb*

3 And whose 1997 book was subtitled "Barking"?

A Robin Smith *B Brad Hogg* *C Jack Russell* *D Simon Hughes*

4 Whose 1999 book was called *White Lightning*?

A Michael Holding *B Darren Gough* *C Brett Lee* *D Allan Donald*

5 Which Australian called his 1993 autobiography *Beyond Ten Thousand*?

A Allan Border *B David Boon* *C Steve Waugh* *D Dean Jones*

6 Which England captain's was called *I Don't Bruise Easily*?

A Mike Atherton *B Brian Close* *C Colin Cowdrey* *D Ted Dexter*

7 Whose 1974 book *Back to the Mark* caused controversy after he wrote that "I try to hit the batsman in the ribcage ... and I want it to hurt so much that [he] doesn't want to face me any more"?

A Jeff Thomson *B Bob Willis* *C Andy Roberts* *D Dennis Lillee*

8 Which controversial bowler's 1961 story was called *Thrown Out*, even though he hadn't been ... yet?

A Geoff Griffin *B Harold Rhodes* *C Charlie Griffith* *D Ian Meckiff*

9 Whose 1976 autobiography was called *Cricket Rebel*, and included some of his own poems?

A Tony Greig *B Bob Woolmer* *C Ian Chappell* *D John Snow*

10 Steve Marsh called his 2001 autobiography *The Gloves Are Off*. But which earlier Kent wicket-keeper had used the same title for his life story?

A Alan Knott *B Les Ames* *C Godfrey Evans* *D Hopper Levett*

11 Who was stripped of his honorary MCC membership after critical remarks in his 1960 book *Over To Me*?

A Fred Trueman *B Tony Lock* *C Tom Graveney* *D Jim Laker*

The Googly

Which commentator's 1972 autobiography *Sort of a Cricket Person* was erroneously but amusingly titled in one overseas newspaper review as "Sort of a Cricket Peron"?

A Brian Johnston *B Henry Blofeld* *C Jim Swanton* *D Richie Benaud*

Answers on page 187

ZIMBABWE IN TESTS

1 Zimbabwe have staged Tests in Harare and which other town?

A Victoria Falls **B** *Bulawayo* **C** *Mutare* **D** *Kwekwe*

2 In which year did Zimbabwe play their first official Test?

A 1982 **B** *1987* **C** *1992* **D** *1994*

3 Who scored a debut century in Zimbabwe's first Test?

A Kevin Arnott **B** *Andy Flower* **C** *Grant Flower* **D** *Dave Houghton*

4 Who made his Test debut for Zimbabwe in 1998-99, a few hours after receiving his passport, and dismissed Sachin Tendulkar?

A Henry Olonga **B** *Neil Johnson* **C** *Murray Goodwin* **D** *Dirk Viljoen*

5 Who drove through the night to make it to the ground on time after being a late call-up for Zimbabwe's inaugural Test, after an injury to another player?

A Ali Shah **B** *Gary Crocker* **C** *Mark Burmester* **D** *Kevin Arnott*

6 Which 45-year-old bowled 50 overs and took 5 for 86 in Zimbabwe's first official Test?

A Mike Procter **B** *John Traicos* **C** *Richie Kaschula* **D** *Dennis Streak*

7 Who scored 142 and 199 not out in the same Test, against South Africa in 2001-02?

A Andy Flower **B** *Mark Vermeulen* **C** *Stuart Carlisle* **D** *Grant Flower*

8 Who scored 119 on his Test debut for Zimbabwe against West Indies in July 2001, a month before his 18th birthday?

A Tatenda Taibu **B** *Trevor Madondo* **C** *Hamilton Masakadza* **D** *Dion Ebrahim*

9 Who scored 148 not out against England at Trent Bridge in 2000, in what turned out to be his last Test for Zimbabwe?

A Andy Flower **B** *Alistair Campbell* **C** *Neil Johnson* **D** *Murray Goodwin*

10 Who was the first Zimbabwean to take eight wickets in a Test innings, with 8 for 109 against New Zealand at Bulawayo in 2000-01?

A Adam Huckle **B** *Bryan Strang* **C** *Heath Streak* **D** *Paul Strang*

11 And which spinner was the first bowler to take 10 wickets in a Test for Zimbabwe?

A Paul Strang **B** *Brian Murphy* **C** *Adam Huckle* **D** *Andy Whittall*

The Googly

Zimbabwe's team against New Zealand at Harare in 1997-98 included three sets of brothers, a Test first. Which of the following duos did *not* play in that match?

A Andy and Grant Flower **B** *Bryan and Paul Strang* **C** *Andy and Guy Whittall*
D *Gavin and John Rennie*

Answers on page 187

WORLD SERIES CRICKET

1 In which year did Kerry Packer sign up 50 of the world's best cricketers?

A 1970 B 1974 C 1977 D 1981

2 Who was captain of his Australian XI?

A Bill Lawry B Richie Benaud C Greg Chappell D Ian Chappell

3 And who was the skipper of his World XI?

A Asif Iqbal B Eddie Barlow C Tony Greig D Viv Richards

4 What did Packer call his international matches?

A Super Tests B Real Tests C Champion Tests D Ultimate Tests

5 On which TV channel did Packer screen the games?

A ABC B Sky TV C Channel Nine D Star TV

6 Which respected commentator raised eyebrows by leading the coverage for the matches, which were disapproved of by the cricket authorities?

A John Arlott B Richie Benaud C Brian Johnston D Tony Cozier

7 Which young Australian batsman had his jaw broken in an early World Series Cricket match?

A Ian Davis B Peter Toohey C Gary Gilmour D David Hookes

8 Which Australian opening batsman came out of retirement to play for Packer?

A Bill Lawry B Ian Redpath C Alan Turner D Rick McCosker

9 Graeme Pollock and which other South African were prevented from joining World Series Cricket because they had never played county cricket?

A Vintcent van der Bijl B Barry Richards C Jimmy Cook D Denys Hobson

10 Which player pulled out of his Packer contract, and captained West Indies while his former team-mates were banned from traditional cricket?

A Alvin Kallicharran B Faoud Bacchus C Gus Logie D Deryck Murray

11 Which bowler took 79 wickets in Packer's "Tests", and 355 in official ones?

A Andy Roberts B Jeff Thomson C Imran Khan D Dennis Lillee

The Googly

Why were the West Indians uncomfortable about the coloured outfits they had to wear for Packer's floodlit games?

A They attracted moths and bugs B They were bright pink
C They were very shiny and reflected the lights D They were nylon and made them itch

Answers on page 188

MIXED BAG 3

1 Which county won the inaugural Twenty20 Cup in England in 2003?
A Surrey B Sussex C Warwickshire D Worcestershire

2 And which county beat the defending champions to win the Twenty20 Cup final in 2004?
A Kent B Lancashire C Leicestershire D Warwickshire

3 Which allrounder, who won ten England one-day caps, became Gloucestershire's player/coach in 2004?
A Mark Alleyne B Kim Barnett C Craig Spearman D Dougie Brown

4 Who was 12th man for Australia in a Test in 1989-90, but didn't actually make his debut until 1997-98?
A Martin Love B Andy Bichel C Damien Fleming D Darren Lehmann

5 Which itinerant county bowler, then with Northamptonshire, batted for 12 successive innings in 1990 without scoring a single run?
A Jim Griffiths B Mike Selvey C Mark Robinson D Richard Davis

6 Which New Zealander hit 68 not out, to break the record score by a No. 11 in Tests, against Pakistan at Auckland in 1972-73?
A David O'Sullivan B Richard Collinge C Bob Cunis D Hedley Howarth

7 Which Australian batsman scored more than 1000 first-class runs on the 1993 tour of England, but couldn't force his way into the Test team?
A Justin Langer B Dean Jones C Matthew Hayden D Damien Martyn

8 And who had the same experience in 1950 – more than 1000 runs for the West Indian tourists, but no Test appearances on that trip?
A Ken Trestrail B Ken Rickards C Roy Marshall D Andy Ganteaume

9 Which man, who captained Australia twice in 1965-66, played hockey for them at the 1956 Olympics?
A Bob Cowper B Brian Booth C Peter Burge D Norman O'Neill

10 Which American topped the English first-class bowling averages in 1908, with 81 wickets at 11.01?
A John Thayer B Bart King C George Kirsch D Richard Newhall

11 Which Englishman played a record 30 Tests after his 40th birthday?
A Jack Hobbs B Bob Taylor C Patsy Hendren D Tom Graveney

The Googly

What did Chandu Sarwate and Shute Banerjee achieve for the Indian tourists against Surrey at The Oval in 1946, which had never been done in first-class cricket before (and wasn't repeated in the 20th century)?
A They each took all ten wickets in an innings B Batting at No. 10 and 11, they both scored centuries C They both took hat-tricks in the same innings D While batting together they ran an all-run nine, including some overthrows

Answers on page 188

WOMEN'S CRICKET

1 Which former England captain was the first woman elected to MCC's committee, in 2004?

A Mollie Hide B Janette Brittin C Carole Hodges D Rachael Heyhoe-Flint

2 Which Australian captain scored the first double-century in any one-day international, at the 1997-98 Women's World Cup?

A Lyn Larsen B Belinda Clark C Belinda Haggett D Lindsay Reeler

3 Who captained England to World Cup victory in 1993?

A Carole Hodges B Karen Smithies C Clare Taylor D Jo Chamberlain

4 Which New Zealander scored the first double-century in a women's Test, in 1996?

A Rebecca Rolls B Kirsty Flavell C Debbie Hockley D Emily Drumm

5 Which daughter of a famous playwright scored 102 in a Test for England v India in 1986?

A Avril Starling B Jackie Court C Sarah Potter D Amanda Stinson

6 Who broke the record for the highest Test score by a woman with 242 for Pakistan against West Indies in March 2004?

A Sajjida Shah B Kiran Baluch C Jemima Khan D Shaiza Khan

7 Which New Zealander became the first woman to play in 100 one-day internationals, in 1999?

A Emily Drumm B Sarah Illingworth C Maia Lewis D Debbie Hockley

8 What was the name of Terry Alderman's sister, who also played Tests for Australia?

A Annette Alderman B Belinda Alderman C Christina Alderman D Denise Alderman

9 Which Test cricketer's wife played her only one-day international in the 1977-78 World Cup?

A Donna Greig, wife of Tony B Jane Border, wife of Allan C Lindsay Lamb, wife of Allan D Karen Hadlee, wife of Richard

10 Which woman scored a hundred and took ten wickets in a Test in 1957-58, 22 years before a man managed this feat?

A Rachael Heyhoe-Flint B Enid Bakewell C Miriam Knee D Betty Wilson

11 Which Australian woman player dismissed Brian Lara in a charity match in 1994, and later posed nude (apart from some strategically placed cricket balls) for a magazine?

A Lisa Keightley B Joanne Broadbent C Catherine Fitzpatrick D Zoe Goss

The Googly

What did Denise Annetts – a one-time holder of the women's Test record with an innings of 193 in 1987 – believe was the reason for her exclusion from the Australian side in 1994?

A She was a lesbian B She wasn't a lesbian C She had posed naked for a magazine D She had rebuffed the advances of the (male) coach

Answers on page 188

BANGLADESH IN TESTS

1 Which was the second city in Bangladesh, after Dhaka, to stage a Test match?

   A Mymensingh B Sylhet C Chittagong D Rajshahi

2 In which year did Bangladesh play their first official Test?

   A 1992 B 1997 C 2000 D 2002

3 Who scored a century for Bangladesh in that debut Test?

   A Aminul Islam B Habibul Bashar C Shahriar Hossain D Mehrab Hossain

4 And who captained Bangladesh in that first Test?

   A Akram Khan B Khaled Mahmud C Khaled Mashud D Naimur Rahman

5 Who took a hat-trick for Bangladesh against Pakistan at Peshawar in 2003?

   A Alok Kapali B Mashrafe Mortaza C Enamul Haque D Mohammad Rafique

6 Who, shortly before his 17th birthday, scored 114 on his Test debut for Bangladesh in Colombo in September 2001?

   A Mohammad Sharif B Mohammad Ashraful C Hannan Sarkar D Alok Kapali

7 Who was the first to score 2000 runs in Tests for Bangladesh – before anyone else had reached 1000?

   A Akram Khan B Habibul Bashar C Javed Omar D Al-Shahriar Rokon

8 Who made a century, batting No. 9, against West Indies in St Lucia in May 2004?

   A Khaled Mahmud B Mohammad Rafique C Mushfiqur Rahman D Tapash Baisya

9 Which foreign coach took over for Bangladesh's tour of Australia in 2003?

   A John Dyson B Bob Woolmer C Trevor Chappell D Dav Whatmore

10 Who took 6 for 3 for West Indies against Bangladesh at Dhaka in 2002-03?

   A Jermaine Lawson B Tino Best C Corey Collymore D Fidel Edwards

11 Who carried his bat against Zimbabwe on his Test debut at Bulawayo in 2000-01?

   A Al-Shahriar Rokon B Mehrab Hossain C Javed Omar D Hannan Sarkar

The Googly

In the days before Bangladesh's independence Pakistan staged Tests in Dhaka (then known as Dacca). Play in Pakistan's penultimate home Test there, in 1968-69, was abandoned after the crowd invaded the pitch, leaving which England batsman stranded on 96, four short of what would have been his first Test century?

A Dennis Amiss B Alan Knott C Colin Milburn D David Lloyd

Answers on page 188

THE OVAL

1 Which county plays its home matches at The Oval?

A Essex B Middlesex C Surrey D Sussex

2 What's the end opposite the pavilion at The Oval called?

A Archbishop Tenison's End B Gasholder End C Vauxhall End D Nursery End

3 Whose 366 for Lancashire in 1990 broke the record for the highest first-class score at The Oval?

A Mike Atherton B Gehan Mendis C Graeme Fowler D Neil Fairbrother

4 Who held the previous record of 364, which remained the best Test score at The Oval?

A Viv Richards B Len Hutton C Don Bradman D Garry Sobers

5 Who owns The Oval?

A Foster's B The Prince of Wales C Surrey CCC D The Queen

6 In which year did The Oval stage the first Test ever played in England?

A 1864 B 1877 C 1880 D 1886

7 Which early Surrey favourite, known as "The Guv'nor", carried his bat for 357 out of 811 against Somerset at The Oval in 1899?

A Bobby Abel B Billy Brockwell C Tom Hayward D Walter Read

8 Who, in 1973, was the first Englishman to make a century on Test debut at The Oval?

A John Hampshire B Phil Sharpe C Frank Hayes D Tony Greig

9 Which former Surrey batsman scored 300 against Surrey at The Oval in 1958?

A Bill Edrich B Freddie Brown C Bernie Constable D Raman Subba Row

10 What was The Oval used as during the Second World War?

A A launching-ground for barrage balloons B Water reservoir for London
C Prisoner-of-war camp D Venue for morale-boosting sporting events

11 Which Surrey player won what turned out to be his only Test cap at The Oval in 1979?

A Alan Butcher B Graham Roope C Ian Greig D Robin Jackman

The Googly

Which sporting event was staged for the first time at The Oval in 1872?

A The FA Cup final B The first international rugby match
C The first All-England lawn tennis tournament (it found a permanent home at Wimbledon in 1877) D The Olympic track and field events

Answers on page 188

ENGLAND v PAKISTAN

1 In which year did England first play Pakistan in an official Test?

   A 1936 B 1947 C 1952 D 1954

2 Who captained Pakistan to victory in England in 1987?

   A Javed Miandad B Wasim Akram C Imran Khan D Salim Malik

3 Which bowler took 9 for 56 at Lahore in 1987-88?

   A Abdul Qadir B Ian Botham C Imran Khan D Devon Malcolm

4 In which city did these two teams meet in a World Cup final?

   A London (Lord's) B Melbourne C Calcutta D Lahore

5 Who made a century in each of the three Tests in the 1967 series in England?

   A Geoff Boycott B Basil D'Oliveira C Ken Barrington D John Edrich

6 Who scored 260 as Pakistan passed 700 at The Oval in 1987?

   A Ijaz Ahmed B Imran Khan C Mudassar Nazar D Javed Miandad

7 Who made his highest Test score of 205 against Pakistan at Lahore in 1961-62?

   A Peter Parfitt B Tom Graveney C Mike Smith D Ted Dexter

8 And who made his highest Test score of 205 against England at Old Trafford in 1992?

   A Aamir Sohail B Basit Ali C Salim Malik D Rameez Raja

9 Who carried his bat for England at Lord's in 1992?

   A Alec Stewart B Mike Atherton C Graham Gooch D Bill Athey

10 Which Pakistani came in as a nightwatchman at Lord's in 1962, and scored a century?

   A Intikhab Alam B Nasim-ul-Ghani C Javed Burki D Shuja-ud-Din

11 Who was the first Englishman to score 1000 runs in Tests against Pakistan?

   A David Gower B Geoff Boycott C Tom Graveney D Graham Gooch

The Googly

What fate befell Dennis Amiss, Majid Khan and Mushtaq Mohammad during the 1972-73 Pakistan-England Test at Karachi?

*A They all bagged pairs B They were all absent ill after eating dodgy prawns
C They were all dismissed for 99 D They were all given out lbw by Shakoor Rana*

Answers on page 188

WEST INDIAN DOMESTIC CRICKET

1 What was the trophy for the inter-island championship from 1965-66 to 1987-88?

A Shell Shield B Worrell Trophy C The Punchbowl D The Trinidad Trophy

2 Which island won the first two inter-island championships, and then challenged the Rest of the World to a game?

A Antigua B Barbados C Jamaica D Trinidad

3 Which team won the regional competition for the first time in 1989-90, by which time it was known as the Red Stripe Cup?

A Guyana B West Indies "B" C Leeward Islands D Windward Islands

4 Which man shared in two partnerships of more than 500 for Barbados in the 1940s?

A Everton Weekes B John Goddard C Clyde Walcott D Frank Worrell

5 On which Caribbean island would you be if you were watching a game at the Beausejour Stadium in Gros Islet?

A Anguilla B St Lucia C Grenada D Dominica

6 And where would you be if you were at Queen's Park in St George's?

A Antigua B Barbuda C Grenada D St Vincent

7 Whose 344 not out for Jamaica against a touring English team in 1931-32 remains the highest first-class score in the West Indies outside a Test match?

A Learie Constantine B Clifford Roach C Clarence Passailaigue D George Headley

8 Which future Test captain broke the record for inter-island cricket with 324 for Trinidad v British Guiana in 1946-47?

A Gerry Gomez B Jeff Stollmeyer C Frank Worrell D John Goddard

9 Omari Banks was the first Test cricketer from which Caribbean island?

A Anguilla B Montserrat C St Kitts D Nevis

10 And Darren Sammy, who made his one-day debut in 2004, was the first international cricketer from which island?

A Grenada B Guadeloupe C St Lucia D St Vincent

11 Which side won all their seven matches in the 2003-04 Carib Beer Series, and then won the final too?

A Leeward Islands B Barbados C Guyana D Kenya

The Googly

Which Englishman took all ten wickets in an innings for an International XI against a West Indian XI at Kingston in 1982-83 – they cost him 175 runs, the most expensive ten-wicket haul in first-class history?

A John Emburey B Norman Gifford C Eddie Hemmings D Phil Edmonds

Answers on page 188

SPONSORS

1 Who took over as the title sponsors of English Test matches in 2001?

    A Vodafone B NatWest C npower D Lucozade

2 Who took over as title sponsors of the County Championship in 2002?

    A Frizzell Insurance B BT Cellnet C Fosters Lager D Direct Line Insurance

3 Which product did Denis Compton famously endorse in the 1950s?

    A Colgate toothpaste B Brylcreem C Compo rations D Hovis

4 Who were the first sponsors of the County Championship, in 1977?

    A Embassy B John Player C Rowntrees D Schweppes

5 Which company sponsored Test matches in England from 1978 to 2000?

    A Coopers & Lybrand B Tetley Bitter C Cornhill Insurance D Cable & Wireless

6 Which company sponsored the County Championship from 1984 to 1998?

    A Abbey National B Britannic Assurance C Canon D Barclays Bank

7 Who replaced John Player as sponsors of the Sunday League in 1987?

    A AXA Equity & Law B Holsten C Norwich Union D Refuge Assurance

8 Which website sponsored the County Championship in 2001?

    A Lastminute.com B Amazon C Cricinfo D Google

9 One of the oldest cricket sponsorships provides an award for the fastest century of the English summer. What is the trophy called?

    *A The Rapid Cup B The Milburn Medal C The Walter Lawrence Trophy
D The Venus Rosewater Dish*

10 Which Indian company sponsored the World Cup in 1987?

    A Hero Honda B Wills C Reliance D Tata

11 And which Australian company sponsored the World Cup in 1992?

    A Ansett B Benson & Hedges C Channel 9 D Qantas

The Googly

Which company ended a long-standing cricket sponsorship in 1980, after market research showed that their name was more associated with cricket than with their core product?

A National Power B Benson & Hedges C Cornhill D Gillette

Answers on page 188

THE SYDNEY CRICKET GROUND

1 Which state plays its home matches at the SCG?

A New South Wales B Queensland C South Australia D Victoria

2 Who scored 277, his first Test century, at Sydney in 1992-93, and later named his first child after the city?

A Steve Waugh B Brian Lara C Sachin Tendulkar D Gary Kirsten

3 Don Bradman and which of his team-mates made 234 against England at Sydney in 1946-47?

A Arthur Morris B Sid Barnes C Keith Miller D Lindsay Hassett

4 Who surprised even himself by taking 7 for 46 (and 4 for 50) in the Australia-West Indies Test at the SCG in 1988-89?

A Steve Waugh B Allan Border C Greg Chappell D Viv Richards

5 In which year did the SCG stage its first Test match?

A 1877 B 1879 C 1882 D 1894

6 Who took 12 wickets in the 1993-94 Sydney Test, but finished up on the losing side?

A Shane Warne B Glenn McGrath C Allan Donald D Fanie de Villiers

7 Whose 287, on his debut in 1903-04, was still the highest individual Test score at the SCG 100 years later?

A Victor Trumper B Warwick Armstrong C "Tip" Foster D Archie MacLaren

8 Which side won a controversial World Cup semi-final at the SCG in 1991-92?

A Australia B England C Pakistan D South Africa

9 Who scored a century in each innings of his first-class debut, at the SCG in 1940-41?

A Arthur Morris B Keith Miller C Jack Moroney D Jim Burke

10 Which West Indies wicket-keeper made the only first-class century of his career in the 1960-61 Sydney Test?

A Gerry Alexander B Deryck Murray C Jackie Hendriks D David Allan

11 How was Stephen Gascoigne, the legendary big-mouthed barracker of the Sydney Hill, better known?

A Blabba B Gabba C Jabba D Yabba

The Googly

Why was it particularly appropriate that Australia's Syd Gregory should score the first Test double-century at the SCG – 201 in 1894-95?

A He was born on the ground B He had attended every match there since he was 11 C His initials were SCG D His father designed the pavilion

Answers on page 189

ENGLAND v SRI LANKA

1   In which year did these countries first meet in an official Test match?
    A 1978 B 1982 C 1986 D 1991

2   Who captained England in that first Test?
    A Mike Brearley B Bob Willis C Chris Cowdrey D Keith Fletcher

3   And who captained Sri Lanka?
    A Anura Tennekoon B Bandula Warnapura C Arjuna Ranatunga D Duleep Mendis

4   Who took 16 wickets as Sri Lanka won at The Oval in 1998?
    A Muttiah Muralitharan B Suresh Perera C Chaminda Vaas D Kumar Dharmasena

5   And who scored the first double-century in these Tests in the same match?
    A Aravinda de Silva B Graeme Hick C John Crawley D Sanath Jayasuriya

6   Who was England's captain when Sri Lanka beat them for the first time, in Colombo in 1992-93?
    A Mike Atherton B Alec Stewart C Graham Gooch D Mike Gatting

7   Who made his Test debut for England against Sri Lanka at Lord's in 1988, and scored 94?
    A Robert Bailey B Kim Barnett C Jack Russell D Robin Smith

8   Whose 190 in 636 minutes against England in 1984 was the longest innings ever played at Lord's at the time?
    A Aravinda de Silva B Sidath Wettimuny C Ranjan Madugalle D Duleep Mendis

9   Who was England's captain when they came from behind to win the 2000-01 series in Sri Lanka 2-1?
    A Mike Atherton B Alec Stewart C Nasser Hussain D Michael Vaughan

10 Who scored 201 not out against England at Galle in 2000-01?
    A Marvan Atapattu B Mahela Jayawardene C Tillakaratne Dilshan
    D Hashan Tillakaratne

11 And whose 122 in that match was his first Test century for England?
    A Andrew Flintoff B Mark Butcher C Marcus Trescothick D Michael Vaughan

The Googly

What delayed the after-match presentation ceremony following England's victory over Sri Lanka at Lord's in 1988?

A The match ended suddenly and the presentation party was still eating lunch
B The wrong name was engraved on the Man of the Match medallion
C The BBC insisted on waiting until the daily screening of Neighbours was over
D Sri Lanka's manager locked his team in the dressing-room for a dressing-down

Answers on page 189

MIXED BAG 4

1 Which team won a Test match inside two days in 2000?

  A Australia B England C India D South Africa

2 Who made the fastest authentic hundred in first-class cricket, in 35 minutes in 1920?

  A Ted Alletson B Percy Fender C Lionel Tennyson D Jim Smith

3 Who, in the course of setting another record, scored 390 runs in a single day's play in 1994?

  A Graeme Hick B Brian Lara C Sachin Tendulkar D Matthew Hayden

4 Who scored two hundreds in a first-class match on a record eight occasions?

  A Walter Hammond B Don Bradman C Sunil Gavaskar D Zaheer Abbas

5 Who took 6 for 58 on his Test debut in 1987-88, and 5 for 21 in his first one-day international the following week?

  A Curtly Ambrose B Waqar Younis C Chetan Sharma D Tony Dodemaide

6 Who scored three Test centuries for Pakistan in the 1980s, two of them over 200?

  A Asif Mujtaba B Qasim Omar C Mansoor Akhtar D Taslim Arif

7 Who, in 1979-80, was the first man to score 150 in both innings of a Test?

  A Aravinda de Silva B Allan Border C Sunil Gavaskar D Duleep Mendis

8 Amir Khan, Britain's boxing silver-medallist at the 2004 Athens Olympics, is the cousin of which England cricketer?

  A Usman Afzaal B Sajid Mahmood C Vikram Solanki D Owais Shah

9 Who took a wicket in each of his first three overs for England, in a one-day international against India in September 2004?

  A Alex Wharf B James Anderson C Martin Saggers D Gareth Batty

10 Who, during 2004, became the first player under 21 to captain a side in a Test match?

  A Graeme Smith B Alok Kapali C Tatenda Taibu D Ramnaresh Sarwan

11 Who was caught by the wicket-keeper in all eight of his innings in the 1956 Ashes series?

  A Peter May B Peter Richardson C Colin McDonald D Neil Harvey

The Googly

England's team against Australia at Sydney in 1886-87 included a record six players from the same county – which one?

A Lancashire B Nottinghamshire C Surrey D Yorkshire

Answers on page 189

AUSTRALIA v NEW ZEALAND

1 When was the first official Test played between these two countries?
A 1886 B 1926 C 1946 D 1966

2 Who captained Australia for the only time in that match?
A Charlie Macartney B Bill Brown C Keith Miller D Ray Lindwall

3 How many years then elapsed before Australia played New Zealand in another Test?
A 4 B 12 C 15 D 28

4 Who took 9 for 52 (and caught the other batsman) at Brisbane in 1985-86?
A Craig McDermott B Lance Cairns C Richard Hadlee D Geoff Lawson

5 Who scored 1500 runs in 23 Tests against New Zealand, at an average of 51.72?
A Allan Border B David Boon C Mark Waugh D Steve Waugh

6 Who scored 247 not out and 133 for Australia at Wellington in 1973-74?
A Ian Redpath B Doug Walters C Greg Chappell D Ian Chappell

7 Who scored 50 and took 6 for 58 on his debut for Australia at Melbourne in 1987-88?
A Greg Matthews B Peter Sleep C Peter Taylor D Tony Dodemaide

8 Which former South Australia batsman captained New Zealand in that series?
A Andrew Jones B Jeremy Coney C Jeff Crowe D Martin Crowe

9 Who scored a century in each innings for New Zealand at Christchurch in 1973-74?
A John Parker B John Morrison C Bevan Congdon D Glenn Turner

10 Who scored a hundred on debut for New Zealand at Perth in 2001-02?
A Mark Richardson B Lou Vincent C Mathew Sinclair D Scott Styris

11 Who was out for 99 for Australia in the same match?
A Shane Warne B Adam Gilchrist C Martin Love D Darren Lehmann

The Googly

What was unusual about the Australian fast bowler Bruce Reid's first Test wicket against New Zealand, at Wellington in 1985-86?

A It was a stumping B The batsman was his cousin C It was the first dismissal to be confirmed by a TV replay D It came from his first ball of the match, and he bowled 51 more overs without taking another one

Answers on page 189

OLD TRAFFORD

1 Which county plays its home games at Old Trafford?

A Lancashire *B Nottinghamshire* *C Warwickshire* *D Yorkshire*

2 Who scored 114 in the 2004 Old Trafford Test, despite breaking a finger during his innings?

A Andrew Flintoff *B Marcus Trescothick* *C Chris Gayle* *D Graham Thorpe*

3 Which Lancastrian captained England against New Zealand at Old Trafford in 1994, and scored 111?

A Mike Watkinson *B Mike Atherton* *C Neil Fairbrother* *D David Lloyd*

4 Which 45-year-old played in the 1976 Old Trafford Test?

A Garry Sobers *B Brian Close* *C John Edrich* *D Ray Illingworth*

5 Whose 311 in 1964 was the first triple-century in a Test at Old Trafford?

A Bob Simpson *B Ken Barrington* *C John Edrich* *D Ted Dexter*

6 Who took a hat-trick for England against West Indies at Old Trafford in 1995?

A Angus Fraser *B Craig White* *C Dominic Cork* *D Darren Gough*

7 In which year was the first Test match played at Old Trafford?

A 1880 *B 1884* *C 1890* *D 1899*

8 Who scored a hundred before lunch on the first day of the 1902 Old Trafford Test?

A Gilbert Jessop *B Victor Trumper* *C Archie MacLaren* *D Reggie Duff*

9 Whose 312 in a county match in 1996 established a new first-class record for Old Trafford?

A Mike Hussey *B Malachy Loye* *C Neil Fairbrother* *D Jason Gallian*

10 Who was the first man to score a century on Test debut at Old Trafford, for India in 1959?

A Abbas Ali Baig *B Nawab of Pataudi junior* *C Hanumant Singh* *D Kripal Singh*

11 Which bowler, who died in 2004, took an all-lbw hat-trick in a county match at Old Trafford in 1963?

A Jack Flavell *B Brian Statham* *C Len Coldwell* *D David Smith*

The Googly

After which legendary cricket writer and *Wisden* contributor, who made his name writing for the *Manchester Guardian*, is the press-box at Old Trafford named?

A John Arlott *B Jim Swanton* *C Neville Cardus* *D John Woodcock*

Answers on page 189

INDIAN DOMESTIC CRICKET

1 What's the name of the first-class competition for India's state teams?

   A Gandhi Trophy B Bedi Bowl C Kapil Cup D Ranji Trophy

2 Which team won that competition 15 years running from 1958-59?

   A Holkar B Bombay C Karnataka D Delhi

3 What's the name of the first-class competition for India's zonal teams?

   A Deodhar Trophy B Rohinton-Baria Shield C Gopalan Trophy D Duleep Trophy

4 Which famous player made his last Ranji Trophy appearance aged 61, in 1957-58, and scored 52?

   A Vijay Merchant B Vijay Hazare C C.K. Nayudu D Lala Amarnath

5 Who hit 230 on his first-class debut for Mysore in 1967-68, and made a century on Test debut two years later as well?

   A Hanumant Singh B Gundappa Viswanath C Sunil Gavaskar D Mohinder Amarnath

6 Who scored 340 for Bombay against Bengal in February 1982?

   A Sunil Gavaskar B Ghulam Parkar C Gundappa Viswanath D Dilip Vengsarkar

7 Which Delhi batsman played only one Test for India, despite an overall first-class average of more than 67?

   A Ajay Sharma B Bhupinder Singh C Ashok Malhotra D Gursharan Singh

8 Which side won the Ranji Trophy for the first time in 2001-02?

   A Assam B Baroda C Railways D Services

9 Which fringe Indian player took all 10 for 46 for East Zone against South Zone at Agartala in 2000-01?

   A Nikhil Chopra B Murali Kartik C Paras Mhambrey D Debashish Mohanty

10 Who made his first-class debut for Punjab in 1987-88, when he was 13, and scored 94?

   A Vinod Kambli B Sachin Tendulkar C Ajay Jadeja D Dhruv Pandove

11 Which left-arm spinner took 589 wickets, most of them for Bombay, but never won a Test cap as Bishan Bedi was blocking his way?

   A Aloke Bhattacharjee B Padmakar Shivalkar C Ramesh Shukla D Rajinder Goel

The Googly

What record was set by Rajeev Nayyar during his 271 for Himachal Pradesh against Jammu & Kashmir at Chamba in 1999-2000?

A Highest innings at altitude B Highest score in Indian domestic cricket
C First first-class innings longer than 1000 minutes D Highest score by an opener carrying his bat

Answers on page 189

MIXED BAG 5

1 Who were the only two West Indians on the 2004 tour of England with the same first name?

   A Lara and Lawson B Collymore and Collins C Smith and Bravo D Smith and Sammy

2 Where did Australia, India and Pakistan compete in a one-day tournament in August 2004?

   A Dubai B Holland C Canada D Denmark

3 Who once scored five successive centuries in Tests – and was controversially given run out for 90 in his next innings?

   A Alan Melville B Don Bradman C Jack Fingleton D Everton Weekes

4 Who scored 224, 227, 125, 4 and 120 in successive Test innings in 1992-93, but played only 17 Tests in all and never made any other centuries?

   A Basit Ali B Brendon Kuruppu C Vinod Kambli D John F. Reid

5 Who collected a record five successive ducks in Test matches during 1985?

   A Azeem Hafeez B Greg Thomas C Ewen Chatfield D Bob Holland

6 What is the only animal to have had its obituary in *Wisden*?

   A Bosser, the horse that used to pull the roller at The Oval B C. Gull, a bird killed by an accurate off-drive at the MCG C Beefy, an Aberdeen Angus presented to Ian Botham D Peter, the Lord's cat

7 Which South African wicket-keeper scored 606 runs – including all three of his Test centuries – in the 1966-67 series against Australia?

   A John Waite B Dennis Lindsay C Ray Jennings D Dennis Gamsy

8 Which Australian took 104 Test wickets, and 106 in one-day internationals, the last of them in the 1999 World Cup final?

   A Craig McDermott B Michael Bevan C Paul Reiffel D Damien Fleming

9 Who played 88 Tests, including 12 on tour in England where he took 47 wickets, but never played against England in a home Test?

   A Allan Donald B Terry Alderman C Imran Khan D Malcolm Marshall

10 Which Australian captain finished up with exactly 1000 runs to go with his 109 Test wickets?

   A Warwick Armstrong B Ian Johnson C Ray Lindwall D Monty Noble

11 Who, in 1993-94, was dismissed by the first ball he faced in a Test – and later by the first ball he faced in a one-day international as well?

   A Phil Tufnell B Gary Kirsten C Heath Streak D Glenn McGrath

The Googly

According to his obituary in *Wisden* 1946, what sporting innovation did Kenneth Gandar-Dowar, a noted allround sportsman, try to introduce to Britain from Africa in the 1930s?

   A Orienteering B Game shooting at Lord's C Racing cheetahs, as a more exciting alternative to greyhounds D Triathlon

Answers on page 189

GROUNDS AROUND THE WORLD 2

1 Which Pakistan city has staged Tests at the Bagh-i-Jinnah and the Gaddafi Stadium?

  A Karachi **B** *Lahore* **C** *Multan* **D** *Rawalpindi*

2 Which was the first ground in the world to host 100 Test matches?

  A Melbourne **B** *Lord's* **C** *Sydney* **D** *The Oval*

3 And which was the first ground in the world to host 100 one-day internationals?

  A Melbourne **B** *Lord's* **C** *Sharjah* **D** *Kolkata*

4 Where in Pakistan did the famous flare-up between Mike Gatting and the umpire Shakoor Rana take place in 1987-88?

  A Karachi **B** *Lahore* **C** *Faisalabad* **D** *Gujranwala*

5 Which ground on mainland Europe staged a World Cup match in 1999?

  A Amstelveen, Amsterdam **B** *Rotterdam* **C** *Copenhagen* **D** *Versailles*

6 Which Test ground in Sri Lanka is really the home ground of a local school, Trinity College?

  A Asgiriya Stadium, Kandy **B** *Premadasa Stadium, Colombo* **C** *Tyronne Fernando Stadium, Moratuwa* **D** *Dambulla Stadium*

7 On which ground did Mark Taylor score the first Test triple-century in Pakistan, in 1998-99?

  A Karachi **B** *Lahore* **C** *Peshawar* **D** *Rawalpindi*

8 On which ground did Canada's John Davison take 17 wickets in a first-class match in 2004?

  A Hollywood **B** *Boston* **C** *New York* **D** *Fort Lauderdale*

9 Which ground, where the teams traditionally stayed overnight at a nearby biscuit factory, became in 1977-78 only the second to stage a one-day international in Pakistan, even though by 2004 it still hadn't hosted a Test?

  A Sialkot **B** *Sahiwal* **C** *Sargodha* **D** *Sheikhupura*

10 Which "offshore" country staged its inaugural official one-day tournament in August 2002?

  A Algeria **B** *Morocco* **C** *Tunisia* **D** *Denmark*

11 The home town of Inzamam-ul-Haq has staged Tests at the Ibn-e-Qasim Bagh Stadium and at a new ground named after the city – where is it?

  A Multan **B** *Quetta* **C** *Sheikhupura* **D** *Rawalpindi*

The Googly

Where is the Brockton Point ground, of which Don Bradman wrote: "This is without question the most beautiful cricket ground in the world ... I cannot imagine a more delightful place for cricket"?

A Adelaide **B** *San Diego, California* **C** *Vancouver, Canada* **D** *Edinburgh, Scotland*

Answers on page 189

WISDEN CRICKETER OF THE 20TH CENTURY: SHANE WARNE

1 With which Australian state side did Warne make his first-class debut?

   A New South Wales B Queensland C South Australia D Victoria

2 What is Warne's middle name, which is also his father's name?

   A Keith B Kenneth C Hollywood D Kerry

3 Which English county side has Warne captained?

   A Essex B Hampshire C Middlesex D Sussex

4 Who did Warne dismiss with his "Ball of the Century" – his first delivery in an Ashes Test, against England at Old Trafford in 1993?

   A Mike Atherton B Mike Gatting C Graham Gooch D David Gower

5 Which shirt number did Warne sport in one-day international cricket?

   A 1 B 8 C 23 D 69

6 Against which country did Warne start his Test career in 1991-92, taking a modest 1 for 150?

   A India B New Zealand C Pakistan D Sri Lanka

7 Who was Warne's captain in that first Test?

   A Allan Border B Steve Waugh C Mark Taylor D David Boon

8 Who was Warne's 500th Test wicket, in Sri Lanka in March 2004?

   A Russel Arnold B Hashan Tillakaratne C Chaminda Vaas D Muttiah Muralitharan

9 Why did Warne miss the 2003 World Cup?

   A He was injured B He was banned C He had retired from one-day cricket
   D He wasn't selected

10 Which batsman did Warne dismiss 14 times in Tests between 1993 and 2003?

   A Alec Stewart B Graham Thorpe C Sachin Tendulkar D Aravinda de Silva

11 Who was the third victim in Warne's Test hat-trick against England at the MCG in 1994-95?

   A Jack Russell B Darren Gough C Devon Malcolm D Phillip DeFreitas

The Googly

Early in his career Ian Healy joked that Shane Warne enjoyed a balanced diet – how exactly did he describe it?

A Chips with everything B Extra everything C A cheeseburger in each hand
D A large pie and large chips

Answers on page 189

GROUNDS IN INDIA

1 In which city would you be watching Test cricket at the Chinnaswamy Stadium?
A Mumbai (Bombay) **B** *Bangalore* **C** *Kolkata (Calcutta)* **D** *Delhi*

2 And where is the functionally named Sector 16 Stadium, which staged a Test in 1990-91?
A Chandigarh **B** *Vadodara (Baroda)* **C** *Cuttack* **D** *Sialkot*

3 Where is the Feroz Shah Kotla Test ground?
A Ahmedabad **B** *Mumbai (Bombay)* **C** *Kolkata (Calcutta)* **D** *Delhi*

4 On which ground did Saeed Anwar break the record for the highest score in one-day internationals, with 194 in 1996-97?
A Chandigarh **B** *Mumbai (Bombay)* **C** *Chennai (Madras)* **D** *Delhi*

5 Where is the Nehru Stadium, where Kenya created a World Cup shock by defeating West Indies in 1996?
A Hyderabad **B** *Pune* **C** *Cuttack* **D** *Visakhapatnam*

6 Test cricket in Bombay started at the Gymkhana ground, then moved to the Brabourne Stadium ... to which ground did it switch in 1974-75?
A Wankhede Stadium **B** *Maidan Ground* **B** *Cricket Club of India* **D** *Nehru Stadium*

7 In which city did Tests start at Chepauk, move to the Corporation Stadium for around ten years, and then return to Chepauk, which is now called something else?
A Vadodara (Baroda) **B** *Mumbai (Bombay)* **C** *Chennai (Madras)* **D** *Kolkata (Calcutta)*

8 At which ground did India finally win their first Test match, after almost 20 years of trying, in 1951-52?
A Kanpur **B** *Mumbai (Bombay)* **C** *Chennai (Madras)* **D** *Kolkata (Calcutta)*

9 Where did Bhausaheb Nimbalkar score 443 not out, the first quadruple-century in Indian first-class cricket, in 1948-49?
A Hyderabad **B** *Pune* **C** *Pataudi* **D** *Nagpur*

10 Who scored the first official Test century on Indian soil, at Bombay in 1933-34?
A Lala Amarnath **B** *Bryan Valentine* **C** *C.K. Nayudu* **D** *Douglas Jardine*

11 Where is Burlton Park, which staged one Test in 1982-83, in which Aunshuman Gaekwad compiled a sedate 201 in 671 minutes?
A Jaipur **B** *Jullundur* **C** *Cuttack* **D** *Rajkot*

The Googly
The University Ground at Lucknow staged the second Test between India and Pakistan in 1952-53. What was unusual about that match?
A The students prepared the pitch **B** *A coconut-matting pitch was used* **C** *It was the only first-class match ever played there* **D** *There was an extra rest day for the Queen's Coronation*

Answers on page 190

NEAR-MISSES

1 Who once made 299 not out in a Test, before running the last man out?

    A Mohammad Azharuddin *B Don Bradman* *C Bob Simpson* *D Denis Compton*

2 And who was once out for 299 in a Test?

    A Hanif Mohammad *B Don Bradman* *C Martin Crowe* *D Brian Lara*

3 Who was left stranded on 99 not out for South Africa against England at Headingley in 2003?

    A Andrew Hall *B Shaun Pollock* *C Mark Boucher* *D Monde Zondeki*

4 Who was left stranded on 99 when his brother, acting as runner for the No. 11, was run out in a Test in 1994-95?

    A Gary Kirsten *B Steve Waugh* *C Jeff Crowe* *D Andy Flower*

5 Who scored 92 on his Test debut, and 90 in his first one-day international, for New Zealand in 1993-94?

    A Nathan Astle *B Stephen Fleming* *C Craig McMillan* *D Bryan Young*

6 Which Australian was twice out for 99 in Tests in 1997?

    A Matthew Elliott *B Greg Blewett* *C Michael Slater* *D Steve Waugh*

7 Which England captain made his highest Test score of 99 against South Africa at Trent Bridge in 1947?

    A Freddie Brown *B Norman Yardley* *C Ken Cranston* *D George Mann*

8 Who was run out for 99 for New Zealand against England at Christchurch in 1991-92 – and never did score a Test century?

    A Blair Pocock *B Blair Hartland* *C Shane Thomson* *D Dipak Patel*

9 And which of his team-mates, in that same match, was only the second man to be stumped for 99 in a Test?

    A John Wright *B Mark Greatbatch* *C Jeff Crowe* *D Martin Crowe*

10 Who scored 99 on his Test debut for Pakistan against South Africa at Lahore in 2003-04?

    A Asim Kamal *B Mohammad Hafeez* *C Imran Farhat* *D Taufeeq Umar*

11 Who, when he was out for 99 at Lord's in 1960, was the first part of the controversial South African fast bowler Geoff Griffin's hat-trick?

    A Peter Walker *B Bob Barber* *C Mike Smith* *D Jim Parks*

The Googly

Who scored 99, 98 and 97 in successive Test innings for Australia in 1901-02?

A Victor Trumper *B Monty Noble* *C Clem Hill* *D Joe Darling*

Answers on page 190

ENGLAND v ZIMBABWE

1 In which year did these two sides first meet in an official Test?

A 1996 *B 1998* *C 2000* *D 2001*

2 And what was the unusual result of that first Test?

A Abandoned *B A tie* *C Called off due to unfit pitch* *D Drawn, with the scores level*

3 Where was that game played?

A Harare *B Bulawayo* *C Chester-le-Street* *D Lord's*

4 Who was the England coach who claimed "We flippin' murdered 'em" after that match?

A Duncan Fletcher *B Ray Illingworth* *C Micky Stewart* *D David Lloyd*

5 Who took a hat-trick against England in a one-day international at Harare in 1996-97?

A Henry Olonga *B Eddo Brandes* *C Pommie Mbangwa* *D Paul Strang*

6 Who took 5 for 73 on his debut for England against Zimbabwe at Lord's in 2003?

A James Anderson *B Anthony McGrath* *C Simon Jones* *D Richard Johnson*

7 And who took 6 for 33 on his Test debut, in the next Test at Chester-le-Street?

A James Anderson *B James Kirtley* *C Steve Harmison* *D Richard Johnson*

8 Which Zimbabwe-born player scored 101 against them at Lord's in 2000?

A Trevor Penney *B Ronnie Irani* *C Graeme Hick* *D Nick Knight*

9 And who took 5 for 15 for England in that same Test?

A Alex Tudor *B Ed Giddins* *C Andy Caddick* *D Darren Maddy*

10 Who took 6 for 19 for Zimbabwe in a one-day international against England at Cape Town in 1999-2000?

A Heath Streak *B Andy Blignaut* *C Henry Olonga* *D Pommie Mbangwa*

11 Where did Zimbabwe inflict an embarrassing defeat on England in the 1992 World Cup?

A Albury *B Ballarat* *C Berri* *D Mackay*

The Googly

What was unusual about Mark Ealham's haul of 5 for 15 in a one-day international against Zimbabwe at Kimberley in 1999-2000?

A All five wickets were lbw *B All five were caught at slip* *C They were his first five wickets in international cricket* *D They were taken with the first balls of five consecutive overs*

Answers on page 190

DOMESTIC CRICKET AROUND THE WORLD

1 Which country's domestic first-class tournament is called the Quaid-e-Azam Trophy?
A Sri Lanka B Bangladesh C Pakistan D Kenya

2 What was the original name of the domestic competition in New Zealand?
A Plunket Shield B Bledisloe Cup C Cook Cup D Hadlee Trophy

3 Who was run out for 499 in a domestic match in Pakistan in 1958-59?
A Imtiaz Ahmed B Hanif Mohammad C Maqsood Ahmed D Waqar Hasan

4 Who scored a hundred in just 34 balls for South Australia against Victoria at the Adelaide Oval in 1982-83?
A Andrew Hilditch B Wayne Phillips C Bob Zadow D David Hookes

5 Who, with innings of 385 and 355 in the 1950s, was the first man to score two triple-centuries in New Zealand domestic cricket?
A John Reid B Bert Sutcliffe C Murray Chapple D Walter Hadlee

6 What is the first-class domestic competition in Zimbabwe called?
A Mugabe Trophy B Logan Cup C Rhodes Bowl D ZimSun Cup

7 In which city might you watch a match at Maitland Place or Maitland Crescent?
A Auckland B Bangalore C Colombo D Delhi

8 Which future Test opener scored twin hundreds on his debut for New South Wales against Queensland in 1940-41?
A Arthur Morris B Sid Barnes C Jack Moroney D Jim Burke

9 Which Sri Lankan-born player once scored a half-century in English county cricket in eight minutes, after being fed full-tosses to expedite a declaration?
A Aravinda de Silva B Stanley Jayasinghe C Clive Inman D Glen Chapple

10 Which New Zealander, playing for Canterbury in 2002-03, extended his maiden first-class century to 301 not out?
A Matthew Hart B Peter Fulton C Michael Papps D Richard Jones

11 Who, playing for Sargodha against Gujranwala in Pakistan in 2000-01, was out for 394 – the nearest anyone had come to a first-class quadruple-century without getting there?
A Naved Anjum B Naved Latif C Rashid Latif D Haroon Rashid

The Googly

Vasbert Drakes was dismissed "timed out" in a domestic match in South Africa in 2002-03. What was his excuse for missing his turn to bat?
A He was stuck in the toilet B He had gone shopping C His plane had been delayed and he hadn't reached the ground D He had lost his bat

Answers on page 190

AUSTRALIA v WEST INDIES

1 Which trophy is at stake when these sides meet?

   A The Bradman Cup *B The Wisden Trophy* *C The Frank Worrell Trophy*
   D The Border Medal

2 In what year did Australia and West Indies contest the first tied Test match?

   A 1960 *B 1965* *C 1968* *D 1973*

3 Who scored a record five centuries in the 1954-55 series?

   A Arthur Morris *B Neil Harvey* *C Clyde Walcott* *D Everton Weekes*

4 Who scored 206 for Australia at Port-of-Spain in 2002-03?

   A Matthew Hayden *B Justin Langer* *C Ricky Ponting* *D Adam Gilchrist*

5 Who captained the West Indian side whitewashed 5-0 in Australia in 2000-01?

   A Jimmy Adams *B Brian Lara* *C Carl Hooper* *D Courtney Walsh*

6 Who took a hat-trick for West Indies at Bridgetown in 2002-03?

   A Omari Banks *B Tino Best* *C Corey Collymore* *D Jermaine Lawson*

7 And who took a hat-trick for West Indies at Brisbane in 1988-89?

   A Malcolm Marshall *B Curtly Ambrose* *C Courtney Walsh* *D Patrick Patterson*

8 Who took a hat-trick, which included his 300th Test wicket, at Perth in 2000-01?

   A Shane Warne *B Glenn McGrath* *C Curtly Ambrose* *D Courtney Walsh*

9 Who captained Australia in the West Indies in 1964-65 – and again in 1977-78?

   A Bill Lawry *B Bob Simpson* *C Ian Chappell* *D Doug Walters*

10 Who scored the first double-century for West Indies against Australia, 219 in his native
Barbados in 1954-55?

   A Clyde Walcott *B Garry Sobers* *C Clairmonte Depeiza* *D Denis Atkinson*

11 Which West Indian, at Sydney in 1930-31, was the first to dismiss Don Bradman for a duck
in a Test match?

   A Mannie Martindale *B Herman Griffith* *C Learie Constantine* *D Jack Grant*

The Googly

What was unusual about Merv Hughes's hat-trick for Australia against West Indies at Perth
in 1988-89?

   A All the victims were left-handers *B It was spread over three different overs*
   C All the victims were Antiguans *D It was the first Test hat-trick by someone with*
a moustache

Answers on page 190

WISDEN

1 Who, in 1850, founded the company that still publishes *Wisden*?

    A Norman Wisden   *B John Wisden*   *C W.G. Wisden*   *D Al Manack*

2 In which year did the *Wisden Almanack* first appear?

    A 1850   *B 1852*   *C 1864*   *D 1877*

3 The 2003 *Wisden* was the first one to feature a photograph on the cover – of whom?

    A Ricky Ponting   *B Michael Vaughan*   *C Nasser Hussain*   *D Shane Warne*

4 Which team plays against England for the Wisden Trophy?

    A Australia   *B New Zealand*   *C South Africa*   *D West Indies*

5 Who returned to edit *Wisden* in 2004 after a three-year absence?

    A Matthew Engel   *B Graeme Wright*   *C Christopher Martin-Jenkins*   *D Tim de Lisle*

6 For which English county did John Wisden play most of his cricket?

    A Essex   *B Middlesex*   *C Surrey*   *D Sussex*

7 Wisden was a member of the first English team to make an overseas tour, in 1859. Where did they go?

    A Australia   *B France*   *C America and Canada*   *D Malta*

8 Which American-born cricket-lover liked Wisden so much he bought the company in 1993?

    A Paul Getty   *B Victor Kiam*   *C Christopher Ondaatje*   *D Victor Blank*

9 An Australian *Wisden* was published for the first time in 1998 – what colour was its cover?

    A Yellow   *B Green*   *C Green and gold*   *D Orange*

10 On which sport, other than cricket, did Wisden publish an Almanack for three years during the 1920s?

    A Football   *B Tennis*   *C Rugby Union*   *D Golf*

11 Which famous war artist designed the woodcut of two top-hatted cricketers, which has featured on the cover of *Wisden* since 1938?

    A Eric Ravilious   *B Paul Nash*   *C Edward Bawden*   *D David Hockney*

The Googly

What unique bowling feat did John Wisden achieve for the North against the South at Lord's in 1850?

    A He took all ten wickets for no runs   *B He took two hat-tricks in one innings*
    C He took all ten wickets, all bowled   *D He took five wickets with five successive balls*

Answers on page 190

ANSWERS – PAGES 12-18

Slow starters – from page 12

1 A – Graham Gooch
2 B – Shane Warne
3 C – Bobby Simpson
4 B – Jeff Thomson
5 D – Ray Illingworth
6 B – Ken Rutherford
7 C – Jimmy Cook
8 D – Malcolm Marshall
9 D – Merv Hughes
10 B – Mike Brearley
11 D – Dave Nourse
Googly D – Len Hutton (his partner in his first Test was Jim Parks senior)

England v West Indies: The Wisden Trophy 2004 – from page 13

1 C – Robert Key
2 B – Dwayne Bravo
3 B – Michael Vaughan
4 C – Graham Gooch (in 1990)
5 D – George Headley (in 1939)
6 A – Shivnarine Chanderpaul
7 B – Marcus Trescothick
8 C – Chris Gayle
9 A – Ashley Giles
10 B – Stephen Harmison
11 D – Shivnarine Chanderpaul
Googly C – His father Colin in the first row of the upper tier of the stand (he dropped it into Michael Vaughan's mother's lap)

Ian Botham – from page 14

1 C – Cheshire
2 A – Australia
3 C – Worcestershire
4 D – Headingley, Leeds
5 B – Queensland
6 B – India
7 D – Sunil Gavaskar
8 C – Hampshire
9 B – "Lord" Tim Hudson
10 B – Bruce Edgar
11 A – Australians
Googly D – Most sixes (80)

Strange but true – from page 15

1 B – The England team had to catch the boat home
2 A – A total eclipse
3 D – A bomb scare (Dickie Bird famously sat on the covers to protect the pitch)
4 D – The death of King George VI
5 C – A general election
6 B – He "streaked" naked across the ground
7 D – Supporters claiming he had been wrongly arrested dug up the pitch
8 C – Robin Jackman
9 A – Anderson Cummins (the protesters carried banners saying "No Cummins, No Goings")
10 A – Aftab Gul
11 A – They played a one-day international
Googly C – A batch of substandard balls that kept going out of shape (inferior-quality balls were inadvertently supplied, but they were used through each first innings to be fair to both sides; England had used eight balls by the time Australia reached 200, and the Aussies later used seven)

The Ashes – from page 16

1 C – The Lord's Museum
2 B – The Oval
3 B – 1882
4 D – Fred "Demon" Spofforth
5 C – The *Sporting Times*
6 B – Bill Woodfull
7 B – Ray Illingworth
8 D – David Gower
9 A – Allan Border
10 C – Archie MacLaren
11 B – Bill Voce
Googly B – She married Bligh (and, on his death, bequeathed the Ashes urn to MCC)

Wisden Cricketer of the 20th Century: Don Bradman – from page 17

1 C – 99.94
2 D – Worcester
3 B – Bowral
4 D – 100
5 D – Headingley, Leeds
6 B – Eric Hollies
7 B – Bill Ponsford
8 B – Sid Barnes
9 A – Jack Ryder
10 C – Melbourne
11 D – 299 not out (his last batting partner was run out)
Googly B – North America (Bradman had just got married, and took his new wife on the tour, which included 51 matches in 76 days. The Don played in all 51 games, and comfortably led the runscorers: for the bowlers "Chuck" Fleetwood-Smith took 238 wickets at 7.5)

West Indies v India – from page 18

1 C – Sunil Gavaskar
2 B – Narendra Hirwani
3 A – Kiran More
4 C – Gordon Greenidge
5 B – Roy Gilchrist
6 A – Rohan Kanhai
7 D – Nawab of Pataudi junior (the appointed captain, Nari Contractor, had his skull fractured during the tour)
8 C – Jack Noreiga
9 A – Abey Kuruvilla
10 D – Kapil Dev
11 B – Bruce Pairaudeau
Googly A – Five batsmen were absent hurt (it was a spiteful pitch; India's captain Bishan Bedi had declared in the first innings after six wickets had fallen, to spare the tail from further injury from West Indies' fast bowlers)

ANSWERS – PAGES 19-27

The men in white coats – from page 19
1 D – Dickie Bird
2 D – David Shepherd
3 B – Steve Bucknor
4 B – Brent
5 C – Peter Willey
6 D – Steve Dunne
7 A – Swaroop Kishen
8 C – Frank Chester
9 C – Col Egar
10 B – Eric Tindill
11 A – Bill Alley
Googly A – He was a Test selector at the time

Datelines – from page 20
1 C – 1971
2 B – 1877
3 D – 1963
4 B – 1975
5 D – 1973
6 A – 1994
7 A – 1930
8 B – 1787
9 D – 1998
10 D – 2003
11 B – 1912
Googly B – 1930 (Andrew Sandham scored 325 in April, then Don Bradman made 334 in July)

Better than average – from page 21
1 D – Don Bradman
2 B – Stuart Law
3 C – Richard Hadlee
4 B – Geoff Boycott
5 B – Garry Sobers
6 A – George Lohmann
7 B – Graeme Pollock
8 C – Vijay Merchant
9 A – Graham Gooch
10 B – Bill Johnston
11 C – Herbert Sutcliffe (Bradman's average after his first Test was 9.50, and didn't pass 60 until his fourth Test; Sutcliffe's first Test innings was 64, and his average remained above 61 until his last Test, when it dipped to 60.73)
Googly B – Jim Standen (64 wickets at 13.00 for Worcestershire; kept goal for West Ham)

Australia v Pakistan – from page 22
1 B – Matthew Hayden
2 C – Sarfraz Nawaz
3 C – One wicket
4 D – Imran Khan
5 A – Intikhab Alam
6 D – Damien Fleming
7 B – Salim Malik
8 B – Billy Ibadulla
9 B – Max Walker
10 B – Taslim Arif
11 D – Dwight Eisenhower
Googly C – Colombo

Hampshire – from page 23
1 D – Shane Warne
2 B – Philip Mead
3 C – Colin Ingleby-Mackenzie
4 C – Chris Tremlett
5 A – Derek Shackleton
6 A – Bournemouth
7 B – Robin Smith
8 C – 2001
9 C – Mark Nicholas
10 A – Johnny Arnold
11 B – Lionel Tennyson
Googly D – Hampshire won by 155 runs (they scored 521 in their follow-on, then bowled Warwickshire out for 158)

The Ashes 1985 – from page 24
1 A – Allan Border
2 D – Paul Downton
3 A – Tim Robinson
4 A – Allan Border
5 B – Bob Holland
6 C – Wayne Phillips (he hit the ball down into Allan Lamb's foot, and it bounced up to be caught by David Gower)
7 B – Jeff Thomson
8 B – Les Taylor
9 D – David Gower
10 A – Graham Gooch
11 D – Dirk Wellham
Googly D – Simon O'Donnell

Doubling up – from page 25
1 C – Kepler Wessels
2 A – Gavin Hamilton
3 D – Nawab of Pataudi senior
4 A – Jeff Wilson
5 B – Brian McKechnie
6 C – Kepler Wessels
7 B – Jonty Rhodes
8 C – Clive van Ryneveld
9 C – Sammy Guillen
10 D – Billy Midwinter
11 A – Flavian Aponso
Googly C – Played Davis Cup tennis

Wisden Cricketer of the 20th Century: Garry Sobers – from page 26
1 B – Barbados
2 D – 365 not out
3 A – Kingston, Jamaica
4 C – Malcolm Nash
5 C – Nottinghamshire
6 C – 90
7 C – Conrad Hunte
8 C – Melbourne
9 C – Frank Worrell
10 D – David Holford
11 C – South Australia
Googly B – Trevor Bailey

The 1975 World Cup – from page 27
1 D – West Indies
2 C – Clive Lloyd
3 C – Clive Lloyd
4 A – Rohan Kanhai
5 C – Five
6 B – New Zealand
7 B – Gary Gilmour
8 D – East Africa
9 A – Alvin Kallicharran
10 B – Glenn Turner
11 A – Alan Turner
Googly C – Rohan Kanhai

ANSWERS – PAGES 28-36

India v Pakistan – from page 28
1 C – Virender Sehwag
2 A – Anil Kumble
3 B – Mudassar Nazar
4 D – Zaheer Abbas
5 C – Kapil Dev
6 B – 12
7 C – 18
8 A – Haseeb Ahsan
9 C – Kris Srikkanth
10 A – Asif Iqbal
11 D – Deepak Shodhan
Googly A – They said the Indian captain (Sunil Gavaskar) had sworn at them

Worcestershire – from page 29
1 D – Duncan Fearnley
2 D – Basil D'Oliveira
3 B – Vikram Solanki
4 C – Reg Perks
5 D – Don Kenyon
6 D – Tom Moody
7 B – Roy Booth
8 A – Stourbridge
9 A – Roly Jenkins
10 D – Nantie Hayward
11 B – Norman Gifford
Googly B – Ben Smith

Datelines 2 – from page 30
1 D – 2004
2 B – 1977
3 B – 1947
4 D – 2003
5 C – 1977
6 A – 1993
7 B – 1934
8 C – 1999
9 C – 1899
10 D – 1984
11 C – 1970
Googly C – 1939 (it was supposed to be a two-year experiment, but the Second World War intervened)

Australia in Tests – from page 31
1 C – Melbourne
2 B – Kim Hughes
3 C – Darren Lehmann
4 D – Dennis Lillee
5 A – Neil Harvey
6 B – Michael Slater
7 D – Lindsay Hassett
8 C – Bob Cowper
9 B – Len Pascoe (he was born in Macedonia)
10 D – Darwin
11 A – Clarrie Grimmett
Googly C – Ross Edwards

English domestic cricket – from page 32
1 D – Yorkshire
2 C – Surrey
3 C – Sussex
4 B – Lancashire
5 A – Durham
6 C – Glamorgan
7 C – Warwickshire
8 B – Gloucestershire
9 D – Yorkshire
10 B – Devon
11 C – 1968
Googly C – Hedley Verity (Yorkshire)

Wisden Cricketer of the 20th Century: Viv Richards – from page 33
1 A – Antigua
2 C – Isaac
3 A – Football (soccer)
4 A – Glamorgan
5 C – The Oval
6 C – Old Trafford, Manchester
7 B – Mali
8 B – India
9 C – Warwickshire
10 B – West Indies and South Africa
11 D – David "Syd" Lawrence
Googly C – Trevor McDonald (who did a similar book on Clive Lloyd)

The 1979 World Cup – from page 34
1 D – West Indies
2 C – Clive Lloyd
3 B – Viv Richards
4 C – Collis King
5 A – India
6 C – Canada
7 D – Joel Garner
8 C – Canada
9 A – New Zealand and Pakistan
10 B – Gordon Greenidge
11 A – Asif Iqbal
Googly C – Mike Hendrick

One-day specialists – from page 35
1 A – Andrew Symonds
2 A – Adam Gilchrist
3 D – Simon O'Donnell
4 D – Yuvraj Singh
5 B – Gavin Larsen
6 C – Ricardo Powell
7 C – Ian Gould
8 B – Brendon Kuruppu
9 D – Shahid Afridi
10 C – Trevor Jesty
11 D – Dave Callaghan
Googly D – Garry Sobers

The first Tied Test – from page 36
1 B – Brisbane
2 D – Richie Benaud
3 B – Frank Worrell
4 A – Garry Sobers
5 A – Alan Davidson
6 C – Norman O'Neill
7 A – Gerry Alexander
8 A – Alan McGilvray
9 D – Wes Hall
10 D – Joe Solomon
11 A – Ian Meckiff
Googly B – Bob Simpson (he was Australia's coach in 1986-87)

ANSWERS – PAGES 37-45

Grounds around the world – from page 37
1 D – Sydney
2 C – Melbourne
3 B – Headingley, Leeds
4 B – Trent Bridge, Nottingham
5 C – Kingston, Jamaica
6 C – Sharjah
7 B – Bloemfontein
8 B – Canterbury
9 A – St John's, Antigua
10 C – New Zealand
11 C – Headingley, Leeds
Googly D – Bangabandhu National Stadium, Dhaka (home Tests for Pakistan and Bangladesh, the neutral final of the Asian Test Championship in 1998-99, plus several ODIs)

Datelines 3 – from page 38
1 C – 1999
2 D – 1992
3 C – 1996
4 A – 1990
5 C – 1930
6 C – 1956
7 A – 1987
8 A – 1954
9 C – 1993
10 C – 1880
11 A – 1975
Googly C – 1988 (they were Mike Gatting, John Emburey, Chris Cowdrey and Graham Gooch. Emburey was the only one to have two matches in charge)

Wicket-keepers – from page 39
1 B – Rod Marsh
2 A – Adam Gilchrist
3 B – Ian Healy
4 C – Jack Russell
5 D – Wasim Bari
6 A – Adam Parore
7 B – Bert Oldfield
8 B – Bob Taylor
9 B – Wayne James
10 C – Richard Blakey
11 D – Dave Richardson
Googly C – Bruce French

Durham – from page 40
1 B – David Graveney
2 D – Dean Jones
3 C – The Riverside
4 C – David Boon
5 D – Simon Hughes
6 D – Yorkshire
7 B – Shoaib Akhtar
8 D – Simon Brown
9 B – Colin Milburn
10 A – Lumley Castle
11 D – Anthony McGrath
Googly C – It cost 483 runs, the most expensive miss in first-class history: Brian Lara had 18 at the time and ended up with 501

Wisden Cricketer of the 20th Century: Jack Hobbs – from page 41
1 C – The Oval
2 C – Cambridgeshire
3 B – Berry
4 C – Herbert Sutcliffe
5 C – Tom Hayward
6 A – Andy Sandham
7 A – Arthur Jones (Francis Fane captained in the first three Tests, as Jones was unwell)
8 C – Percy Chapman (Jack White captained in the final Test)
9 B – 47 (1930)
10 B – Melbourne
11 D – 98 (some sources show 199 centuries, 100 of them after his 40th birthday)
Googly A – The Master's Club ("The Master" was Hobbs's usual nickname)

New Zealand v India or Pakistan – from page 42
1 C – Inzamam-ul-Haq
2 D – John Wright
3 B – Bruce Taylor
4 C – Majid Khan
5 D – Chris Pringle
6 D – Mathew Sinclair
7 D – Rodney Redmond
8 B – Javed Miandad
9 A – Mohammad Nazir
10 B – Surinder Amarnath
11 B – Vinoo Mankad
Googly C – Mohammad Wasim

Test bowling records – from page 43
1 D – Jim Laker
2 C – Anil Kumble
3 C – Muttiah Muralitharan and Shane Warne
4 A – Allan Donald
5 C – Chris Cairns
6 C – Sonny Ramadhin
7 B – Sydney Barnes
8 A – Terry Alderman
9 C – Chris Old
10 C – Upul Chandana
11 C – Clarrie Grimmett
Googly C – Carl Hooper

The Ashes 1986-87 – from page 44
1 C – Mike Gatting
2 C – Chris Broad
3 B – Ian Botham
4 C – Jack Richards
5 B – Peter Taylor
6 B – Bruce Reid
7 C – Tim Zoehrer
8 C – Geoff Marsh
9 C – John Emburey
10 A – James Whitaker
11 D – Gladstone Small
Googly C – The first staging of the America's Cup yachting in Australia (at Fremantle near Perth. The competition was called the Perth Challenge, and the players wore specially designed nautical-themed coloured kit)

The 400 club – from page 45
1 C – Brian Lara
2 B – Graeme Hick
3 A – Bill Ponsford
4 D – Run out
5 B – Graham Gooch (333 and 123 in 1990)
6 D – Don Bradman
7 C – Taunton
8 D – Archie MacLaren
9 B – Bhausaheb Nimbalkar
10 C – Somerset
11 A – Aftab Baloch
Googly C – Bob Woolmer (taken to watch Hanif as a boy in 1958-59, Warwickshire's coach for Lara's innings in 1994)

ANSWERS – PAGES 46-54

South African domestic cricket – from page 46

1 C – Currie Cup
2 D – Transvaal
3 C – Castle Cup
4 D – Orange Free State
5 B – Transvaal
6 D – Graeme Pollock
7 D – Daryll Cullinan
8 B – Orange Free State
9 B – Eastern Province
10 C – Daryll Cullinan
11 B – Steve Jefferies

Googly C – The ball landed in the frying pan and was unusable (*Wisden* says: "Daryll Cullinan hit a six into a frying pan ... it was about ten minutes before the ball was cool enough for the umpires to remove the grease. Even then, [the bowler] was unable to grip the ball and it had to be replaced.")

Un-straight arms – from page 47

1 A – Muttiah Muralitharan
2 C – James Kirtley
3 B – Geoff Griffin
4 C – Ian Meckiff
5 B – Ernie Jones
6 C – Henry Olonga
7 B – Grant Flower
8 D – David Gower
9 B – Tony Lock
10 C – Charlie Griffith
11 B – Jayananda Warnaweera

Googly D – He impersonated Bartlett's bowling action – and was no-balled for throwing himself

The 1983 World Cup – from page 48

1 B – India
2 D – Kapil Dev
3 A – Mohinder Amarnath
4 B – Kris Srikkanth
5 D – Dickie Bird
6 B – Kapil Dev
7 D – David Gower
8 C – Vic Marks
9 D – Duncan Fletcher
10 C – India
11 C – Trevor Chappell

Googly C – Ken MacLeay

England in Tests – from page 49

1 B – Nasser Hussain
2 C – Colin Cowdrey
3 B – The Oval
4 B – W.G. Grace
5 D – Devon Malcolm
6 A – Mike Atherton
7 C – Ken Barrington
8 B – Godfrey Evans
9 D – Graham Gooch
10 A – Len Hutton
11 A – Alec Bedser

Googly C – They won after following on (India later did it against Australia as well)

The Ashes 1989 – from page 50

1 A – David Gower
2 B – Mark Taylor
3 C – 29
4 A – Terry Alderman
5 C – Steve Waugh
6 D – Ted Dexter
7 A – Angus Fraser
8 D – Mike Atherton
9 A – Mark Taylor
10 C – Trevor Hohns
11 C – Greg Campbell

Googly A – Alan Igglesden

Plucked from obscurity – from page 51

1 B – Peter Taylor
2 A – Tauseef Ahmed
3 D – Fidel Edwards
4 C – Waqar Younis
5 C – Mike Whitney
6 B – Basil D'Oliveira
7 C – Tom Cartwright
8 C – Colin Cowdrey
9 D – Ehteshamuddin
10 C – George Gunn
11 C – John Watkins

Googly C – He'd never kept wicket before (*Wisden* reported that "only when he had accepted the terms offered and joined the ship at Adelaide was the discovery made that he had never kept wicket in his life")

Sri Lanka in Tests – from page 52

1 B – Arjuna Ranatunga
2 C – Sanath Jayasuriya
3 B – Sidath Wettimuny
4 D – Nuwan Zoysa
5 A – Aravinda de Silva
6 B – Muttiah Muralitharan
7 D – Duleep Mendis
8 C – Kandy
9 B – Thilan Samaraweera
10 C – Wettimuny (Mithra and Sidath)
11 A – Amal Silva

Googly B – The worst bowling average (Wijesuriya's was 293.00, Lewis's is 318.00; both were briefly surpassed in 2003 by Bangladesh's Khaled Mahmud, but he spoiled it by taking another wicket)

Media men – from page 53

1 D – Kerry Packer
2 B – Richie Benaud
3 C – Jim Swanton
4 C – Christopher Martin-Jenkins
5 C – The Guardian
6 C – Peter West
7 B – Bill Lawry
8 B – Bill Frindall
9 B – Brian Johnston
10 B – Brian Murgatroyd
11 A – John Woodcock

Googly B – Henry Blofeld (the England manager, David Clark, asked him to "Try to get to bed before 12". He did, but next morning Micky Stewart left his sickbed to play)

The Ashes 1990-91 – from page 54

1 C – Graham Gooch
2 A – Allan Lamb
3 B – Bruce Reid
4 D – Phil Tufnell
5 A – Mark Waugh
6 B – John Morris
7 A – Mike Atherton
8 B – Phil Newport
9 D – Mark Taylor (the first occasion was at Adelaide too)
10 C – Craig McDermott
11 B – Wayne Larkins

Googly C – Peter Cantrell

ANSWERS – PAGES 55-63

Strange birthplaces: England – from page 55

1 C – Adam Hollioake
2 D – Ted Dexter
3 B – Freddie Brown
4 D – Mike Denness
5 A – Tony Lewis
6 C – Geraint Jones
7 D – Phillip DeFreitas
8 A – Allan Lamb
9 D – Phil Edmonds
10 D – Dermot Reeve
11 C – Pelham Warner
Googly B – Robin Jackman (born in India, played for England, banned from Guyana for playing in South Africa)

Derbyshire – from page 56

1 B – Kim Barnett
2 D – Queen's Park
3 C – Michael Di Venuto
4 A – Bob Taylor
5 C – Donald Carr
6 D – Dominic Hewson
7 B – Barry Wood
8 B – Eddie Barlow
9 B – Les Jackson
10 B – Chris Bassano
11 C – 1936
The **Googly** C – His false teeth ("wrapped in a hanky", according to his obituary in *Wisden* 1988), as it was a spiteful pitch: the match, although in June, had been interrupted by snow

One big moment – from page 57

1 B – Bob Massie
2 C – Charles Bannerman
3 A – Arthur Milton
4 D – David Lloyd
5 D – Dirk Wellham
6 B – Billy Griffith
7 A – Nilesh Kulkarni
8 C – Mick Malone
9 A – Taslim Arif
10 B – Praveen Amre
11 B – John Warr
Googly A – Arthur Coningham

Grounds in Australia – from page 58

1 D – Sydney
2 C – Perth
3 B – Brisbane
4 A – Hobart
5 C – Perth
6 C – Canberra
7 C – Melbourne (307 by Bob Cowper)
8 A – Exhibition Ground
9 D – Don Bradman
10 B – Bowral
11 B – Brisbane
Googly A – Two balls (after a late start India made 1 for 0 off 0.2 overs, then it rained again)

Screen tests – from page 59

1 B – Ian Botham
2 C – Clare Connor
3 A – Phil Tufnell
4 B – Bodyline
5 D – David Gower
6 B – Jim Troughton (his grandfather Patrick was television's second Doctor Who)
7 D – Lagaan
8 C – Charters and Caldicott
9 A – Wondrous Oblivion
10 B – Aubrey Smith
11 C – Fred Trueman
Googly B – Mike Whitney

Essex – from page 60

1 B – Graham Gooch
2 A – Ilford
3 D – Andy Flower
4 C – Brian Taylor
5 B – Jack Russell (v South Africa at Durban, 1922-23)
6 C – 1979
7 C – John Lever
8 C – Southend
9 A – Percy Perrin
10 D – Johnny Douglas
11 A – David Acfield
Googly B – To wear a moustache

Brian Lara – from page 61

1 C – Trinidad
2 A – St John's, Antigua
3 B – Graham Thorpe
4 C – Darrell Hair
5 B – Durham
6 C – Keith Piper
7 C – Sydney
8 A – He was caught at slip
9 D – Sri Lanka
10 D – South Africa
11 D – Desmond Haynes
Googly C – Anderson Cummins

The Ashes 1993 – from page 62

1 C – Graham Gooch
2 A – Michael Slater
3 C – Mike Gatting
4 D – Peter Such
5 D – Allan Border
6 A – Mark Waugh
7 A – Mike Atherton
8 C – Martin McCague
9 B – Graham Thorpe
10 A – Angus Fraser
11 B – Robin Smith
Googly D – They were both born in New Zealand

Carrying the bat – from page 63

1 D – Desmond Haynes
2 C – Graham Gooch
3 C – Jimmy Cook
4 B – Geoff Boycott
5 B – Glenn Turner
6 D – Frank Worrell
7 B – Bill Woodfull
8 B – Bill Brown
9 B – Len Hutton
10 B – Bernard Tancred
11 C – Cyril Wood
Googly D – He opened but was the last man out in both innings

ANSWERS – PAGES 64-72

Surrey – from page 64
1 B – John Major
2 A – Alistair Brown
3 D – Douglas Jardine
4 B – Jack Hobbs
5 C – Mark Ramprakash
6 D – Andy Sandham
7 C – Stuart Surridge
8 A – Guildford
9 C – John Edrich
10 C – Roy Swetman
11 D – Pat Pocock
Googly C – Bob Willis and
Geoff Howarth

The 1987 World Cup – from page 65
1 A – Australia
2 C – Calcutta
3 A – Allan Border
4 B – David Boon
5 D – Graham Gooch
6 C – Craig McDermott
7 D – Viv Richards
8 C – Chetan Sharma
9 B – Jeff Crowe
10 A – Bill Athey
11 D – Greg Dyer
Googly C – Andrew Zesers

Grounds in New Zealand – from page 66
1 A – Auckland
2 D – Dunedin
3 C – Christchurch
4 A – Auckland (by Walter
       Hammond)
5 D – Wellington
6 C – New Plymouth
7 A – Napier
8 A – Hamilton
9 B – Taupo
10 A – Lincoln
11 B – Timaru
Googly B – It forms a giant
traffic roundabout

Short but sweet – from p67
1 D – David Steele
2 B – Ed Giddins
3 B – Barry Richards
4 B – Kim Barnett
5 C – John Hampshire
6 C – Chetan Sharma
7 A – Ali Bacher
8 A – Archie Jackson
9 C – Raman Subba Row
10 C – Grahame Corling
11 C – Wajahatullah Wasti
Googly C – Clive Rice

Hat-tricks – from page 68
1 D – Matthew Hoggard
2 A – Shane Warne
3 B – Harbhajan Singh
4 A – James Anderson
5 C – Chaminda Vaas (against
       Bangladesh)
6 A – Jimmy Matthews
7 A – Andy Blignaut
8 B – Jalaluddin
9 C – Javagal Srinath
10 D – Wes Hall
11 B – Willie Bates
Googly C – It included three
kings (his grandfather Edward
VII, his father George V, and
his brother Edward VIII, later
the Duke of Windsor. *Wisden*
observed that this made him
"the best Royal cricketer since
Frederick, Prince of Wales, in
1751")

What's in a name? – from page 69
1 B – Durham
2 D – Yorkshire
3 D – Surrey
4 B – Bob Willis
5 B – Sussex (brothers Tony
       and Mike Buss)
6 B – Murray
7 C – Surrey (1848-67)
8 B – Greenidge
9 D – Worcestershire (1919-31,
       and later their president)
10 B – Robert Kennedy
11 A – Glamorgan (1951-55)
Googly C – Michael Slater
(Brendon Julian was actually
No. 356, but he and the
Australian Board eventually
agreed to swap numbers with
Slater)

Mixed bag – from page 70
1 B – Viv Richards
2 D – Dennis Lillee
3 A – Holland
4 D – Rachael Heyhoe-Flint
5 B – Bill Ponsford
6 C – Lee Germon
7 C – Jim Higgs
8 B – Grant Flower
9 B – Michael Bevan
10 A – Graeme Fowler
11 D – David Green (the highest
       of his 14 half-centuries
       was 85)
Googly B – Shoaib Mohammad
(the previous record was set by
his father Hanif Mohammad
and Hanif's brother Wazir)

Geoffrey Boycott – from page 71
1 A – Australia
2 B – Michael Holding
3 C – Barnsley
4 B – 1964
5 B – Fred Titmus (John
       Edrich pulled out
       injured shortly before
       the start)
6 B – India
7 C – Surrey
8 B – Herbert Sutcliffe (112)
9 C – Northern Transvaal
10 B – He bowled with his cap
       on back to front
11 C – Nottinghamshire
Googly D – Graham Roope

More hat-tricks – from page 72
1 D – Doug Wright
2 B – Mike Procter
3 A – Albert Trott
4 B – Stephen Harmison
5 D – Dean Headley
6 C – Wasim Akram
7 B – Marcus Trescothick
8 C – Jack Russell (one catch
       off Courtney Walsh and
       two off David Lawrence)
9 C – Charlie Parker
10 B – Kevan James
11 C – Tony Pigott
Googly B – It was the first hat-
trick completed on a Sunday in
English first-class cricket

ANSWERS – PAGES 73-81

The Ashes 1994-95 – from page 73

1 C – Mark Taylor
2 A – Shane Warne
3 D – Michael Slater
4 D – Steven Rhodes
5 C – Graeme Hick
6 D – Darren Gough
7 C – He had chicken-pox
8 B – Greg Blewett
9 D – Mike Gatting
10 B – Steve Waugh
11 C – Chris Lewis
Googly D – Australia "A" (whose matches – including the finals – didn't count as official one-day internationals. Some players turned out for both Australia and Australia "A")

Glamorgan – from page 74

1 A – Alan Jones
2 D – Don Shepherd
3 C – Matthew Maynard
4 C – Simon Jones
5 A – Maurice Turnbull
6 B – David Hemp
7 B – 1948
8 C – Tony Lewis
9 B – Pontypridd
10 B – Steve James
11 B – Majid Khan
Googly C – Colwyn Bay (it's in north Wales, a long way from Glamorgan's base in Cardiff)

The Waughs – from page 75

1 B – Steve (by four minutes from Mark)
2 A – Headingley, Leeds
3 C – Rodger
4 C – Steve Waugh
5 C – Somerset
6 B – Kent
7 D – Mark Taylor
8 D – West Indies (Melbourne, 2000-01)
9 C – Gary Kirsten
10 D – Western Australia
11 C – Kingston, Jamaica
Googly C – Ireland (Steve against Australia A in 1998, Mark two one-day games against Zimbabwe in 2000)

Fielding records (not wicket-keeping) – from page 76

1 B – Frank Woolley
2 C – Greg Chappell
3 D – Viv Richards
4 A – Walter Hammond
5 A – Allan Border
6 A – Mohammad Azharuddin
7 B – Jonty Rhodes
8 B – Bob Simpson
9 C – Jack Gregory
10 C – Viv Richards
11 B – Walter Hammond
Googly B – Micky Stewart (Tony Brown of Gloucestershire equalled the record in 1966)

West Indies in Tests – from page 77

1 B – Weekes, Worrell and Walcott
2 C – Guyana
3 D – Dwayne Smith
4 C – Conrad Hunte
5 B – Lance Gibbs
6 A – Clive Lloyd
7 C – Junior Murray
8 B – Courtney Browne
9 A – Seymour Nurse
10 A – Alf Valentine
11 B – Faoud Bacchus
Googly B – He was allergic to grass

The Ashes 1997 – from page 78

1 B – Nasser Hussain
2 A – Adam and Ben Hollioake
3 D – Mark Taylor
4 C – Greg Blewett
5 B – Mark Butcher
6 D – Glenn McGrath
7 D – Dean Headley
8 C – Matthew Elliott
9 A – Ricky Ponting
10 B – Mike Smith
11 C – Shaun Young
Googly C – Brian Close

Lord's Cricket Ground – from page 79

1 A – Thomas Lord
2 C – Nursery End
3 A – Graham Gooch (333 v India)
4 D – The Gherkin (because it looks rather like one)
5 C – Egg and bacon (some prefer "unwearable")
6 A – The first Twenty20 Cup match there
7 B – 1814
8 A – Gubby Allen
9 C – Denis Compton
10 C – George Headley
11 A – About the size of a tall man in a top hat
Googly D – He went down too many stairs and ended up in the basement toilets

Gloucestershire – from page 80

1 C – Craig Spearman
2 A – Walter Hammond
3 D – Gloucester
4 B – Jonty Rhodes
5 A – David Allen
6 C – David "Syd" Lawrence
7 A – Zaheer Abbas
8 A – Arthur Mailey
9 D – Tom Pugh
10 C – David Shepherd
11 A – Gilbert Jessop
Googly C – Jack Crapp

Nicknames – from page 81

1 B – Fred Trueman
2 B – Ian Botham
3 B – Joel Garner
4 D – David Lloyd
5 C – Clive Lloyd
6 C – Glenn McGrath
7 C – Graeme Fowler
8 A – Warwick Armstrong
9 C – Martin Crowe
10 C – Jeremy Coney
11 B – Bill Lawry
Googly B – Mark Waugh

ANSWERS – PAGES 82-90

Kent – from page 82
1 D – Tich Freeman
2 B – Muttiah Muralitharan
3 C – Colin Cowdrey
4 D – Matthew Fleming
5 B – Mark Benson
6 A – Frank Woolley
7 A – Aravinda de Silva
8 D – Dartford
9 A – Arthur Fagg
10 C – Steven Marsh
11 A – Bill Ashdown
Googly B – He drove the wrong way down a one-way street (but fortunately met a cricket-loving policeman, who let him off when he explained)

Fast starters – from page 83
1 A – Graeme Hick
2 B – W.G. Grace
3 A – Glenn Turner
4 D – Don Bradman
5 B – Bill Edrich
6 A – Mike Atherton
7 B – Brian Close
8 D – Derek Underwood
9 A – Joe Solomon
10 C – Charlie Hallows
11 A – Len Hutton
Googly B – Bob Simpson

The Ashes 1998-99 – from page 84
1 C – Mark Taylor
2 B – Alec Stewart
3 C – He was recovering after a shoulder operation
4 A – Alan Mullally
5 C – Stuart MacGill
6 A – Alex Tudor
7 A – Alec Stewart
8 D – Darren Gough
9 D – Warren Hegg
10 D – Dean Headley
11 C – Matthew Nicholson
Googly B – Ian Healy

Marvellous middle names: England – from page 85
1 D – David Gower
2 B – Mike Smith
3 A – Gubby Allen
4 D – Peter May
5 D – Fred Trueman
6 C – Nick Knight
7 C – Nick Cook
8 A – Ed Giddins
9 C – Clive Radley
10 A – Gilbert
11 B – Joey Benjamin
Googly B – John William Henry Tyler

The 1992 World Cup – from page 86
1 D – Pakistan
2 B – Melbourne
3 A – Imran Khan
4 D – Wasim Akram
5 C – Martin Crowe
6 B – New Zealand
7 A – Australia
8 B – Richie Richardson
9 D – Dipak Patel
10 B – David Boon
11 D – Phil Simmons
Googly C – Wasim Akram

More strange birthplaces – from page 87
1 C – Clarrie Grimmett
2 D – George Headley
3 D – Mathew Sinclair
4 B – Henry Olonga
5 A – Roger Twose
6 B – Basil D'Oliveira
7 C – Bob Crisp
8 B – Robin Singh
9 C – Lall Singh
10 A – Afghanistan
11 B – Kuwait
Googly C – John Traicos (born in Egypt, played for South Africa and Zimbabwe)

South Africa in Tests – from page 88
1 D – Gary Kirsten
2 A – Ali Bacher
3 B – Jacques Rudolph
4 C – Hugh Tayfield
5 D – Kepler Wessels (Rice captained them in their first official one-day international)
6 A – Paul Adams
7 A – Dave Richardson
8 B – Colin Bland
9 A – Andrew Hudson
10 D – Dudley Nourse
11 D – Durban
Googly C – Lee Irvine

One-day international batting records – from page 89
1 D – Sachin Tendulkar
2 B – Viv Richards
3 B – Saeed Anwar
4 B – Shahid Afridi
5 B – Dennis Amiss
6 A – Zaheer Abbas
7 D – Sanath Jayasuriya
8 C – Jacques Kallis
9 B – Nick Knight
10 C – Javed Miandad
11 B – Geoff Boycott
Googly C – Sunil Gavaskar

Lancashire – from page 90
1 B – Brian Statham
2 B – Stuart Law
3 A – Iain Sutcliffe
4 D – David Hughes
5 B – Graeme Fowler
6 C – Chris Schofield
7 C – Glen Chapple
8 C – Blackpool
9 A – Andrew Kennedy
10 C – Leonard Green
11 D – Ted McDonald
Googly D – Sonny Ramadhin (whose daughter married the former Lancashire fast bowler Willie Hogg)

ANSWERS – PAGES 91-99

**Sachin Tendulkar –
from page 91**
1 C – 16
2 D – Pakistan
3 B – Vinod Kambli
4 B – Old Trafford,
 Manchester
5 D – Rahul Dravid
6 A – Ramesh
7 D – Namibia
8 B – New Zealand
9 A – Australia
10 D – Kris Srikkanth
11 B – Viv Richards
Googly D – Steve Waugh

**The 1996 World Cup –
from page 92**
1 C – Sri Lanka
2 C – Lahore
3 B – Arjuna Ranatunga
4 A – Aravinda de Silva
5 C – Kenya
6 B – Sanath Jayasuriya
7 A – Keith Arthurton
8 D – United Arab Emirates
9 D – Mark Waugh
10 D – Nolan Clarke
11 A – Nathan Astle
Googly C – Sri Lanka won by
default when the crowd rioted
after India collapsed

**Initially speaking –
from page 93**
1 C – Colin Cowdrey
2 C – Chaminda (W.P.U.J.C.)
 Vaas
3 B – Mike Smith
4 A – Aravinda de Silva
5 C – Alan Knott
6 B – Stuart MacGill
7 D – Peter May
8 B – Gubby Allen
9 B – Roland Holder
10 C – "Chud" Langton
11 A – Chris Duckworth
Googly B – He collected Test
cricket's fastest pair (inside 120
minutes for both innings)

**New Zealand in Tests –
from page 94**
1 B – Richard Hadlee
2 A – Ian Smith
3 C – John Bracewell
4 A – John Reid
5 B – Trevor Franklin
6 D – Dunedin
7 A – Glenn Turner
8 A – Geoff Allott
9 C – Scott Styris
10 B – Peter Petherick
11 D – Dick Motz
Googly D – He never finished
on the winning side

**Who said that? –
from page 95**
1 A – Jonathan Agnew
2 D – Fred Trueman
3 B – John Bracewell
4 B – Don Bradman
5 A – Angus Fraser
6 C – Ian Chappell
7 C – Robert Mugabe
8 C – Neville Cardus
9 C – Meat Loaf
10 A – Arthur Mailey
11 D – Tommy Docherty
Googly D – Groucho Marx

**Pakistan's Mohammad
brothers – from page 96**
1 D – Wazir
2 C – Sadiq
3 A – Northamptonshire
4 B – Gloucestershire
5 D – Zaheer Abbas
6 C – Shoaib Mohammad
7 A – Raees
8 B – Mushtaq
9 C – Nazar
10 A – Khan
11 C – Junagadh (in Gujarat)
Googly D – New Zealand

**England's one-cap wonders
– from page 97**
1 A – Alan Butcher
2 C – Alan Wells
3 B – Andy Lloyd
4 C – Paul Parker
5 B – Mark Benson
6 C – Ken Palmer
7 B – Neil Williams
8 B – Joey Benjamin
9 D – Andy Ducat
10 A – Norman Oldfield
11 C – Charles "Father"
 Marriott
Googly C – John Stephenson

**Leicestershire –
from page 98**
1 C – Brad Hodge
2 B – Ray Illingworth
3 C – Virender Sehwag
4 A – Jonathan Agnew
5 B – Ken Higgs
6 D – Oakham School
7 D – David Gower
8 B – Paul Nixon
9 A – James Whitaker
10 D – Cyril Wood
11 C – George Geary
Googly A – He played county
cricket (for Leicestershire v
Derbyshire, scoring 51 not out
and completing his century the
next day; they clinched the
Championship title during his
innings) then nipped up the
road to play for Doncaster
Rovers against Brentford (they
drew 1-1)

**The Chappells –
from page 99**
1 A – Ian
2 C – Melbourne
3 B – He scored a century in
 each innings
4 B – Bangladesh
5 C – Vic Richardson
6 C – Perth
7 D – Sydney
8 D – Somerset
9 C – Wellington
10 C – Bob Simpson
11 B – Baseball
Googly B – Rod Marsh and
Dennis Lillee

ANSWERS – PAGES 100-107

The Ashes 2001 – from page 100
1 C – Mike Atherton
2 A – Adam Gilchrist
3 B – Mark Butcher
4 A – Adam Gilchrist
5 B – Usman Afzaal
6 C – Simon Katich
7 B – Mark Ramprakash
8 B – Glenn McGrath (Warne took 31)
9 C – Jimmy Ormond
10 D – Justin Langer
11 A – Mike Atherton
Googly D – Three ducks waddling behind the bowler's arm (Blewett was lbw to James Brinkley for 3)

More middle names – from page 101
1 C – George
2 B – Michael Bevan
3 B – Vinoo Mankad
4 C – Jock Cameron
5 C – Everton Matambanadzo
6 D – Kepler Wessels
7 B – Neil Hawke
8 D – Duncan Sharpe
9 C – Jack Badcock
10 B – Jack Richards
11 B – Murphy Su'a
Googly C – Chris Kuggeleijn (he was of Dutch extraction)

India v Australia 2000-01 – from page 102
1 B – Sourav Ganguly
2 A – Border-Gavaskar Trophy
3 B – Adam Gilchrist
4 D – Rahul Dravid
5 C – 16
6 A – Ajit Agarkar
7 B – Harbhajan Singh
8 B – Twice (both by England against Australia, at Sydney in 1894-95 and Headingley in 1981)
9 D – Samir Dighe
10 D – Matthew Hayden
11 A – Steve Waugh
Googly C – Peter Willey

Marvellous middle names: West Indies – from page 103
1 D – Garry Sobers
2 B – Kenny Benjamin
3 C – Colin Croft
4 A – Curtly Ambrose
5 B – Eldine Baptiste
6 D – Darren Sammy
7 B – Tino Best
8 B – Frank Worrell
9 A – Gerry Alexander (his real first name was Franz)
10 D – Easton McMorris
11 B – Collie Smith
Googly D – Nixon McLean

Richie Benaud – from page 104
1 A – New South Wales
2 D – West Indies
3 B – 2000 runs/200 wickets
4 C – Colin McDonald
5 C – Ian Craig
6 A – Peter May
7 D – France
8 C – Neil Harvey
9 D – John
10 B – It came after he had been dropped for the next Test (after this the Australian practice of sometimes announcing the next Test side mid-match was shelved)
11 D – 500 (he got there in 2004)
Googly C – He took all 20 wickets in a two-innings game (10 for 30 and 10 for 35 for Penrith Waratahs against St Marys)

Keeping it in the family – from page 105
1 B – Mark Waugh
2 D – Dean Headley
3 C – Martin Crowe
4 A – Mohinder Amarnath
5 C – Adam and Ben Hollioake
6 D – Mudassar Nazar
7 A – Arnie Sidebottom (Ryan is his son)
8 B – Middlesex
9 B – Pat Pocock
10 D – David Lloyd (Graham is his son)
11 C – Pedro Collins and Fidel Edwards
Googly C – Fred Tate

Northamptonshire – from page 106
1 C – Allan Lamb
2 D – Phil Jaques
3 B – Freddie Brown
4 C – Frank Tyson
5 B – Michael Hussey
6 D – David Steele
7 C – Luton
8 A – Raman Subba Row
9 C – Gloucestershire
10 B – David Larter
11 A – Vallance Jupp
Googly B – They beat Leicestershire by an innings and 153 runs in May 1939 (the local paper enthused: "Northants break a bad spell")

England v West Indies: The Wisden Trophy 2000 – from page 107
1 A – Jimmy Adams
2 B – First ground to stage 100 Tests
3 C – Andy Caddick
4 B – Matthew Hoggard
5 A – Marcus Trescothick
6 A – Alec Stewart
7 A – Andy Caddick
8 A – Curtly Ambrose
9 A – Mike Atherton
10 B – Mahendra Nagamootoo
11 C – Craig White
Googly C – John Hampshire (in 1969 he had scored 107 on his Test debut at Lord's: in 2000 he umpired the memorable Lord's Test)

ANSWERS – PAGES 108-115

Middlesex – from page 108
1 D – Fred Titmus
2 B – Mike Brearley
3 C – Denis Compton
4 C – Chad Keegan
5 C – Angus Fraser
6 A – Phil Edmonds
7 B – Southgate
8 D – Patsy Hendren
9 A – Gubby Allen
10 B – Mann (Frank and George)
11 D – Pelham Warner
Googly B – Alec Douglas-Home (as "Lord Dunglass". He was a handy fast bowler who won his 2nd XI cap for Middlesex)

The Ashes 2002-03 – from page 109
1 C – Michael Vaughan
2 B – Simon Jones
3 C – Steve Waugh
4 D – Matthew Hayden
5 D – James Foster
6 A – Andy Caddick
7 A – 11 (a record)
8 C – Martin Love
9 C – Craig White
10 C – Craig White (his brother-in-law is Darren Lehmann)
11 C – Chris Silverwood
Googly B – They stopped sledging (insulting) him

India in Tests – from page 110
1 B – Sunil Gavaskar
2 C – Kapil Dev
3 D – Sunil Gavaskar
4 C – Laxman Sivaramakrishnan
5 A – Ajit Wadekar
6 C – Farokh Engineer
7 B – Nawab of Pataudi junior
8 C – Cuttack
9 A – Abbas Ali Baig
10 D – Dilip Doshi (the first was Clarrie Grimmett)
11 C – Madhav Mantri
Googly B – They were 0 for 4, the worst Test start (Fred Trueman, on his debut, took seven wickets in the match)

Bodyline – from page 111
1 D – Douglas Jardine
2 C – Bill Woodfull
3 A – Harold Larwood
4 B – Bert Oldfield
5 C – He was ill
6 C – Stan McCabe
7 C – Bill Bowes
8 A – Gubby Allen
9 B – Freddie Brown
10 B – Bert Ironmonger
11 C – Hugh Buggy (the word "Bodyline" appeared in his copy in the *Melbourne Herald* on the first day of the first Test)
Googly C – Harold Larwood

W.G. Grace – from page 112
1 D – Doctor
2 C – Gloucestershire
3 C – The Coroner
4 D – Three (W.G., E.M. and G.F.)
5 B – London County
6 C – Crystal Palace
7 C – 50
8 A – Wilfred Rhodes
9 C – He scored 1000 runs in May
10 A – Gentlemen
11 B – Bowls
Googly C – He ran an extra three runs with the ball still stuck (according to *Wisden* 1916, eventually "he was stopped, and Jupp asked him to give up the ball, but this he wisely declined to do, as he might have been adjudged out for handling the ball")

One-cap wonders from around the world – from page 113
1 B – Stuart Law
2 B – Gavin Hamilton
3 C – Robin Singh
4 A – Andy Ganteaume
5 B – Banerjee
6 B – Iain Butchart
7 B – Tertius Bosch
8 A – Tony Howard
9 B – Victor Stollmeyer
10 B – John Rutherford
11 C – Ken Eastwood
Googly C – She dropped her knitting, and he was out while she picked it up

Debut hundreds – from page 114
1 A – Andrew Strauss
2 B – Mohammad Azharuddin
3 C – Gundappa Viswanath
4 D – David Sales
5 D – Desmond Haynes
6 B – Ali Naqvi
7 B – Kepler Wessels
8 B – Peter Bowler
9 A – Andy Flower
10 B – Bruce Taylor
11 C – Greg Chappell
Googly C – Keith Miller (181 for Victoria v Tasmania in 1937-38, then 102* for Nottinghamshire v Cambridge University in 1959)

The 1977 Centenary Test – from page 115
1 B – Tony Greig
2 B – Greg Chappell
3 D – David Hookes
4 D – Dennis Lillee
5 B – Rick McCosker
6 C – Kerry O'Keeffe
7 B – Rod Marsh
8 A – Dennis Amiss
9 A – Alan Knott
10 C – Chris Old
11 D – Jack Ryder
Googly B – Hans Ebeling

ANSWERS – PAGES 116-122

Australian domestic cricket – from page 116

1 B – Lord Sheffield
2 B – Pura (Milk) Cup
3 C – Victoria (against NSW)
4 A – New South Wales
5 D – Western Australia
6 B – Jamie Siddons
7 C – Clarrie Grimmett
8 B – Don Bradman
9 C – Stuart Law
10 D – Tim Wall
11 C – Martin Love
Googly C – Retired "out" (he walked off believing he'd been caught in the gully, but at the end of the day the umpire informed him it hadn't been a catch)

Somerset – from page 117

1 D – Viv Richards
2 B – Brian Close
3 B – Ian Blackwell
4 A – Bill Alley
5 B – Brian Rose
6 D – Brian Langford
7 D – Weston-super-Mare
8 C – Brian Close
9 C – Harold Gimblett
10 D – Marcus Trescothick
11 C – Colin McCool
Googly C – Brian Rose

The 1999 World Cup – from page 118

1 A – Australia
2 B – Steve Waugh
3 C – Shane Warne
4 A – Allan Donald
5 B – Alec Stewart
6 C – Gavin Hamilton
7 D – Rahul Dravid
8 B – Saqlain Mushtaq
9 A – Geoff Allott
10 C – Henry Olonga
11 A – Saeed Anwar
Googly B – Herschelle Gibbs, who dropped the ball in the act of throwing it up in celebration; Waugh went on to score a matchwinning century, Australia qualified after all, and went on to win the World Cup

Mind the gap – from page 119

1 B – Martin Bicknell
2 D – Younis Ahmed
3 D – George Gunn
4 C – Mike Gatting
5 D – Martin Donnelly
6 D – Tommy Spencer
7 C – Philip Mead
8 C – George Carew
9 D – Derek Shackleton
10 A – Alan Melville (one in 1938-39, then three more after the War in 1947)
11 D – Les Jackson
Googly B – He played for South Africa (in their last three Tests before excommunication in 1969-70) and then Zimbabwe (in their first four Tests in 1992-93)

Jim Laker – from page 120

1 D – Yorkshire
2 A – Old Trafford, Manchester
3 C – Tony Lock
4 B – Jim Burke
5 C – Neil Harvey
6 A – The Australians again (for Surrey at The Oval)
7 C – Tony Lock
8 D – West Indies (Bridgetown 1947-48)
9 C – Jim McConnon
10 A – Essex
11 C – Clyde Walcott
Googly C – 8 for 2 (from 14 overs, with 12 maidens. The two runs he conceded reputedly included "one off the mark" for his Surrey team-mate Eric Bedser. *Wisden* observed that "the young batsmen opposed to Laker did not possess the ripe experience needed to cope with his skill under conditions so suited to his bowling")

Ever-present – from page 121

1 A – Allan Border
2 A – Mike Atherton
3 C – Sunil Gavaskar
4 A – Tony Greig
5 A – Alan Knott
6 B – Kapil Dev
7 C – John Reid
8 C – Alistair Campbell
9 C – Sachin Tendulkar
10 C – Colin Cowdrey
11 C – David Constant
Googly C – Ken Suttle (for Sussex; Binks made 412 for Yorkshire between 1955 and 1969, and didn't miss one between his debut and his retirement)

Sussex – from page 122

1 B – K.S. Ranjitsinhji
2 A – Chris Adams
3 B – John Snow
4 A – Mushtaq Ahmed
5 D – Ted Dexter
6 D – Eastbourne
7 C – 1963
8 D – Maurice Tate
9 B – Kepler Wessels
10 B – John Langridge
11 A – Alan Oakman
Googly C – His wedding. He needn't have bothered: the ceremony was set for the fourth scheduled day of the match, at Wellington, and New Zealand won inside three days

ANSWERS – PAGES 123-130

Headingley '81 –
from page 123
1 C – Mike Brearley (replaced Ian Botham)
2 C – 500-1
3 D – John Dyson
4 D – Rod Marsh (beat Alan Knott's record)
5 B – Bob Taylor (beat John Murray's record)
6 C – Ian Botham
7 D – Ian Botham
8 B – Bob Willis
9 C – Trevor Chappell
10 D – Graham Dilley
11 B – Once (England beat Australia at Sydney in 1894-95)
Googly B – Jack Gregory (100 and 7 for 69 for Australia at Melbourne in 1920-21)

England v Australia –
from page 124
1 B – Melbourne
2 A – Australia won by 45 runs
3 A – Allan Border
4 C – Rod Marsh
5 C – Mark Taylor
6 D – Dennis Lillee
7 D – Graham Thorpe
8 C – Tom Graveney
9 B – Barry Jarman
10 D – Jack Hobbs
11 B – Syd Gregory
Googly A – He said he wanted to know who they were playing

Grounds in the West Indies –
from page 125
1 A – Georgetown, Guyana
2 C – Kingston, Jamaica
3 A – St John's, Antigua
4 C – Kingston, Jamaica
5 A – St John's, Antigua
6 B – Bridgetown, Barbados
7 C – Kingston, Jamaica
8 C – Grenada (the Old and New Queen's Park grounds in St George's)
9 B – Bridgetown, Barbados
10 A – Georgetown, Guyana
11 A – Arnos Vale, St Vincent
Googly C – Peter Willey (1980-81)

Mixed bag 2 –
from page 126
1 B – Sachin Tendulkar
2 B – Brian Statham
3 B – It was made of aluminium
4 A – Andrew Symonds
5 C – Tatenda Taibu (2004)
6 D – South Africa (beat Australia in the final)
7 B – Jason Gallian
8 A – Michael Hussey
9 C – Wilf Slack
10 C – 1962
11 B – Jahangir Khan (his son was Majid Khan, and his nephews Javed Burki and Imran Khan)
Googly A – It took him 96 minutes to get off the mark

A funny way to go –
from page 127
1 D – Graham Gooch
2 A – Steve Waugh
3 B – Mohinder Amarnath
4 C – Len Hutton
5 B – Handled the ball
6 D – Michael Vaughan
7 A – Andrew Hilditch
8 B – Vinoo Mankad
9 D – Dean Jones
10 B – Roy Fredericks
11 B – It hit short leg (Eric Freeman) on the head and ballooned 30 yards to square leg
Googly D – Absent bathing (Peebles wrote, in *Spinner's Yarn*: "As our batsmen were soon well entrenched I went with a couple of local lads to bathe in a nearby river. The time passed more quickly than we calculated and, when I got back, we were in the field and I was soundly and properly berated by Ronny [Stanyforth, MCC's captain]"

England v South Africa –
from page 128
1 B – Kepler Wessels
2 C – Graeme Smith
3 A – Mike Atherton
4 C – Denis Compton
5 D – Allan Donald
6 C – Marcus Trescothick
7 D – Peter Kirsten
8 B – Peter May
9 D – Peter van der Merwe
10 C – Steve Elworthy
11 A – None (unusual for such a short time-span)
Googly B – Pat Symcox

The 2003 World Cup –
from page 129
1 C – Ricky Ponting
2 D – Kenya and Sri Lanka
3 B – Brett Lee (against Kenya)
4 B – Steve Bucknor and David Shepherd
5 A – Sachin Tendulkar
6 D – Chaminda Vaas
7 B – Bangladesh
8 C – Sri Lanka
9 C – Rudi van Vuuren
10 D – Andy Bichel
11 D – Namibia
Googly D – John Davison

Warwickshire –
from page 130
1 A – Nick Knight
2 B – Mike Smith
3 A – Dennis Amiss
4 B – Bob Wyatt
5 C – Collins Obuya
6 D – Norman Gifford
7 A – Stratford-upon-Avon
8 B – John Whitehouse
9 D – Tom Dollery
10 B – Neil Smith
11 C – Combined Services
Googly B – He took off his pads and bowled – and took a hat-trick (the first three wickets in Essex's second innings as they chased 203 to win. Smith's figures were 21-10-36-4, but Essex hung on for a draw at 141 for 9)

ANSWERS – PAGES 131-139

**Test match firsts –
from page 131**
1 A – Allan Border
2 C – Courtney Walsh
3 C – Colin Cowdrey
4 C – Sunil Gavaskar
5 A – Richard Hadlee
6 C – Rod Marsh
7 D – Garry Sobers
8 C – Fred Trueman
9 D – Walter Hammond
10 D – Walter Hammond
11 B – Johnny Briggs
Googly C – Ian Botham

**Pakistan in Tests –
from page 132**
1 A – Wasim Akram
2 A – Hanif Mohammad
3 B – Imran Khan
4 B – Wasim Bari
5 B – Wasim Akram
6 A – Zaheer Abbas
7 D – Fazal Mahmood
8 B – Faisalabad
9 C – Nazar Mohammad
10 D – Yasir Hameed
11 C – Imtiaz Ahmed
Googly D – Khizar Hayat

**Bookworms –
from page 133**
1 D – Steve Waugh
2 A – Mike Brearley
3 D – Douglas Jardine
4 A – Peter Roebuck
5 B – Richie Benaud
6 C – Frances Edmonds
7 C – Jack Fingleton
8 D – Simon Hughes
9 A – Jack Iverson
10 B – Ed Smith
11 B – Peter West
Googly C – Cricketers who
committed suicide

Yorkshire – from page 134
1 C – Craig White
2 B – Fred Trueman
3 A – Matthew Hoggard
4 B – Sachin Tendulkar
5 C – Herbert Sutcliffe
6 A – Ray Illingworth
7 C – Wilfred Rhodes
8 C – Sheffield
9 D – Norman Yardley
10 C – Paul Jarvis
11 C – Martyn Moxon
Googly C – He was born in
France rather than Yorkshire
(in Nice, of parents from
Bradford; he was the last
person born outside Yorkshire
to play for them until the
home-only policy was relaxed
in the 1990s)

**World Cup: general –
from page 135**
1 B – Javed Miandad
2 D – Imran Khan
3 B – Wasim Akram
4 D – Graham Gooch
5 C – Tom Moody
6 C – Graeme Hick
7 D – Darren Lehmann
8 B – Pramodya
Wickremasinghe
9 C – Michael Bevan
10 B – Barry Hadlee
11 B – Swansea
Googly A – Aasif Karim

**England v West Indies –
from page 136**
1 B – The Wisden Trophy
2 A – Sonny Ramadhin and Alf
Valentine
3 C – Michael Holding
4 D – David Gower
5 C – Viv Richards
6 B – Grant (Jackie and Rolph)
7 A – Peter Loader
8 C – Chris Cowdrey
9 A – Andy Sandham
10 C – Richard Illingworth
11 D – John Hampshire
Googly B – It was his first first-
class century outside his native
island (Jamaica)

**Slow starters 2 –
from page 137**
1 C – Imran Khan
2 A – Marvan Atapattu
3 C – Mudassar Nazar
4 B – Trevor Bailey
5 B – New Zealand
6 B – Bill Lawry
7 A – Geoff Allott
8 C – Derek Underwood
9 C – Wilfred Rhodes
10 B – Brendon Kuruppu
11 C – M.L. Jaisimha
Googly C – Sunil Gavaskar

**African grounds –
from page 138**
1 B – Johannesburg
2 A – Port Elizabeth
3 B – Johannesburg
4 B – Benoni
5 D – Durban
6 C – Centurion
7 C – East London
8 B – Bulawayo Athletic Club
9 D – Nairobi Gymkhana
10 D – Lindsay Kline
11 D – Potchefstroom
Googly D – Graeme Hick

**One-day international
bowling records –
from page 139**
1 D – Wasim Akram
2 C – Chaminda Vaas
3 A – Fidel Edwards
4 A – Aqib Javed
5 A – Ashish Nehra
6 D – Winston Davis
7 C – Courtney Walsh
8 A – Joel Garner
9 C – Rikki Clarke
10 A – Geoff Arnold
11 D – Saqlain Mushtaq
Googly A – Alan "Froggy"
Thomson

ANSWERS – PAGES 140-148

Nottinghamshire –
from page 140
1 B – Kevin Pietersen
2 B – Franklyn Stephenson
3 A – Jason Gallian
4 B – Bruce Dooland
5 C – George Gunn
6 D – Worksop
7 C – Larwood and Voce
8 B – Paul Franks
9 A – Reg Simpson
10 B – Chris Broad
11 A – Keith Miller
Googly C – Lord's was being
used for the Eton v Harrow
match

Eden Gardens, Kolkata –
from page 141
1 A – 1987
2 A – Australia
3 B – V.V.S. Laxman
4 C – Harbhajan Singh
5 C – Lance Klusener
6 B – Saeed Anwar
7 B – 1934
8 B – Rohan Kanhai
9 D – Sri Lanka
10 C – Pankaj Roy
11 B – Gursharan Singh
Googly D – Everton Weekes
(162 and 101 in 1948-49)

England v New Zealand –
from page 142
1 B – 1930
2 D – 48 (they didn't win one
until 1977-78)
3 D – John Edrich
4 D – Richard Hadlee
5 B – Mark Richardson
6 A – Nathan Astle
7 B – Alex Tudor
8 D – Geoff Howarth
9 A – Maurice Allom
10 B – Brian Close
11 C – Tony Lock
Googly A – He was knighted
(and appeared on the new
electronic scoreboard as "Sir R.
Hadlee", as there wasn't room
for his full name)

Cricketer-footballers –
from page 143
1 C – Geoff Hurst
2 D – Denis Compton
3 C – Viv Richards
4 B – Gary Lineker
5 A – Andy Goram
6 C – Graham Cross
7 A – Steve Bucknor
8 D – Willie Watson
9 C – Tony Cottey
10 C – "Tip" Foster
11 B – Phil Neville
Googly B – They were both
played on Christmas Day

England v India –
from page 144
1 C – Graham Gooch
2 B – Ian Botham
3 D – Rahul Dravid
4 A – Fred Trueman
5 B – Sourav Ganguly
6 A – John Lever
7 D – David Lloyd
8 C – 1932
9 D – Douglas Jardine
10 C – Yajurvindra Singh
11 A – Bapu Nadkarni
Googly C – Eddie Hemmings

The Melbourne Cricket
Ground – from page 145
1 C – Steve Waugh
2 B – Virender Sehwag
3 D – Derek Randall
4 D – Hugh Trumble
5 A – 1877
6 A – Graham Yallop
7 C – Olympic Games
8 C – Colonial Stadium
(Docklands)
9 C – Bob Cowper
10 C – 1992
11 C – Gary Cosier
Googly B – A Billy Graham
crusade (approximately
130,000 in 1959)

The ICC Trophy –
from page 146
1 B – Sri Lanka (not then a
Test-playing country)
2 C – Ole Mortensen
3 D – Zimbabwe
4 D – Dermot Reeve
5 D – Zimbabwe
6 A – Sew Shivnarine
7 A – Holland
8 C – Nolan Clarke
9 D – United Arab Emirates
10 B – Steve Tikolo
11 D – Holland
Googly D – Ireland

Autobiographies –
from page 147
1 B – Dickie Bird
2 B – Ian Botham
3 C – Jack Russell
4 D – Allan Donald
5 A – Allan Border
6 B – Brian Close
7 D – Dennis Lillee
8 D – Ian Meckiff (who was
no-balled out of the
game in 1963-64)
9 D – John Snow
10 C – Godfrey Evans
11 D – Jim Laker
Googly C – Jim Swanton

Zimbabwe in Tests –
from page 148
1 B – Bulawayo
2 C – 1992
3 D – Dave Houghton
4 B – Neil Johnson
5 B – Gary Crocker
6 B – John Traicos
7 A – Andy Flower
8 C – Hamilton Masakadza
9 D – Murray Goodwin
10 D – Paul Strang
11 C – Adam Huckle
Googly C – Andy and Guy
Whittall (Andy was 12th man –
but in any case he and Guy
Whittall are cousins, not
brothers)

ANSWERS – PAGES 149-156

World Series Cricket – from page 149

1 C – 1977
2 D – Ian Chappell
3 C – Tony Greig
4 A – Super Tests
5 C – Channel Nine
6 B – Richie Benaud
7 D – David Hookes
8 B – Ian Redpath
9 D – Denys Hobson
10 A – Alvin Kallicharran
11 D – Dennis Lillee
Googly B – They were bright pink (the colour worn by gay men in the Caribbean)

Mixed bag 3 – from page 150

1 A – Surrey
2 C – Leicestershire
3 A – Mark Alleyne
4 D – Darren Lehmann
5 C – Mark Robinson (seven of the 12 innings were not-outs)
6 B – Richard Collinge
7 C – Matthew Hayden
8 C – Roy Marshall
9 B – Brian Booth
10 B – Bart King (for the touring Gentlemen of Philadelphia team)
11 B – Bob Taylor
Googly B – Batting at No. 10 and 11, they both scored centuries

Women's cricket – from p151

1 D – Rachael Heyhoe-Flint
2 B – Belinda Clark
3 B – Karen Smithies
4 B – Kirsty Flavell
5 C – Sarah Potter
6 B – Kiran Baluch
7 D – Debbie Hockley
8 D – Denise Alderman (later Mrs Emerson)
9 D – Karen Hadlee, (then) wife of Richard
10 D – Betty Wilson
11 D – Zoe Goss
Googly B – She wasn't a lesbian (she told ABC TV she had been omitted from a tour of New Zealand because she was heterosexual and married; questions were asked in the New South Wales parliament)

Bangladesh in Tests – from page 152

1 C – Chittagong
2 C – 2000
3 A – Aminul Islam
4 D – Naimur Rahman
5 A – Alok Kapali
6 B – Mohammad Ashraful
7 B – Habibul Bashar
8 B – Mohammad Rafique
9 D – Dav Whatmore
10 A – Jermaine Lawson
11 C – Javed Omar
Googly B – Alan Knott

The Oval – from page 153

1 C – Surrey
2 C – Vauxhall End
3 D – Neil Fairbrother
4 B – Len Hutton
5 B – The Prince of Wales (it's part of the Duchy of Cornwall, which is why Surrey's badge is the Prince of Wales feathers)
6 C – 1880
7 A – Bobby Abel
8 C – Frank Hayes
9 D – Raman Subba Row
10 C – Prisoner-of-war camp
11 A – Alan Butcher
Googly A – The FA Cup final (The Wanderers beat the Royal Engineers 1-0)

England v Pakistan – from page 154

1 D – 1954
2 C – Imran Khan
3 A – Abdul Qadir
4 B – Melbourne (in 1992)
5 C – Ken Barrington
6 D – Javed Miandad
7 D – Ted Dexter
8 A – Aamir Sohail
9 A – Alec Stewart
10 B – Nasim-ul-Ghani
11 A – David Gower
Googly C – They were all dismissed for 99 (the first such threesome in Test history)

West Indian domestic cricket – from page 155

1 A – Shell Shield
2 B – Barbados
3 C – Leeward Islands
4 D – Frank Worrell
5 B – St Lucia
6 C – Grenada
7 D – George Headley
8 B – Jeff Stollmeyer
9 A – Anguilla
10 C – St Lucia
11 B – Barbados
Googly C – Eddie Hemmings

Sponsors – from page 156

1 C – npower
2 A – Frizzell Insurance
3 B – Brylcreem
4 D – Schweppes
5 C – Cornhill Insurance
6 B – Britannic Assurance
7 D – Refuge Assurance
8 C – Cricinfo
9 C – The Walter Lawrence Trophy
10 C – Reliance
11 B – Benson & Hedges
Googly D – Gillette

ANSWERS – PAGES 157-165

The Sydney Cricket Ground – from page 157

1 A – New South Wales
2 B – Brian Lara
3 B – Sid Barnes
4 B – Allan Border
5 C – 1882
6 A – Shane Warne
7 C – "Tip" Foster
8 B – England
9 A – Arthur Morris
10 A – Gerry Alexander
11 D – Yabba

Googly A – He was born on the site of the ground (in 1870 – his father was the groundsman there) and died within throwing distance of it in 1929

England v Sri Lanka – from page 158

1 B – 1982
2 D – Keith Fletcher
3 B – Bandula Warnapura
4 A – Muttiah Muralitharan
5 D – Sanath Jayasuriya
6 B – Alec Stewart
7 C – Jack Russell
8 B – Sidath Wettimuny
9 C – Nasser Hussain
10 A – Marvan Atapattu
11 C – Marcus Trescothick

Googly C – The BBC insisted on waiting until the daily screening of *Neighbours* was over

Mixed bag 4 – from page 159

1 B – England (v West Indies at Headingley)
2 B – Percy Fender
3 B – Brian Lara (on his way to 501 not out)
4 D – Zaheer Abbas
5 D – Tony Dodemaide
6 B – Qasim Omar
7 B – Allan Border
8 B – Sajid Mahmood
9 A – Alex Wharf
10 C – Tatenda Taibu
11 B – Peter Richardson

Googly B – Nottinghamshire (Billy Barnes, Wilfred Flowers, William Gunn, William Scotton, Mordecai Sherwin and the captain Arthur Shrewsbury)

Australia v New Zealand – from page 160

1 C – 1946
2 B – Bill Brown
3 D – 28 (not till 1973-74)
4 C – Richard Hadlee
5 A – Allan Border
6 C – Greg Chappell
7 D – Tony Dodemaide
8 C – Jeff Crowe
9 D – Glenn Turner
10 B – Lou Vincent
11 A – Shane Warne

Googly B – The batsman was his cousin (New Zealand's John F. Reid)

Old Trafford – from page 161

1 A – Lancashire
2 D – Graham Thorpe
3 B – Mike Atherton
4 B – Brian Close
5 A – Bob Simpson
6 C – Dominic Cork
7 B – 1884
8 B – Victor Trumper
9 D – Jason Gallian
10 A – Abbas Ali Baig
11 A – Jack Flavell

Googly C – Neville Cardus

Indian domestic cricket – from page 162

1 D – Ranji Trophy
2 B – Bombay (later Mumbai)
3 D – Duleep Trophy
4 C – C.K. Nayudu
5 B – Gundappa Viswanath
6 A – Sunil Gavaskar
7 A – Ajay Sharma
8 C – Railways
9 D – Debashish Mohanty
10 D – Dhruv Pandove
11 B – Padmakar Shivalkar

Googly C – First first-class innings longer than 1000 minutes (1015 in all, beating Hanif Mohammad's old record of 970)

Mixed bag 5 – from page 163

1 C – Smith and Bravo
2 B – Holland
3 D – Everton Weekes
4 C – Vinod Kambli
5 D – Bob Holland
6 D – The 1965 *Wisden* solemnly observed that Peter Cat's "ninth life ended on November 5, 1964"
7 B – Dennis Lindsay
8 C – Paul Reiffel
9 C – Imran Khan
10 B – Ian Johnson
11 D – Glenn McGrath

Googly C – Racing cheetahs, as a more exciting alternative to greyhounds

Grounds around the world 2 – from page 164

1 B – Lahore
2 B – Lord's
3 C – Sharjah
4 C – Faisalabad
5 A – Amstelveen, Amsterdam
6 A – Asgiriya Stadium, Kandy
7 C – Peshawar
8 D – Fort Lauderdale
9 B – Sahiwal
10 B – Morocco
11 A – Multan

Googly C – Vancouver, Canada

Wisden Cricketer of the 20th Century: Shane Warne – from page 165

1 D – Victoria
2 A – Keith
3 B – Hampshire
4 B – Mike Gatting
5 C – 23
6 A – India
7 A – Allan Border
8 B – Hashan Tillakaratne
9 B – He was banned (he had failed a drug test after taking a slimming tablet given to him by his mother)
10 A – Alec Stewart
11 C – Devon Malcolm

Googly C – A cheeseburger in each hand

ANSWERS – PAGES 166-171

Grounds in India – from page 166

1 B – Bangalore
2 A – Chandigarh
3 D – Delhi
4 C – Chennai (Madras)
5 B – Pune
6 A – Wankhede Stadium
7 C – Chennai (Madras; it's now called the M.A. Chidambaram Stadium)
8 C – Chennai (Madras)
9 B – Pune
10 B – Bryan Valentine (Lala Amarnath scored India's first in the second innings of the same match)
11 B – Jullundur
Googly C – It was the only first-class match ever played at the ground

Near-misses – from page 167

1 B – Don Bradman
2 C – Martin Crowe
3 A – Andrew Hall
4 B – Steve Waugh
5 B – Stephen Fleming
6 B – Greg Blewett
7 B – Norman Yardley
8 D – Dipak Patel
9 A – John Wright
10 A – Asim Kamal
11 C – Mike Smith
Googly C – Clem Hill

England v Zimbabwe – from page 168

1 A – 1996
2 D – Drawn, with the scores level
3 B – Bulawayo
4 D – David Lloyd
5 B – Eddo Brandes
6 A – James Anderson
7 D – Richard Johnson
8 C – Graeme Hick
9 B – Ed Giddins
10 C – Henry Olonga
11 A – Albury
Googly A – All five wickets were lbw

Domestic cricket around the world – from page 169

1 C – Pakistan
2 A – Plunket Shield
3 B – Hanif Mohammad
4 D – David Hookes
5 B – Bert Sutcliffe
6 B – Logan Cup
7 C – Colombo
8 A – Arthur Morris
9 C – Clive Inman (1965)
10 B – Peter Fulton
11 B – Naved Latif
Googly C – His plane had been delayed and he hadn't reached the ground

Australia v West Indies – from page 170

1 C – The Frank Worrell Trophy
2 A – 1960
3 C – Clyde Walcott
4 C – Ricky Ponting
5 A – Jimmy Adams
6 D – Jermaine Lawson
7 C – Courtney Walsh
8 B – Glenn McGrath
9 B – Bob Simpson
10 D – Denis Atkinson
11 B – Herman Griffith
Googly B – It was spread over three different overs (last ball of one over, first ball of next to end the first innings, first ball of second innings)

Wisden – from page 171

1 B – John Wisden
2 C – 1864
3 B – Michael Vaughan
4 D – West Indies (the trophy was presented to mark the publication of the 100th Almanack, in 1963)
5 A – Matthew Engel
6 D – Sussex
7 C – America and Canada (Wisden hated the choppy boat crossing, and suggested the Atlantic was in need of the heavy roller)
8 A – Paul Getty
9 B – Green
10 C – Rugby Union
11 A – Eric Ravilious
Googly C – He took all ten wickets, all bowled